David Toop is a musician, author and music curator. This, his first book, is now in its third edition. His latest work, *Exotica: Fabricated Soundscapes in a Real World*, was published in summer, 1999. Since the publication of *Ocean of Sound* in 1995 he has recorded five solo albums, including *Screen Ceremonies*, *Pink Noir* and *Spirit World*. He lives in London.

From the reviews of the first edition:

'An excellent genealogy of New York City's premier street sound.'   *New Statesman*

'David Toop has done more justice to the rap scene than Hollywood ever could. A word of praise, too, for the excellent black and white photographs of Patricia Bates.'
West Indian World

'*The Rap Attack* will not only put you in touch with the most innovative music of the last decade but will also give you a fair insight into the creative input of the Black American for the last century and more, and then tie it up neatly with a comprehensible bow at the end—most rewarding.'
The Wire

'*The Rap Attack* is "down by law" for understanding the roots of rappers in America—past, present and future.'
Gary Byrd, DJ

'David Toop rolls away the stones to uncover a hidden world of B Boys, Hip Hoppers and Planet Rockers, where time is caught in a frantic loop, and where taste is a matter of "if it fits, use it".'
Charlie Gillett

'Records the vertiginously metamorphic nature of Afro-American culture.'
Greg Tate, *The Village Voice*

'The most authoritative book yet on the New York street phenomenon. Recommended.'   *Record Mirror*

DAVID TOOP

RAP
ATTACK 3

AFRICAN RAP TO GLOBAL HIP HOP

OCM 40752952

Library of Congress Catalog Card Number: 98–89857

A catalogue record for this book is available from the
British Library on request

The right of David Toop to be identified as the author
of this work has been asserted by him in accordance
with the Copyright, Designs and Patents Act 1988

Copyright © David Toop 1984, 1991, 2000

This third revised, expanded and updated edition
first published in 2000 by
Serpent's Tail, 4 Blackstock Mews, London N4 2BT

Website: www.serpentstail.com

All photographs by Patricia Bates unless otherwise
credited

Printed by Legoprint - Italy

10 9 8 7 6 5 4 3 2

Contents

End-troducing

By way of explanation, this is the third edition of Rap Attack, the book I wrote at the beginning of 1984 and then updated in 1991. The story now ends at the beginning of the first section – Millennial Tension: Octopus People Invasion – then goes back to the beginning and ends, regrettably, with a photo of Vanilla Ice. Confusing? No more so than a six turntable mix created live in the heat of the moment. The historic photographs in Rap Attack 1 were taken by Patricia Bates. As ever, my thanks to her.

David Toop
London, July 1999

Millennial tension

1999: a 20th anniversary for hip hop. In 1979, a small underground movement of modest means and ambitions broke through into the wider world. Originating in Bronx clubs, school gymnasiums and street parties, this new music of reanimated funk breaks and spoken rhymes was released on record for the first time, predominantly through small labels in Harlem and New Jersey. As the disco era collapsed on the dancefloor from an overdose of cocaine, sex and non-stop party action, hip hop took over.

The first big hit was 'Rapper's Delight' by The Sugarhill Gang, released in October 1979 on Joe and Sylvia Robinson's Sugarhill Records label. Newly formed after the demise of their previous label, All Platinum, Sugarhill was assisted in the early days by the late Morris Levy, owner of Roulette Records and the so-called 'godfather of American music'. Long suspected of Mafia associations, Levy was finally convicted of conspiracy to commit extortion two years before his death in 1990. Despite the shady connections, 'Rapper's Delight' was an auspicious beginning, both for Sugarhill and for the future of hip hop.

'Sylvia brought this to me,' Joe Robinson told me in 1992. 'A 15-minute record on a 12-inch disc. No 15-minute record has ever got played on the radio, so I said, what am I gonna do with this? But all I had to do with it was get one play anywhere and it broke. Radio was difficult at first but you only needed one play.' Frankie 'Love Man' Crocker was one of the powerful radio DJs who resisted. Despite having recorded a single for Sylvia and Joe's Turbo label, Crocker decided to block the record at New York's WBLS, where he was programme director. 'Frankie is the kind of guy,' said Joe Robinson, 'if he don't hear something as a hit he's not gonna play it and that's it. But eventually he had to play it.' Robinson credits a DJ named Jim Gates at WESL in St Louis with giving 'Rapper's Delight' one of its biggest breaks. 'I shipped it to him, a dub,' he said. 'He played that and they jammed all the phone lines at the station for the next 12 hours. First time I've ever seen anything like that happen. I just rolled up my sleeves and went to work.'

The runaway success of 'Rapper's Delight' was a catalyst for many events that would shape the long-term future of hip hop. The creater of Tommy Boy Records, Tom Silverman, was distributing sale-or-return copies of his magazine, *Disco News*, to New York record stores at the time. 'I saw what Sugarhill was doing and the games they were playing with their artists,' he says. 'I thought if these guys are doing it I can do it. It wasn't like they were experts. They didn't really know what they were doing. They were just doing it.'

Thanks to a tip given by a dance-music promoter, Silverman checked out a strange phenomenon. 'She said there was this place in Downstairs Records,' says Silverman, 'which at the time was on 6th Avenue, in the subway. You had to go down a step right before you got into the subway, down off of 6th Avenue near 42nd Street. There was this record shop and they used to be an oldies record store. They had current records but they had an enormous oldies section and they knew about all the doo-wops and everything. I used to go down there when I was in high school to buy doo-wops, so I knew the place. But she said they had an annex right next to them where you could go and buy these b-boy records. I'd never heard the term before in 1979. I said, "Well what's that?" And she said, "They're paying a lot of money and they're buying these records just for like 10 seconds of the record. Then they mix 'em together and make that beat go on for like five minutes or so."

'I went down to the place and I saw this little annex. Maybe it was a room that was about 8 feet by 10 feet, if that big, or maybe even 6 by 8. It had a three and a half foot counter and the guy had a turntable behind it. All over the wall he had 45s. Some of them were bootlegs, some of them were original. Then they had some albums too. I remember seeing The Eagles' *The Long Run* album there. The guy would write on them, you know, "Rare break beat, Bob James 'Mardi Gras'." There was "Son Of Scorpio" and stuff like that. All these weird records. Some of them were cut-out records that they probably bought for 99 cents. They were selling them for 19 dollars in 1979.

'And there'd be these black kids that would come in that were about 15 years old, or maybe 14. There'd be two or three of them and they'd chip in together and buy the record as a group so they could share it for DJing. I didn't know who any of these little kids were but the room was always filled with these little kids and they were mostly from the Bronx. That's where Kool Herc was, that's where Grandmaster Flash was, and Afrika Bambaataa. They were taking breaks from rock records and that's when I really got interested in going to T Connection to go and hear Bambaataa DJing.'

Silverman drove up to the Bronx where he found the club, an upstairs room on White Plains Road. 'Nobody was drinking and people were just sort of standing around,' he remembers. 'Not really anybody was dancing. There were people on the dancefloor but they weren't really moving that much. There was a very small stage that almost never was used because all the action was in the DJ booth.

'Bambaataa was DJing but a lot of the time he was just picking the records and giving them to Jazzy Jay or Red Alert who were the two DJs that he had at the time. They would put the records on. They were spinning these records. A lot of them had scratched-out labels so you couldn't see what they were and I realised this was one of the sources of where these kids were finding out about these records. I heard 'em playing Kraftwerk. The invitations would say, "James Brown tribute" and it would say, "Invited guests Kraftwerk". None of these people were ever there but kids would turn out. I remember Whiz Kid was playing bass on the stage once while the music was going and then somebody else was up there rapping. That was the first time I heard people actually rapping to these breakbeats. Most of the time it was just beats going on and on and there was no MC.

'Bambaataa would mix different things. Like he used "Mary Mary" by The Monkees, "The Big Beat" by Billy Squier, just dun-daa-duh-dun-dun-dak. Jazzy Jay was more of a technician. Bambaataa was the master of records. He owned the records and could programme the music. It was amazing. I was immediately comfortable and immediately witnessing a merging of cultures. There were no white people in the place and the average age was around 16, 17, something like that. I was probably around 23, 24. I went right up there and I got with him afterwards and talked to him about this and other things.'

These club nights were relatively private events, uncompromised by the usual demands from promotors or record companies. After 'Rapper's Delight', nothing would ever be the same. This was certainly true for the rappers themselves, many of whom lived out the rags-to-riches cliche to the full. As Doug Wimbish, bass player on most Sugarhill tracks, told me in 1984, 'Here you have rappers, that one guy was flipping pizzas the week before, which I bought a slice off of. The other guy's trying to get his high school diploma, another guy's sleeping on a bench selling roses. The next week they're all making beaucoup cash. It's like a dream comes true overnight. One week we're in station wagons. The next week we're on Lear jets.' This story continues unchanged, except the rewards are now far greater. The distance to fall is far greater also, and rappers such

as L.L. Cool J have joined the culture of confession with autobiographies that detail both the ups and downs of sudden wealth and fame.

By 1984, pundits were writing obituaries for hip hop, a passing fad that would surely become a footnote in music history. That was the year when I researched and wrote the first edition of this book. In the same year, the story of hip hop was mutated into an all-singing, all-dancing romance by Hollywood; as is so often the case, the deadly effects of this trivialisation were counterbalanced by the explosive emergence of an underground alternative. Run-D.M.C., The Beastie Boys and Def Jam Recordings were a reaction against the populist trend in hip hop at the time. Ironically, this consciously hardcore stance moved rap up to a higher level of profitability and public acceptance. Stadium concerts, sponsorship, MTV rotation and multi-million dollar record deals ensued, with Russell Simmons, the co-founder of Def Jam, going on to become the first great mogul of the rap industry.

By 1990, when I wrote the second edition of the book, the future looked somewhat bleak. The urgently interlocked sonic and textual density of Public Enemy had been displaced by gangsta rap from Los Angeles, a more conventional approach to hip hop that drew upon slightly different histories and cultural references, yet captured the changing mood with a force that was unstoppable. Already, there were signs that the enduring myths of players and gangsters, the hardboiled fictions and documentations of reality voiced through the rhymes of gangsta rappers, were being enacted in the runnings of their record companies or in their own less-than-private lives.

As if to mask this development, a sanitised pop hip hop had broken through to the core MTV audience and its commercial sponsors, led by M.C. Hammer and Vanilla Ice. Hammer and Ice seemed set to dominate rap for the foreseeable future, yet their career trajectories turned out to be as rapid on the downward slope as they had been on the upwave. According to Ronin Ro in his book, *Have Gun Will Travel: The Spectacular Rise and Violent Fall of Death Row Records*, Vanilla Ice's ambitions in the hip-hop business were curtailed by the intimidating owner of Death Row Records, Marion 'Suge' Knight. Having made bogus claims to be a gangster and scooped up songwriting credits for compositions actually created by his DJ, Chocolate, Ice found his credentials tested in the worst way by Knight. Ice alleged that Knight had held him over a fifteenth floor hotel balcony. Whether the story was truthful or not, Ice was later forced in court to assign publishing rights to Chocolate on seven songs of a debut album that had sold 18 million copies.

In the nineties, reality rap was pervaded by an air of unreality as the financial rewards escalated. By 1998, hip hop had overtaken country music to become America's biggest-selling format. With virtually every rap album sporting a 'Parental Advisory – Explicit Content' sticker, hip hop had become the rebellious gesture of choice, an alternative to alternative rock that boasted more attitude, more explicit language, bigger beats and more bass.

The beast shall live

What I'm saying though, back in the day, hip-hop originated with breakdancers, graffiti writers, MCs and most of all the DJs. But here in 1995 selfishness and greed has forced some to neglect those on the wheels of steel. MCs engaging in this type of behaviour see themselves as getting over but in reality they're contributing to the death of true hip-hop.

With five years remaining before the end of the millennium, these melodramatic words, spoken on Kool DJ E.Q.'s track, 'Death of Hip-Hop', had signalled the emergence of a mutinous cabal, disillusioned with the trajectory of b-boy culture and determined to uphold the values of the old school. As old-school records were repackaged like relics from a bygone era, members of The Sugarhill Gang took advantage of the retro mood, reforming to take nostalgia on the road.

Twenty years earlier, the shock of the new had resonated outwards from the Bronx through New York City's five boroughs, ripples widening to embrace the rest of America, finally reaching the most unlikely corners of the globe. By inventing a new language of musical speech, painting, dance, dress, slang, musical composition, even a succession of musical tools, hip hop's pioneers chopped out their own niche in a world increasingly dominated by global capital.

Hip hop could not be tidied away as a lifestyle, a passing fad to be courted and then brushed aside by hype-sensitive record corporations, art galleries or movie studios. This was a life (potentially both expressive and profitable) that could be lived with some dignity and hope, that crossed boundaries of race, that melted the tribal divisions of genre, that allowed space for a variety of raw yet incandescent talents. As a way of making music, hip hop was an entirely new invention. Only a few pointers to its future innovations lay buried in obscure dreams of the 20th century avant-garde; even they were misleading.

Nobody could predict or anticipate the art of the DJ. With R&B novelty records from the 1960s like Pigmeat Markham's 'Here Comes the Judge', or Dr. Horse's 'Jack, That Cat Was Clean', rapping existed in a form that clearly anticipated the art of the hip-hop MC, whether Lovebug Starsky's old-school party rhymes or Snoop Dogg's malevolent drawl. Yet the notion of creating new music and previously undiscovered sounds from old records, using only a pair of record decks, was as new as any art form could be in the accelerated information blur of the technological 20th century.

Hip hop did not fade away, as its detractors claimed it must. Instead, the music grew and mutated into a war zone of conflicting philosophies, the conscious rappers and the gangstas, culminating in tru-life dramas as the morbid fascinations of gangsta lyrics erupted in shoot-outs and death.

In moments of truce, when the guns fell silent, the stakes became clear. These deaths were not lines from a rhyme or scenes in a video. The potential of hip hop and some of its most talented artists was threatened by a deadly overlap: poetic myths confused with a cynical exploitation of conflicts running deep under life that much, though not all, hip hop purports to document.

California love

What is California love? Somewhere, late on a journey between troubled, bleak, unbalanced, fatherless spirit and violent death, the Eastener – Tupac Amaru '2PAC' Shakur – settled on a golden myth of Hollywood gun law, sex, sun, fun, the gold rush: '. . . wild, wild west,' he rapped on 'California love', 'city of sex . . . money-making machine . . . no dancefloor ever empty . . .'

Fictions, followed hard by facts, struck terror into hearts that claimed to be big. Even the imposing Biggie Smalls, Bad Boy Entertainment artist and Tupac's chief adversary in an overcranked territorial skirmish between East Coast and West Coast rap, acknowledged the aura. 'I felt the darkness when he rolled up that night,' Biggie, the Notorious B.I.G., told *Vibe* magazine, following antagonism at the Soul Train awards, between Los Angeles based Death Row Records and Bad Boy Entertainment from New York, the two rival Empires of hip hop at that time.

Drama, rappers called it, when they meant violent conflict, or heightened life. Life as theatre. Biggie certainly believed in it, equating Tupac's rolling darkness with his cinema role as Bishop, the psychopathic killer in *Juice*. Crazy, but learning to prefer that feeling to the alternative, which was downtrodden misery. Then the Notorious B.I.G. was gunned down. March, 1997, seated in a car at the intersection of Fairfax and Wilshire in Los Angeles, his life was terminated, like Tupac's before him; gunmen firing shots in stationary traffic, in the American way.

The last video of Tupac's life, a promotional clip for 'I Ain't Mad At Cha', makes the cliche of life folding into art loom large. Leaving a building, Tupac is shot. His life fades away in the ambulance. Next we see him welcomed into the afterlife, Miles Davis, Louis Armstrong and Jimi Hendrix playing softly in the heavenly house band, more subdued than those of us still living might hope when we envision music beyond the veil. The video is dedicated to two of the fallen warriors of revolutionary black politics: Geronimo Pratt and Mutula Shakur.

Tupac left Los Angeles, as did Nicholas Cage in *Leaving Las Vegas*, to die in Las Vegas, like a purgative journey from false paradise into the desert. In the evening of his final gundown, he paid court to another troubled, bleak, unbalanced, fatherless spirit. Some way down his own booby-trapped path to redemption, Mike Tyson was in Vegas on 7 September 1996, with intent to destroy a heavyweight named Bruce Seldon. Victim to the slaughter, Seldon fell in one, reasserting Tyson's claim on extreme violence as a route to salvation. Tyson was too fast, hit too hard, Seldon concluded after the fight. Tupac attended – Vegas, heavyweights and celebrity plumage being a rite that shows few signs of decline – and besides, during a spell in prison after a rape conviction, he had intended to join forces with Tyson to offer some kind of help to otherwise doomed young black men. That night, Tupac travelled in the company of Death Row Records boss Marion Suge Knight and their combined entourage, who at some point in the proceedings fought with other members of the crowd. Seldon demolished, they left in a wagon train of 10 cars, heading for Suge Knight's club, 662.

A white Cadillac pulled alongside the correct BMW in this convoy; when the traffic slowed to a halt, two men stepped out to fire on Knight and Shakur. Knight was grazed, though he refused to give any description of the men who were shooting. Tupac was hit four times, dying after a week in University Medical Center, Las Vegas. He was cremated in Brooklyn, a final irony after all the kung fu venoms aimed at New York City; full circle, also, since his life had swung from the Bronx and Harlem, through to Baltimore, Marin City, Los Angeles, Atlanta, back to rest in New York.

Conveniently *dramatised* by gangsta lyrics, a deadly rivalry had flourished between East and West, a war of words, attitude, drawn guns: on the Eastside, Bad Boy Entertainment, Bad Boy CEO Sean 'Puffy' Combs and Biggie Smalls; on the

Westside, out of LA and Vegas, Death Row Records, Death Row CEO Suge Knight and, until 7 September his most valuable artist, Tupac Shakur. In public Knight and Combs downplayed the rivalry, though their actions rarely suggested brotherly love. Perceived by some rappers as legitimate business competition, Suge versus Puffy was a bitter fracas on a minor planet, its crackling small-arms fire a distraction from gang wars raging behind the scenes or the bigger business opportunities available to the legitimised playa. That opportunity was later clinched by Combs, once an employee at Andre Harrell's Uptown label, now mixing business duties with a performance *alter ego* of Puff Daddy and the Family, a family that embraced Lil' Kim and the mediocre, shiny-suited pop-rapper Mase.

Biggie Smalls, the Notorious B.I.G., titled his 1994 album *Ready To Die*, an attempt perhaps, to hold the future to ransom, to express overwhelming depression or simply to spook the opposition. Then came *Life After Death*, which came after death, followed by Puff Daddy's emotionally shallow but financially deep elegy, 'I'll Be Missing You', based around Sting's 'Every Breath You Take'.

Turf battles are enshrined in the origins of hip hop, probably a legacy of the gang territorialism that music and rhymes briefly displaced. As Funky Four's Lil Rodney C had told me in 1984, 'The b boys were strictly in competition.' 'In my death,' Tupac told *Vibe* reporter Kevin Powell, 'people will understand what I was talking about.' So who was Tupac Shakur? He was a successful rapper, a promising film actor, black, defiant, a 25-year-old multi-millionaire (on paper, at least) who had come from nothing. Because of all that and the strange entwining of a dramatic life with a fatalistic outlook, his death carries the symbolic weight accorded to other sudden, premature deaths in the entertainment business. Cathartic in his music, he rapped about abandonment, neglect, burial, shootings, execution, last words and final judgement with a morbid obsession that cried out for help. Ex-Vice President Dan Quayle felt so chilled in his heart by Tupac that he demanded his exclusion from society. Unwittingly, Quayle's judgement synchronised with Tupac's lifelong experience of exclusion, fuelling a stated belief that God, not human society, was his only judge, yet wildly missing the point that in a meritocracy of greed, the pop-gun morality of politicians is deflected by a wave of bank notes.

Tupac's devotion to material success and celebrity, the politics of brand names, the storytelling of media, was striking. Here is what he told Powell at *Vibe* about the events of November 1995, when Tupac was shot after entering the lobby of a Manhattan recording studio. Jewellery worth $40,000 was ripped from his neck. 'I opened my pants,' he said, 'and I could see the gunpowder and the hole in my Karl Kani drawers.' He had been shot five times. A straightforward armed robbery? Tupac suspected a professional hit, a conspiracy. This drama introduced a third solo album – *Me Against the World* – and in established rap tradition, autobiography was written through the medium of sampled television news reports. In quieter moments, Tupac admitted that he suffered nightmares as a symptom of post-traumatic stress, in itself as potent a brand name in the TV confession society as Karl Kani.

The name – Tupac Amaru – was given to him by his mother, Afeni Shakur, during an era when revolutionary acts went hand in hand with a search for re-identification informed by civilisations more ancient than the United States of America. 'They shoulda killed me as a baby,' Tupac raps on *Me Against the World*. Disillusionment was central to his life. He was born in 1971, one month after his mother was released from prison, acquitted of conspiring to bomb police stations and department stores in New York City. At the time of their arrest in 1969, the group of 21 Panthers charged with these crimes released a statement calling for more 'revolutionists who are completely willing and ready at all times to KILL to change conditions'. Afeni Shakur had joined the Black Panther Party looking for a new day, only to see J. Edgar Hoover's Federal Bureau of Investigation blow the organisation apart for being what was described as a 'highly secret all-Negro, Marxist-Leninist, Chinese Communist-oriented' threat.

So ideals were shattered to be replaced by poverty, drugs, the despair that comes when high optimism goes unfulfilled. 'I saw my friends' brains splattered on the sidewalk by police bullets,' said Black Panther leader Elaine Brown. 'I saw their faces in caskets. Things got so bad that funeral attire became a regular part of our wardrobe. I became paranoid; I learned to look over my shoulder.'

Tupac's family history is convoluted, but a number of prominent Black Panthers, including Geronimo Pratt and Mutula Shakur, figured in his early life. Unsurprisingly, Tupac appears to have been torn in half: family connections and his sympathies for the Panthers' revolutionary action on one side; the material world and its pleasures on the other. We can see that attempts by America's government and its agencies to eliminate the beliefs represented by the Panthers have looped back on themselves. Inevitably, activists would have children and at least one of those children was bound to become a Tupac. As Dan Quayle said, in his deep ignorance, 'no place in our society'. Us and them.

Rappers are chastised for their moral vacuity, though Tupac's writing raised moral issues on every album. 'That's why I'll never be a father, unless you got the time it's a crime to even bother,' he raps on 'Papa'z Song'. The music pulls in two directions. *Strictly 4 My N.I.G.G.A.Z...* squealed its way through an overpowering Bomb Squad influence, booming bass smothering the lyrics, yet falling short of the panic of Public Enemy, the urgency of NWA. By half-way point, the album was lurching in the direction of a blunted, easy-rolling West Coast gangsta mood, Dre-Daz-Snoop style, though always personal and disarmingly confessional.

Overburdened by problems, Tupac recorded the remorseful *Me Against the World*, a collection of slow jams, more and more of those Roger Troutman, Isaac

Hayes, Joe Sample smooth grooves that gangstas love (just like the Mafiosi swooning to Sinatra and Dino). Questioning his own lifestyle, doubting his own ability to stay out of jail, skirting close to self-pity and paranoia: 'Just woke up and screamed fuck the world', 'I see death around the corner, any day.' For a moment, image-wise, low-key clothes, glasses, like the pensive student, but turn it over to see that developing Thug Life outer shell, the back-of-the-head shot like Mike Tyson and on *All Eyez On Me*, rap's first double album, he brandished dollar bills, cigarette, alcohol, transforming into the shining serpent of gold and jewels, armoured in leather and tattooed carapace. In the balance of opposites, the outlaw triumphs.

Tupac's cinema acting adds more confusion to all this. Being a small man, narrow intense face, fluid in states of emotional extremity, the inevitable comparison was James Cagney, the Public Enemy, so brilliant at portraying instability. In John Singleton's *Poetic Justice*, Tupac and Janet Jackson carry most of the screen time, all of the reflective emotional weight. Required to cry, to show remorse, act tender, express grief, show parental love and responsibility, Tupac acquits himself well despite the burden of Singleton's direction, which constantly teeters on the brink of mawkishness. Like other rappers who have acted in films – Ice Cube, Queen Latifah, Ice-T, Tone Loc – he seemed relaxed in front of the camera, looking natural in repose.

In June, 1993, I interviewed Tupac for a profile that would concentrate on his role in *Poetic Justice*. This turned out to be an uncomfortable interview, Tupac withdrawn and reluctant, my questioning increasingly fraught with the tension of the situation. Returning to that interview, hindsight knowledge of Tupac's destiny adds an ominous significance to even the most recalcitrant, minimal answer. He was struggling and striving, he told me more than once. A few months earlier, I had interviewed Janet Jackson, who had gushed about the experience of working on *Poetic Justice*. Tell me your feeling about the film, I asked Tupac.

'It came at a real pertinent time of my life,' he answered. 'I was just turning 21, I was meeting Janet Jackson for the first time, The Last Poets and all these people, and I felt the same way like Janet. It was just overwhelming and after it was all over I really took it all in, the experience. Everybody around me was older than me or more experienced so it was my culture shock.'

He played a single parent in the film, as he put it – 'trying to be responsible in an irresponsible world'. It's interesting that you play a single parent, I suggested, since you've written sympathetic raps on that type of subject.

'Yeah, I'm from a single-parent home,' he replied, 'so I can definitely relate. All my music shows how it's very important when you come from a single home to make yourself whole again because you are coming from a disadvantage.'

I asked if he could tell me about his mother's involvement with the Black Panthers.

'No, not really,' he mumbled. 'I mean, it's my family tree, you know?'

A blank on that one. He was more forthcoming about his student days at the High School of Performing Arts in Baltimore: 'I felt like I was out of place so I wanted to be at a school full of people who felt like they were outta place. I learned a good admiration for the real world 'cause it was different cultures, different people. I saw females kissing females, males kissing males, when I was at that school so it really wasn't a big thing to me when everybody was tripping off homosexuality. I already saw that in my school.'

Did he aspire to working in film, I asked.

'Yeah,' he said, 'but in the school they didn't even think there would be movies for black people. They told me there was not a lot of work out there.'

Did he want to do more? 'Definitely. Very, very, very much so. I can't wait to do more.'

I asked if any particular incident had motivated him to write rhymes.

'Yeah,' he said, 'We didn't have any lights at home in my house. No lights, no electricity, and I had batteries in my radio. I heard 'I'm Bad' by L.L. Cool J for the first time and I was writing rhymes by candlelight and I knew I was gonna be a rapper.'

So you were really struggling then? 'Still struggling,' he murmured.

Our conversation struggled also. I asked him about the Dan Quayle incident. He sighed deeply. 'Oh man, I don't know. I don't really give a fuck what Dan Quayle said. I'm sure you could find it somewhere but I don't give a fuck what he said. My answer's on my record, you know, so I wouldn't have to answer it over and over.'

Now he was writing thug music, he said. 'Music for the masses, the underprivileged. Revolutionary music.' And what was the effect of it? 'Shit, I don't know. I can't really see the effects. I can only keep doing the music.' And what was next? 'More o' the same, more o' the same, more o' the same.'

Tupac wrote this line for *Strictly 4 My N.I.G.G.A.Z. . .*: 'You know my momma used to tell me, "If you can't find something to live for, you'd best find something to die for."' Easy to see how that ethos could evolve into a nihilistic double bind, since living for ideals so clearly did not work, not in his family, nor in his surroundings. But then money, women, expensive cars, champagne, fame and California love led to the same conclusion: penitentiary, violent death, no place in our society. Something to die for.

Death wish

A noose, a hearse, a skull, a gravestone. A corpse draped in the American flag, bare feet up against the camera lens, a label saying 'UNCLE SAM' tied around the big toe. Rap record covers in the nineties.

Death is a constant in the imagery of gangsta rap, with album covers, lyrics and videos dominated by guns, gravestones, funerals and retribution. The law of Hollywood's wild west – all problems can be solved by a gun – were now echoed by rap. 'Hip hop is the '93 blues,' J-Dee of Los

Angeles trio Da Lench Mob told me in that same year. 'It's all our sorrows put on wax. They're just put in a different style. It is the last voice of the black man. This is our church. This is our sermon to the kids. This is our own little meeting ground. We teach everybody through our music. A lot of kids don't like to be told what to do because they've been raised up by parents who don't give a damn about what they do. So how can somebody else's society tell them what to do?'

Locked into gang culture, gangsta rap has been depicted with some justice as unremittingly violent and misogynous. Yet many records of this time stand as fascinating, complex documents made in a period of turbulence that peaked with the Los Angeles riots of 1992. Over loops of The Main Ingredient and George Clinton, Da Lench Mob's 'Guerillas In Tha Mist' sampled the words of L.A.P.D. officer Larry Powell, the policeman who had beaten Rodney King 45 times with his baton. Powell spoke about a call he had received prior to the now famous drunk-driver incident involving King. He described a black family in a domestic incident as being like 'gorillas in the mist'. Overturning Tarzen's supremacy in the jungle, Da Lench Mob's track, produced by Ice Cube, ends with the persecution of African mountain gorillas being used as a metaphor for race war in America.

With video increasingly important to hip hop and black film enjoying a period of resurgence, rap tracks took on the quality of cinema. Tracks such as 'I Seen A Man Die' by Scarface, a sombre, moving life history of a young man dying after being shot, or the lighter shoot-out scenario of 'Regulate' by Warren G, were crime stories condensed into four minutes of audiodrama. 'Just chill 'til the next episode,' said Snoop Doggy Dogg on Dr. Dre's ground-breaking 'Nuthin' But a "G" Thang', as if each rap was an instalment in a TV series.

At this point, although much gangsta rap contrived to shock, the more serious MCs were writing rhymes that seemed a genuine expression of what J-Dee had described as 'all our sorrows put on wax'. Cypress Hill, the Los Angeles trio of DJ Muggs, B-Real and Sen Dog, had released 'How I Could Just Kill A Man' at the beginning of the nineties. A nagging, foggy sound – all crackling squeals, tortured guitar breaks and relentless beats and bass – rolled under lyrics that threw up the challenge: 'Hangin' out the window with my Magnum . . . Here is something you can't understand, how I could just kill a man.' Cut into the brattish vocals was a repeated question – 'What does it all mean?' – sampled from Double D and Steinski's 'Payoff Mix'.

Despite the pertinent questions that loomed out of these stark documentary scenes, gangsta rap's leading practitioners were too volatile, too closely identifiable with their lyrics, to be accepted as the equivalent of an earlier generation of black protest music, typified by Curtis Mayfield and Gil Scott-Heron. Da Lench Mob's recording career, for example, was cut short by attempted murder and murder charges levelled at group members J-Dee and T-Bone. As a counterattack against an explosion of black-on-black violence and drug abuse, many rap artists became involved with Louis Farrakhan's Nation Of Islam. Ice Cube's *Death Certificate* album (the record that ended the record-breaking US chart-topping run of country singer Garth Brooks) showed Cube on the back cover, reading the Nation's newspaper, *The Final Call*, flanked by members of the Fruit of Islam task force.

In 1991, sitting in Mosque Maryan, the Chicago base for Minister Farrakhan and his flock, I listened to the Minister For Youth, rapper Prince Akeem, as he discussed incidents that had caused embarrassment to followers of the Nation of Islam. Shortly after a collaboration with Prince Akeem on his *Coming Down Like Babylon* album, Public Enemy's Flavor Flav had been imprisoned for beating the mother of his children. Big Daddy Kane, a follower of the Islamic splinter group, The Five Percent Nation, was accused of the more trivial charge of posing naked in *Playgirl*. 'They're doing what they're doing,' said Prince Akeem, 'because they're not following the restrictive laws of Islam. I'm learning from them. Flav has been in jail for fighting with his girlfriend. I don't have a girlfriend, so I'll never go to jail for that. Kane has a problem for posing for *Playgirl* magazine. See, that offended a lot of the Muslims. The Muslim community said, "What?" He replied, "I know a lot of brothers that do wrong things." Now that's a weak reply because two wrongs don't make a right.'

Watts interlude

1992. Watts, Los Angeles. I am sitting in the home of Anthony Hamilton, for more than 20 years a member of an obscure yet legendary group of rapping poets called The Watts Prophets. Three of them are here. In one corner of the room is a signed photograph of Nina Simone, and standing by the fireplace is a large stick, given to Anthony by Bob Marley. When Marley visited him in Watts he was advised to take some bodyguards. He took his stick instead.

Anthony, also known as Father Amde, has been a priest in the Ethiopian Orthodox Christian Church since 1979, only the second American to be ordained into the church. During visits to the archbishop in Kingston, Jamaica, he met Marley and became a friend. Shortly before his death, Marley was planning a Watts Prophets album on his Tuff Gong label. That, like many other tantalising opportunities to raise themselves out of obscurity, was snatched away from the Prophets by events beyond their control. Study photographs of Marley's funeral and you will find Anthony Hamilton among the priests, reading a poem over the coffin.

In 1971, The Watts Prophets were hot. They were hot on the West Coast when The Last Poets were hot in New York. Their album – *Rappin' Black In a White World* – was released that year on ALA Records. Stylistically comparable to The Last Poets, Melvin Van Peebles or Bama, The Village Poet's *Ghettoes Of the Mind* album released on Chess the following year, the record was packaged in a cover that montaged photographs of Malcolm X, an electioneering poster for Black Panther founder Bobby Seale, the Watts Towers, desolate ghetto scenes and, prophetically, a young boy wearing an army shirt and holding a gun. Despite being pioneers, revered and sampled by rappers like Poor Righteous Teachers, the Watts Prophets story had become a forgotten episode.

For their first and only album, made back in the days of Afros, The Watts Prophets were a quartet. With pianist and poet/vocalist Dee Dee McNeil having become an established cabaret artist, the group was now a trio of poets: Anthony Hamilton, Richard Dedeaux and Otis O'Solomon. All of them were in their early fifties, the Afros long gone. What had happened to the group? How had they vanished into the LA smog for 20 years?

Initially, they met at the Watts Writers' Workshop, a writers' forum organised by Budd Schulberg, author of *On The Waterfront*, as a gesture of solidarity after the Watts riots of 1965. 'This workshop was unique,' said Anthony. 'It had the full spectrum. It had the ultra-militant writer to the most soft and beautiful love poet.'

'Robert Kennedy came down,' said Otis. 'If you wanted to be politically in with the black community, that was one of your stops.'

What was the effect of this poetry?

'Even in our most vicious and rageful poems,' said Anthony, 'we still were saying it with love. We were just calling what we saw. We didn't know that that was a political thing. Things that we were saying had such a political effect. We didn't mean it like that.'

'Well some things we did mean,' countered Richard. 'See, one thing about that album right there,' he said, pointing at a copy of *Rappin' Black In a White World*, 'there's a very disturbing opening. The album starts off "Ask not what you can do for your country, 'cause what in the fuck has it done for you?" And back then, John Kennedy was a saint.'

'Even black people would roll their eyes,' said Anthony.

'Their mouth would freeze,' laughed Otis.

Presumably, in those repressive times, The Watts Prophets upset a lot of people with lines like that.

'Yes, we did,' Anthony confirmed. 'The FBI finally had that workshop burned to the ground.' Later in our conversation he produced a magazine, *Mother Jones*, which printed the story of Darthard Perry, an FBI informant who confessed to loading up with fuel and then breaking into a garage owned by sixties activist Angela Davis, searching in her papers for a link between Davis and the revolutionary underground. After this, Perry burned the garage to the ground and then went on to set fire to the Writers' Workshop.

Later, The Watts Prophets were courted by a number of record companies and established stars, all of whom jumped back and fell silent after their initial excitement. A&R executives were particularly prone to this syndrome. 'This person,' said Otis, 'we would meet them, they would be highly enthused, very emphatic. But then one day you walk in it's like you met a dead person. You know, the colour's out of their face.

Quincy Jones set one of Otis's poems to music for his *Mellow Madness* album. Stevie Wonder also came to them for contributions to *Songs In the Key of Life*, but in the final roll call they were relegated to a lengthy thank-you list at the back of the album booklet. 'We would see the light and then it would go out,' said Anthony, who, along with the other Watts Prophets, remains convinced that FBI influence was at the root of this concerted freeze-out.

Since cabs are reluctant to come to Watts after nightfall, Anthony drove me back to my hotel. He showed me some of the community centres still active in the area, their outer walls emblazoned with paintings of Malcolm X and Martin Luther King. At one point during the drive he recited a poem he had written as a young man, a stream of frozen anger which placed these stories about FBI dirty tricks into their proper context. Conspiracy theories? Paranoia? No, this wasn't a poem about one person's protest. This was like touching the cold rage of a hidden mass of people. Loose tongues and unwanted prophets who broadcast the wrong messages for the wrong times can still be prime candidates for the role of disposable heroes. Living in the fourth world of the second millennium, blinking in the glare and flicker of baffling images, struggling to translate in Babel, can the word still be so strong?

War zone

As with all mature music genres, hip hop had developed a number of different audiences as stylistic, regional and international differences multiplied. One audience, many of them young, white and middle class, enjoyed the tales of drug deals, drinking, gangbanging, shootings and bitches that were causing despair and dismay amongst a strange alliance of liberals and conservatives; another audience would take guidance from the radical messages of Ice Cube and Public Enemy; a third audience listened to hip hop as the new mainstream pop culture, a trend reflected in the breakthrough of acts such as Naughty By Nature, Coolio, House Of Pain, Kris Kross or Sir Mix-A-Lot and the high-profile launch of *Vibe* magazine in 1992, launched by Quincy Jones Entertainment and Time Publishing Ventures; a fourth audience turned to the bohemian experimentalism of Me Phi Me, dcBASE-HEAD, Disposable Heroes of Hiphoprisy, Digable Planets, The Pharcyde, New Kingdom, P.M. Dawn, Me'Shell NdegeOcello, Freestyle Fellowship, Justin Warfield, Gang Starr, MC Solaar, Divine Styler, the once-more reinvented Beastie Boys or the self-consciously homespun Afrocentric positivism of Atlanta's Arrested Development.

Speaking to me in Oakland in 1992, Disposable Heroes of Hiphoprisy rapper and lyricist Michael Franti seemed disappointed that the group were ignored by rap magazines and hardcore rappers. 'But what is hip hop?' he asked rhetorically, bouncing a water bottle on his open palm. 'It's talking over a beat.' For Franti, hip hop was as much an extension of black poetry and the rhymes of Gil Scott-Heron as it was an expression of current reality. 'Television, the Drug Of the Nation', Hiphoprisy's first single, was a remake of an earlier version by The Beatnigs. Whereas the prototype was thick with preaching fury, shouting and drum violence, the new version wrapped a lovingly malicious embrace around the hallucinatory world of TV.

The parallels with Gil Scott-Heron were interesting. Franti's delivery of lyrics and the way he threaded complex trains of thought around the beats shared some obvious similarities to the man who recorded 'The Revolution Will Not Be Televised'. The perception of both television and revolution had changed dramatically, however, over two decades. 'If there was a revolution,' said Franti, 'the first place it would be shown *would* be on television and it would be the highest ratings ever.' As for Gil Scott-Heron, after a period of personal and artistic decline, he emerged revitalised in 1994 with the *Spirits* album. In the opening track, 'Message To the Messengers', he used his position of respect as a rap originator to speak directly to the new generation of rappers, addressing the issues raised by his original song and relating them to the present. 'Four-letter words or four-syllable words won't make you a poet,' chided Scott-Heron, 'they will only magnify how shallow you are and let everybody know it.'

Oppositions, real or false, that stimulate hype and lifestyle choices also stimulate sales. Acts such as Jeru The Damaja, Main Source, UMC's, Pete Rock & C.L. Smooth, Downtown Science and Gang Starr fell between the cracks of such oppositions. Creating music that was too idiosyncratic or simply too uncontroversial in its excellence to stir up either repressive hysteria or political righteousness, they faced the problem of working within a war zone in which massive sales and exaggerated attitude could win battles for contradictory points of view. If the huge sales of Arrested Development's debut album seemed to encourage hope that the violence, misogyny and materialism of the thug life were losing ground, the massive underground sales of Too Short, rhyming about pimping and pussy, suggested something else.

For Oakland's Too Short, speaking to *The New Beats* author S.H. Fernando Jr., his raps were a 'marketing exercise', using the traditional literary virtues of observation and imagination to make money. Whatever they lacked in 'positive messages' or subtlety, Too Short's records were no more or less of a fantasy than Arrested Development's exhortations to children to 'switch off the television' and 'dig your hands in the dirt'.

A turning point came with Dr. Dre's album for Death Row. Created in chaotic circumstances, *The Chronic* reiterated the importance of marijuana to West Coast rap, a link first made by Cypress Hill on tracks such as 'Something For the Blunted', 'Light Another' and 'Stoned Is the Way Of the Walk'. The featured cast of rappers working with Dre on *The Chronic* included That Nigga Daz, Warren G, Kurupt, Bushwick Bill, Rage, D.O.C. and Snoop Dog, soon to become one of the biggest yet most blighted stars of rap as Snoop Doggy Dogg. With his ice-cool drawling delivery, a direct descendent of Slick Rick's 'La-Di-Da-Di', Snoop was the only rapper present capable of making music out of rhymes that were often puerile, tasteless, vindictive or barely more than an advertisement for Death Row.

As for Dre, his production style was a continuation of the techniques he was using back in the days of N.W.A. and J.J. Fad. Simple, verging on simplistic, the music reshaped seventies soul. Despite lacking the textural density or sensuality of the tracks that inspired it, Dre's formula was extremely effective. Irresistible mid-tempo samples such as Parliament's 'Mothership Connection' and 'P-Funk (Wants To Get Funked Up)', Isaac Hayes's 'Do Your Thing' and Donny Hathaway's score for *Come Back Charleston Blue* were overlaid with bass lines played by Colin Wolfe and heavy beats programmed by Dre.

The music was powerful but Dre seemed to have little of substance to talk about, other than documenting his intake of chronic and sending messages of venom to Eazy-E, his former colleague in N.W.A. Claiming large sums of unpaid royalties for his production work for Eazy-E's Ruthless Records label, Dre used his record to vent spleen against Eazy and manager Jerry Heller. After *The Chronic* had turned into the biggest seller in gangsta rap history, Eazy responded with his own threat of a

gang hit on Dre – 'It's On (Dr Dre) 187UM Killa' – but the feud collapsed and bad feeling turned to reconciliation when Eazy died from Aids-related pneumonia in March 1995.

Having showcased Snoop as the most distinctive new voice in rap and potentially its biggest star, Dr. Dre went on to produce *Doggystyle*. Although the drawl was intact, Snoop had little more to say than his producer. Despite the use of unusual samples such as Edwin Birdsong's 'Rapper Dapper Snapper', the music had been stripped back to the most basic grooves, hardly enlivened by Snoop detailing his daily life, sipping gin, putting on his socks, paying for 'bitches', smoking chronic, partying with parasites and hoes. A few weeks before the spectacularly successful release of *Doggystyle*, Snoop was involved in a shooting incident that ended with the death of a gang member named Philip Woldemariam. As his promotional work for the album began, he was charged with murder with bail posted at $1 million. Although he was finally acquitted in 1995, his career prospects had suffered. 'He was a free man,' wrote Ronin Ro in *Have Gun Will Travel*, 'but now had to deal with a reputation sullied by months of damaging media coverage.'

In 1997, Suge Knight was sentenced to nine years imprisonment for probation violation. Suge began serving his nine-year sentence at the California Men's Colony in San Luis Obispo,' wrote Ronin Ro, 'where he was barred by law from running Death Row, saw half of the label's staff get laid off, and watched creditors like American

Express continue demanding payment. Immediately after his imprisonment, he noticed, the Death Row family disbanded. Where the label once promoted a united front, artists had scattered to the four winds.'

Snoop Doggy Dogg's second album, *The Doggfather*, had sold extremely well, though not in such huge quantities as his debut. After the collapse of Death Row, he became Snoop Dogg and transferred allegiance to a new rap mogul. Recording for No Limit Records, a label owned by the New Orleans based CD, straight-to-video, sports and clothing entrepreneur and rapper Percy 'Master P' Miller, Snoop recorded desultory retreads of his earlier work, including a second-rate remake of 'Gin and Juice'. Without Dr. Dre, the Dogg had lost his creative bite, though his first album for No Limit went platinum in only two weeks. All that Master P touched, from washed-up superstars to total unknowns, turned to gold. This mass-market gift was symbolised by the portrayal of himself as The Colonel, commanding his soldiers – Mystikal, Mercedes, Skull Duggery, Mia X, Steady Mobb'n, Soulja Slim *et al.* – from a gold-plated, diamond-studded tank, masterminding 'the world's #1 independent label'. Returning from his own prison sentence, Dre had left Death Row before its demise. Tired of gangsta rap and insulted by Suge Knight's suggestion that he produce an album for M.C. Hammer in a desperate attempt to revive Hammer's annihilated career, Dre withdrew, harbouring plans to start his own label. His fortunes shot skywards again in 1999 with his production of white rapper Eminem's *The Slim Shady LP*, released on Aftermath. Totally original, bizarre, sick and irritatingly compulsive, Eminem played games with hip hop's amoral, violent image, the aftermath of Death Row and gangsta. On 'Guilty Conscience' he trades lines with Dr. Dre, poking fun at his gangsta past – 'Aha, temper, temper, Mr. Dre, Mr. N.W.A., Mr. AK, comin' straight out of Compton you all better make way.' Dre reasons with him – ''Cause he don't need to go the same route that I went, been there done that' – then reverts to stereotype with 'Ahh fuck it, shoot 'em both Brady, where's your gun at?' Boom! click, Boom!

Mystery of chessboxing

As the West Coast gangstas rode the freeways with impunity, bass bins shuddering with explosions and the pump of shotguns, a new sound and vision rose in the East. From Staten Island came the Wu-Tang Clan, initially a loose collective of rappers and producers looking to build a business platform out of hip-hop: Method Man ('mad different methods'), The Genius 'The GZA', Raekwon ('He's the chef'), Ol' Dirty Bastard ('There's ain't no father . . .'), Ghostface Killah ('Now you see me, now you don't'), U-God ('He's a psychopathic thinker'), Prince Rakeem 'The RZA' ('He the sharpest motherfucker in the whole clan, he always on point, razor sharp') and associates such as Shyheim, aka The Rugged Child, and Inspectah Deck ('he'll take you to court'). Released in 1993 on BMG, their first album, *Enter the*

Wu-Tang (36 Chambers) combined raucous shouted ensemble raps with eerie samples from Shaw Brothers martial arts movies, echoing beats and disembodied piano phrases. Rough, rugged and slightly unhinged, *Enter the Wu-Tang* was a far stranger beast than the majority of Wu-Tang solo projects.

Ghostface Killah's *Ironman* album, for example, set up odd contrasts between the horns and solid beats of The RZA's sixties-soul-flavoured production and Killah's rough-voiced stream-of-consciousness lyrics, images piling up through association, euphony and strange lateral logic. With the bleak nostalgia of 'Can It Be All So Simple' on their first album, built around a wistful sample from the Gladys Knight and The Pips version of 'The Way We Were', Wu-Tang set the template for a convergence of hardcore rap and the new wave of retro-future R&B. After losing its edge with the soft radio format of 'quiet storm' during the 1980s, R&B found a new direction by matching hip hop's grainy production values with vocal styles that jumped back over the years, past Luther Vandross, Freddie Jackson and Anita Baker to an earlier generation of soul singers.

Among the Wu-Tang solo projects, Method Man's 'I'll Be There For You/ You're All I Need To Get By' and Ghostface Killah's 'All That I Got Is You' featured Mary J. Blige and 'Cold World' by Genius featured D'Angelo, anticipating the most potent commercial trend of the late nineties, R&B with a hardcore twist, exemplified by TLC, Lauryn Hill's multiple Grammy-winning album, *The Misedu-cation Of . . .*, Busta Rhymes recording with Janet Jackson, Miss Jones with Big Punisher, Q-Tip with Janet Jackson, Redman with Dru Hill, Funkmaster Flex with Khadejia, Mary J. Blige with Jay-Z, The Roots with Erykah Badu and D'Angelo, Mase with Total, MC Lyte with Gina Thompson and a host of similar fusions and collaborations (or exercises in sweeping up as many record buyers as possible).

At its best, on tracks such as Ghostface Killah's 'The Soul Controller' or Method Man's 'Stimulation', the Wu-Tang style is tamed chaos, samples grating against each other in different keys, circling like smoke in a mix that rarely bothers with integration or resolution, simply letting harps, flutes, saxophones, soul vocals, string sections and tremulous kung fu soundtracks cohabit in hallucinatory rooms of doom. This dissociated atmosphere of queasy strings, plodding beats and Carnival Of Souls organ was used to good effect by RZA on his production work for Gravediggaz, a horror-rap collaboration with Poetic the Grym Reaper and ex-Stetsasonic members Prince Paul and Fruitkwan. 'Like Dr. Octagon and Funkadelic,' wrote Kodwo Eshun in *More Brilliant Than the Sun*, '– right down to the homage "Mommy What's a Gravedigga?" – the mythillogical humour of Gravediggaz lacerates minds inured to sensation, intensifies illness in order to sensitize.'

But as the Wu-Tang releases proliferated and their empire grew to include non-musical business ventures such as clothing lines, the surprise of their music evaporated. Their confrontational rapping style had become standard in the world of multi-million selling Parental-Advisory-stickered albums. West Coast gangsta rap may have fallen off but gangsta attitudes and hardcore language had been absorbed into rap of all kinds. Only Will Smith, his career having evolved from rapper to television actor to one of the biggest young movie stars in Hollywood, continued to turn out records that were happy to be happy.

Beyond the opposition crushing sales of Will Smith's *Big Willie Style*, conscious rappers still battled for supremacy. With their 1995 album, *The Score*, New Jersey trio The Fugees – Lauryn Hill, Wyclef Jean and Pras – sold a record-breaking 17 million copies worldwide. All three used the success as a platform for solo projects and productions that included Wyclef Jean's work on *Can-I-Bus* by Canibus, a disappointing debut for a gifted rapper. From the darkside, guns, sex and drug deals gone bad were represented by imposing characters like Fat Joe and Big Punisher, all following in the heavy footsteps of The Notorious B.I.G.

So-called ghetto pop was exemplified by the fast rapping Jay-Z, whose smart pop hit, 'Hard Knock Life', drew on the talents of veteran producer DJ Mark, 45 King. At face value, Jay-Z appeared to be a lucrative update of what J-Dee from Da Lench Mob had called 'the '93 blues, all our sorrows put on wax', a legacy that linked back to The Watts Prophets and The Last Poets. What was missing, however, was the internal dialogue between polemic, realism and questioning once interwoven in tracks such as Ice Cube's 'It Was a Good Day'. In the early days of hip hop, MCs who had nothing but the clothes on their backs and their verbal skills recorded wish-fulfilment raps about driving a Mercedes and drinking champagne; now rappers with five cars and a mansion were telling hard-luck stories.

Jaz-Z also turned to producer Timbaland for his *Vol. 2 . . . Hard Knock Life* album, only to be overshadowed by the speed and sharpness of Timbaland's beats. After years of murky beats, swamped in blurred, crackling samples from the lower depths, Tim 'Timbaland' Mosley led hip hop into clear air. Like the amplified metabolic rhythms of insects, his minimalist beats pushed vocalists into subtle rhythmic and tonal variations. On rapper and singer Missy Elliott's *Supa Dupa Fly* album from 1997, Missy Elliott dips in and out of the seductive clicks, bangs and empty liftshafts of Timbaland's chop guitars, hissing hi-hats, vocal samples and electronic squeals, 'my hormones jumping like a disco'.

A similar twitchy sophistication, playful, sly and subversive, emerged on the gravel voiced Busta Rhymes's *Extinction Level Event*. Stardom had clearly sobered the Busta Rhymes worldview, adding an apocalyptic survivalist theme to the off-the-wall party rapping of earlier tracks like 'Woo Hah! Got You All In Check'. All cosmic costumes, new-world-order symbols and doom-gloom-civilisation-ending-soon imagery, *Extinction Level Event* still managed some degree of levity, mainly thanks to the creative use of exotic samples such as Dick Hyman's 'Topless Dancers of Corfu', Terry Baxter's 'Early In the Morning', Dr. Buzzard's 'Sunshower', Manu Dibango's 'New Bell' and a string orchestra loop from Bernard Herrmann's soundtrack score for *Psycho*, not to mention a guest appearance by Black Sabbath's Ozzy Osbourne on 'This Means War'. Yet the musical brilliance was undermined by overblown Armageddon scenarios and delusions of grandeur. Similar distasteful passages of self-aggrandisement were everywhere, brought to a controversial head by Nas, rapping 'Hate Me Now' and portraying himself crucified, inflating the natural 'playa hater' paranoia and self-promotion of hip hop to an absurd level.

Far more satisfying were the porno-horror visions of Keith Thornton, aka Kool Keith. Once a member of the influential and underrated Bronx crew UltraMagnetic M.C.'s, Kool Keith now approached each project with a new identity. Erotic Man or Black Elvis, he donned the mask of Dr. Octagon for his 1995 collaboration with Automator, D. Nakamura, Kut Masta Kurt and DJ Q-Bert from the Bay Area turntable crew Invisibl Skratch Piklz. Echoing with eerie bleeps and chimes, groaning under the weight of growling bass lines, the music portrayed chambers of horror, Dr. Octagon prowling the corridors, shining light into dark operating theatres haunted by 'the nurse with voodoo curse', rooms vacated by serial killers. Outside these claustrophobic interiors, the rain was green and the flowers were blue. Straight outta solitary as Dr. Dooom, corrosive with bile, Kool Keith came back in 1999 with *First Come, First Served*, a similarly surreal

excursion through Kool Keith's fantasy life. 'For the love of animals I used to always cut the legs off a roach,' he raps on 'Welfare Love', 'See if he'll stand there on a tissue and give him a piece of toast. That morning he would wake up and be gone.'

Paring down his music to funk basics, Kool Keith was a non-aligned, left-of-centre proponent of a back-to-funk drift in hip hop. In Atlanta, Outkast and Goodie Mob were making music of pathos and depth, steeped in the tradition of Southern soul, George Clinton, Gil Scott-Heron and King Tubby. *Aquemini*, Outkast's third album, was a dazzling, inventive and consistently engaging showcase for the contrasting personalities of rappers Big Boi and Dre. Suffused with melancholy and spirituality, tracks like 'SpottieOttieDopaliscious', 'Return Of the "G"' and 'Aquemini' reaffirmed rap's place in an African-American storytelling tradition. A similar sombre mood permeated Goodie Mob's *Soul Food*, jarring harmonica notes jutting out from the Organized Noize production, a raw seventies funk feel of wah-wah guitars, congas, electric piano and smooth bass, night insects chirping and voices harmonising and reasoning, Goodie Mob's raps delivered with the solemn intensity of a sermon: 'We ain't natural born killas, we are a spiritual people, God's chosen few, think about the slave trade when they had boats with thousands of us on board and we still was praising the Lord – now you ready to die over a coat, a necklace round your throat, that's bullshit Black people you'd better realize, we losin', you better fight and die if you got to get yo' spirit and mind back and we got to do it together, Goodie Mob means "The Good Die Mostly Over Bullshit".'

Octopus people invasion

As a student of hip-hop, the juggler respects the pioneers, but does not romaticize them. The pioneers were inventing hip-hop as they went along, and soon they had lost control of it. Informal values were attached, but there wasn't the luxury to sit down and specify what those values were. The loosely defined values were good for a time when hip-hop's arena was the playground and the train yard. Today hip-hop is the world's predominant youth culture . . . The spirit is still there. It used to be called hip-hop. I don't know what it's called anymore, but whatever it is, it needs to be the new blueprint not only for hip-hop, but for the future of America, suburbs and all.

Bomb the Suburbs, William Upski Wimsatt

1999, memories everywhere, ghosts from 'back in the days', the old, old school: superfluous cover versions of old-school classics; remastered, scholarly, annotated reissues of historic hip hop, illustrated by photographs that conjure the flavour of another century; careers snatched back from the twilight zone, such as Run-D.M.C.'s 'It's Like That', remixed in house style by Jason Nevin, reminding us how innocent even the hardest of yesterday's hardcore now sounds; catching the wave, The Sugarhill Gang reforming to disinter the old days for an audience too young to know if they are cheering original members or a sugar-pill gang of lookalikes.

At the end of 1993, a near-formless and mostly instrumental vinyl 12-inch by an unknown artist called DJ Shadow was released. Twelve minutes long, the track opened with a fragment taken from 'Listen', written by Watts Prophet Anthony Hamilton and recorded for a 1970 poetry album called *The Black Voices: On the Streets In Watts*. With its disconnected beats and vocal samples, 'Influx' sounded like a throwback to live hip-hop jams from the late seventies, though the downbeat, downtempo mood was light years away from the turntable gymnastics of Jazzy Jay, Red Alert, Grand Wizard Theodore or Grandmaster Flash. On the B side, 'Hindsight' was stripped back to little more than beats, bass and noirish atmospherics, like John Barry for the blunted generation.

Recorded in San Francisco, the record was like a reincarnation of 'Beat Bop', the drag-tempo, hallucinatory snapshot of street surrealism recorded by Rammelzee in 1983. With hindsight, 'Beat Bop' now looked like the definitive template for many hip-hop tributaries: the dense psychogeography of Tricky's 'Aftermath'; the glutinous headnodding instrumentals of trip-hop; the 'data streams' of noise, DJ scratching and hip-hop beats coming from New York's Illbient luminaries such as DJ Spooky and DJ Olive.

On his 1996 album, *Endtroducing*, DJ Shadow named one of the tracks 'Why Hip

Hop Sucks In '96'; the music, a melancholy synthesiser wail over a deep funk groove, rivalled Dr. Dre's productions for Death Row, though instead of a Snoop Dogg or Kurupt rapping bitches, gangbanging niggas, killas and 'my mind on my money and my money on my mind', the vocal reverberated plaintively with an answer to the question: 'It's the money . . . money . . . money . . .'

The record business had always revolved around celebrities. With rap becoming big business, there was an inevitable shift of focus to the marketing of personality MCs. Paradoxically, the profound impact of hip-hop innovation was registering in other genres. Musical movements such as drum 'n' bass were founded on the inventive transformation of breakbeats, the short one- or two-bar drum rhythms first cut up on turntables in the South Bronx in the 1970s, then sampled and looped with the advent of digital samplers in the 1980s. Yet drum 'n' bass was separate from hip-hop culture. A distinctly British invention with many sub-genres, drum 'n' bass fed break-beats through an evolutionary time machine to create an entirely new form of music – virtuosic in its programming, frenetic in its pace, often dark and abstract in mood and more likely to draw on Jamaican imagery than Americana.

Pockets of underground resistance were growing among those who had pinned their hopes on the fate of hip hop. These were determined to detach themselves from the excesses of gangsta and claim independence from the corporate record business. As the cover photograph of DJ Shadow's *Endtroducing* showed – a record store interior, young males leafing through racks of vinyl, and the album track notes strewn with rare 7-inch funk singles – artists like Shadow were more interested in the archaeology of beats and breaks than in highrolling and feuding.

Peter Shapiro summed up the counter-trend in *The Wire*: 'This re-emergence of the DJ from the shadows of the stage dovetailed with a developing grass roots movement that set out to establish a "real" HipHop culture, one that would flourish in direct opposition to the materialism and violence that had come to characterise what groups such as Company Flow disparagingly referred to as mainstream "rap". While gangster-entrepreneurs such as Suge Knight, Dr. Dre, Puff Daddy, et al settled into a volatile collusion with the established practices of the record industry, the new turntablists looked back to HipHop's origins as a streetculture with its own language and codes of practice.'

The wheel had turned full circle. Masters of the turntable such as Flash, DJ Premier and Grandmixer D.ST were revered for their innovative skills, the vital role they had played in hip hop's evolution. DJs had, after all, paved the way for MCs, yet star producers and celebrity MCs had reduced them to historical curiosities. In 1995, David Paul expanded his San Francisco-based magazine, *Bomb Hip-Hop*, into record production. His compilation, *Return Of the D.J. Vol. I*, turned out to be a manifesto. A roll call of some of the best new turntablists, including The Beat Junkies, Invisibl Skratch Piklz (Q-Bert,

Disk and Shortkut), Rob Swift, Peanut Butter Wolf, Jeep Beat Collective, Cut Chemist and Mixmaster Mike, the album celebrated noise, experiment, speed of thought and wrist, deep archival knowledge and the unleashed power of cutting and scratching raised to a higher level of virtuosity.

By the time David Paul released *Return Of the D.J. Vol. II* in 1997, distinguished by its inclusion of Kid Koala's 'Static's Waltz', turntablism was a global phenomenon, connected through the worldwide web, mix tapes and mixing battles. The battles and tapes were forms of media that imitated hip hop's original methods of dissemination. The web sites, on the other hand, emphasised how far the music, and the world, had come. Hip hop's original subversion of technological trajectories, its democratisation of creative skills, fitted well with many of the ideals associated with the Internet. As established recording artists grew dissatisfied with the workings of the entertainment business, it seemed fitting that Public Enemy would take the lead in deciding to release an album on the Internet, rather than through conventional distribution channels. Constrained by Def Jam from releasing a 'Bring the Noise' remix on the Public Enemy web site, Chuck D took the radical step of leaving Def Jam and signing his group to an Internet record label called Atomic Pop. 'Technology and hip-hop have always run parallel,' Chuck D told *Guardian* writer Randeep Ramesh. 'For me, seeing a crowd moving to the sounds of a microphone and turntables got me into the business at first. So the net was a natural move.'

In praise of the turntable's new role as a drum, Bill Laswell had compiled *Altered Beats* for Axiom, a collection that crossed the generations by featuring Rob Swift, Prince Paul, DXT, the amazing 'Invasion of the Octopus People' by Invisibl Skratch Piklz (the same track that appeared on *Return Of the D.J. Vol. I*) and from Japan, sedate in this company, DJ Krush. 'Sacred texts are randomly cut-up, or cut and scratched, in Burroughs-Gysin fashion to create collages of rhythm, sound, spoken tongues, noise – whatever is available,' wrote Bill Murphy in his sleevenotes. 'Such a "mad science" possesses the power to open completely unique windows on the world, where the realm of possibilities for new directions in music stretches as far as the mind can conceive . . . and perhaps even further. In the end all we can know with any immediacy is that the quest begins when needle is touched to groove; from there, the DJ defines the journey.'

Solo albums appeared after these compilations, including *Man Or Myth?* by DJ Faust, Rob Swift's *The Ablist*, Peanut Butter Wolf's *My Vinyl Weighs a Ton*, DJ Spinna's *Heavy Beats Volume 1*, Mixmaster Mike's *Anti-Theft Device* and PhonosycographDISK's *Ancient Termites*. Rob Swift, frontman of The X-Men, cites Herbie Hancock's 'Rockit', produced by Bill Laswell and featuring Grandmixer D.ST, as the track that showed him an alternative use for the turntable as a musical instrument. 'I think it's phat,' Swift says on 'Two Turntables And a Keyboard', 'because for the first time you have turntables accompanying a keyboard player.' Turntablism was an improvisation laboratory in which unknown chemicals were being mixed. Perhaps the most varied and consistently creative of these albums was *Ancient Termites*. The creator who had burdened himself with the name PhonosycographDISK and devised track titles like 'Polar Bear Sunskreen', 'Ducks Decay', 'Penguin Burial' and 'Thinking Room Sculpture' was DJ Disk, a member of Invisbl Skratch Piklz. Released on Bomb Hip-Hop in 1998, his album careered wildly through jazz from Louis Armstrong to John Coltrane, easy listening, nursery rhymes, sound effects, stumbling beats, strange atmospheres, squealing metallic feedback and lightning scratches.

In the hands of turntablists, the new beats were complex, the moods oblique, the sources obscure, demanding an equivalent development of fluid, agile MC skills. Images tumbled in streams from crews like Company Flow, flowing in and out of their murky soundscapes. From Brooklyn, the Company Flow MCs Big Jus and El-P with DJ Mr Len rose to the challenge, making their own dense, dystopian instrumentals on *Little Johnny From the Hospital*. In search of a fresh start, groups like Jurassic-5, The Roots and Black Star wrestled with the legacy of hip hop, the demands of an audience spoiled for choice, the need to look forward and yet learn from the past. Meanwhile, hip hop was embedded in the music of artists as radically different as Tricky, Beck or Ozomatli. Versions of hip hop were now an established element in the cultures of France, Brazil, Spain, Germany and Japan, a liberation of local languages, a universal voice with which to air dissatisfactions with domestic politics. Hip-hop style was plundered by fashion designers and fed back to the streets. The strange dreams lived out in school gyms, block parties and a tiny record store annex below 6th Avenue now spread all over the world.

Full circle: the story begins here.

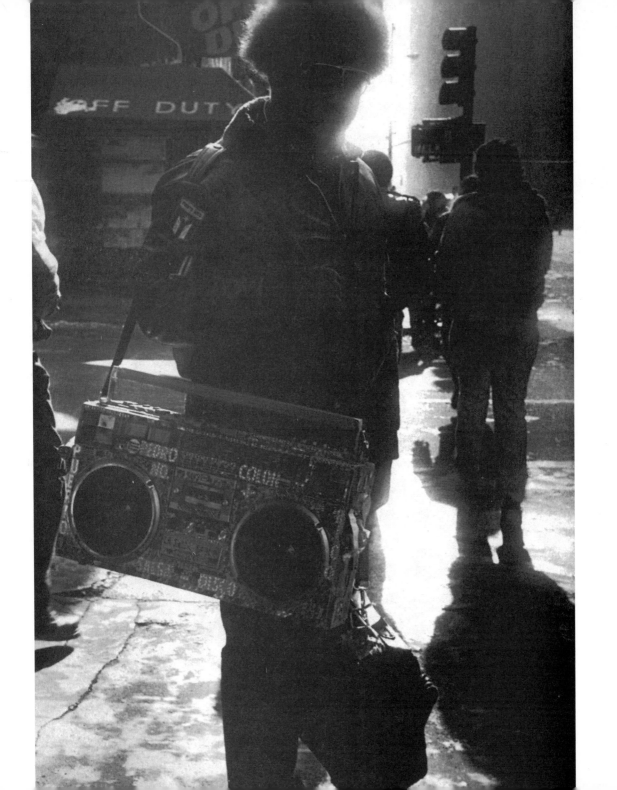

STUDS AND GLOVES AT DANCETERIA

1. On the corner

Ten thirty p.m. on a cold Saturday night in January and three b boys are working their pitch near Times Square, New York City. The spectators have just paid to watch Clint Eastwood blow away a selection of black stick-up men and multi-cultural rapists. They settle down to a few free moments with uptown culture.

Eddie is 10 years old. He has been break-dancing and moonwalking on the streets around this block since he was 6, using a strip of cardboard as a dancefloor. The two others in the crew are 16, one of them huddled in a sheepskin, the other with the top of his head pushed into a stocking. Both of them pat the beat for Eddie with hand-claps, taking turns to rap. Whether I believe their claims that they appeared in Charlie Ahearn's hip-hop movie *Wildstyle* is neither here nor there; the most important thing they want to put across to me is that they know everybody on the block.

On West 52nd and 10th Avenue Daniel Ponce has just finished his first set at Soundscape. The standout number for me is an interpretation of a Beny Moré bolero, played with great sensitivity and facility by saxophonist Paquito D'Rivera. Ponce is a Cuban with a rep as a great bata and conga player. Though his live shows combine Cuban folklore with jazz he is also becoming known for adding the Latin ingredient to beat-box tracks fronted by Herbie Hancock, Material and Grandmixer D.ST –

recordings which combine the innovations of scratch mixing and turntable cutting with the most advanced percussion and key-board technology.

The two extremes of hip hop are the sophisticated cross-cultural fusions which meld the oldest traditions with the freshest of musical technologies or, at the other pole and clinging for life, the bottom line of street survival. They are indicative of the sharp contrasts within its city of origin, New York. Hip hop's home, The Bronx, is an area with a fearsome reputation caricatured by films such as *Bronx Warriors* and *Fort Apache: The Bronx*. Its grim project housing and burnt-out buildings have little of the political and cultural resonance of neighbouring Harlem, let alone the material assets further downtown; it was within The Bronx and, to a lesser extent, Harlem that black youths developed their own alterna-tive to the gang warfare that had risen from the dead in the late 1960s to dominate and divide neighbourhoods north of Central Park.

It was a DJ style which helped to create the lifestyle which came to be known as hip hop. At the beginning of the disco era in the first half of the 1970s, regular disco jocks in clubs were most concerned with the blend between one record and the next – match-ing tempos to make a smooth transition which, at its best, could continually alter the mood on the dancefloor without breaking the flow. At its worst the technique could turn the night into one endless and inevitably boring song.

FRESH BREAKERS AT THE ROXY

In The Bronx, however, the important part of the record was the break – the part of a tune in which the drums take over. It could be the explosive Tito Puente style of Latin timbales to be heard on Jimmy Castor records; the loose funk drumming of countless '60s soul records by legends like James Brown or Dyke and The Blazers; even the foursquare bass-drum-and-snare intros adored by heavy metal and hard rockers like Thin Lizzy and The Rolling Stones. That was when the dancers flew and DJs began cutting between the same few bars on two turntables, extending the break into an instrumental. One copy of a record – forget it.

The dances featuring these off-the-wall mobile jocks, at first held in schools, community centres, house parties and parks,

helped bring former rival gangs together. In the transition from outright war the hierarchical gang structure mutated into comparatively peaceful groups, called crews. Over a period of five years the crews contributed to the development of hip hop. Since nobody in New York City, America or the rest of the world wanted to know about the black so-called ghettoes – the unmentionable areas of extreme urban deprivation – the style was allowed to flourish as a genuine street movement whose presence was felt only through the prominence of one aspect of the culture – graffiti.

White New Yorkers might never have to visit the black or Hispanic parts of town; in that sense graffiti was a visitation upon them. A relic from a past age of streetcorner men and warrior gangs, graffiti had progressed from a scribbled tag (nickname) or club name on the wall to an elaborate art form emblazoned with Magic Marker and spray paint over every available surface of the subway trains and buildings. If the city refused to come to young blacks and Puerto Ricans, then they would go to the city. The rest of the culture was a private affair – truly underground. The DJs teamed up with MCs who provided a show, creating spoken rhymes, catch phrases and a commentary about the DJ, the clientele and themselves over the beats:

When I was born my momma gave birth
to the baddest MC on the goddam earth

A style of dress grew up – a fractured image of cool, combining casual and sports wear – and the dancing was fiercely competitive. Competition was at the heart of hip hop. Not only did it help displace violence and the refuge of destructive drugs like heroin, but it also fostered an attitude of creating from limited materials. Sneakers became high fashion; original music was created from turntables, a mixer and obscure (highly secret) records; entertainment was provided with the kind of showoff street rap that almost any kid was capable of turning on a rival.

In 1979 the b boys and b girls (as they had come to be known) were in for a shock. From seemingly nowhere, two singles were released to send hip hop public. First Fatback, a waning street funk group from Brooklyn, put out a record on Spring with an unknown disc jockey called King Tim III. It was a rap called 'King Tim III

BOMBING THE 6 TRAIN

(Personality Jock)'. Second, The Sugarhill Gang, a trio who were also unknowns, had their 'Rapper's Delight' launched on Sugarhill Records. Though Fatback's record was a success of sorts, its style harked back to the days when radio rapping jocks heated up the airwaves with rhyming jive. 'Rapper's Delight', on the other hand, not only stole MC rapping but also appropriated the idea of using a remake of Chic's huge disco hit 'Good Times' as its backing track. The response from the hip-hop community was a contradictory mixture of resentment and a desire to get in on the action.

During the next few years the rush to sign deals was largely accommodated by relatively small-scale, uptown independents whose guiding lights were familiar names from the past three decades of New York black music. At the centre were Enjoy Records and Sugarhill, with a number of smaller labels – Winley, Sound of New York USA, Holiday – popping up with rap records to underline further the fact that this was the Harlem shuffle.

Sylvia Robinson (Sugarhill), Bobby Robinson (Enjoy), Danny Robinson (Holiday) and Paul Winley (Winley) had all been involved in the New York music scene since the 1950s. With the exception of Sylvia, none of these entrepreneurs had ventured far into the increasingly racially integrated disco market. While the rest of the music industry was being saved (and subsequently near-ruined) by their exploitation of disco, the R&B and doo-wop veterans stood by in contempt or bewilderment, unable to identify with beats-per-

minute, Studio 54 and all the more blatant high-living trappings imposed on the genre. Rapping, by comparison, bore a striking resemblance to the street-corner harmony era. Just as the 115th Street Tin Can Band had honed their routines in their playground at Wadleigh Junior High (later becoming The Harptones) back in 1951 so, 25 years later, it would have been possible to peer through the wire-mesh fence of a similar schoolyard and hear schoolfriends and neighbours struggling to arrange ensemble raps and solo verses in preparation for a block party.

ADVENTURES ON THE WHEELS OF STEEL: GRANDMASTER FLASH AT BROADWAY INTERNATIONAL

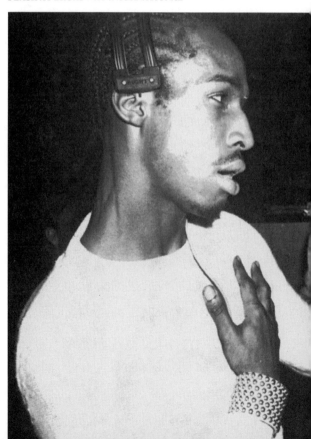

The veterans were now of an age to be able to follow their children. For Sylvia Robinson it was partly the enthusiasm of her son which led her to record The Sugarhill Gang; Paul Winley had his daughter, a 'rap fanatic', to spur him into action, and Bobby Robinson watched his nephew, Spoonie Gee, writing rhymes in the front room of the Robinson apartment. None of these old hands could be attributed with musical genius – their talent had always lain in spotting a certain kind of musical potential. Their record label credits as producer and co-writer might simply indicate

their experience in sharpening a tune for the marketplace (if it wasn't just for fronting the money). Both label owners and rappers depended on skilled and versatile musicians who, like Mickey 'Guitar' Baker (a lynchpin of R&B recordings of the '50s), channelled their abilities as jazz musicians into arrangements which were as tough and as calculatedly direct as they were elementary. In the early days of rap on wax, it was musicians like Pumpkin at Enjoy and Jiggs Chase at Sugarhill who defined a new musical style. In its educated simplicity it was as New York as the rent party stride piano of James P. Johnson, the 'jump' band blues of Louis Jordan or the small-group disco of Chic.

Because most rappers started out with a DJ playing records for musical accompaniment (no live musicians), many rap records are based around the chords and bass lines of popular songs. In the early days they were instrumentals – Herbie Hancock or Bob James – and instrumental sections from vocal discs, but as it became standard to put the backing track of the topside song on the B side of 12-inch singles, so it became easier to make a rap over a hit tune. The practice was nothing new – there are plenty of seven-inch singles which do the same thing – but the length of the tracks on a 12-inch (sometimes over 10 minutes) and the width of the grooves, not to mention the fact that there's more *plastic* to get a hold of, made it easier to cut and scratch mix between two copies. To hear Grandmaster Flash cutting up Barbara Mason's story of living with a cross-dressing gay, 'Another Man', at a roots club like Broadway Inter-

17

national on 146th Street is an education. Like watching transformation effects in modern horror movies like *The Thing* or *The Howling*, the endless high-speed collageing of musical fragments leaves you breathless, searching for reference points. The beauty of dismembering hits lies in displacing familiarity. It gives the same thrill that visitors to Minton's Playhouse must have felt in the 1940s hearing Charlie Parker carve up standards like 'I Got Rhythm'. Parker wrote many tunes in this way, of course, including 'Ornithology', a bebop standard based on the chords of 'How High The Moon'. When Babs Gonzalez added words (as both Eddie Jefferson and King Pleasure did with 'Parker's Mood' and many other jazz tunes

and solos) he was creating one of the many Harlem-based antecedents of rap – jive lyrics superimposed on a dislocated version of a popular tune of the day.

The parallel also applies to reggae toasting, a form of music-making that was strongly influenced by American jive-talking radio disc jockeys and MCs. Although reggae was relatively unknown to most black Americans in the early '70s the links between New York and the Caribbean are strong. In the 1930s almost one-quarter of Harlem's residents were from the West Indies. For Grandmaster Flash, whose parents came from Barbados (his father collected records of both Caribbean music and American swing), it was the 'monstrous' sound system of Kool DJ Herc which dominated hip hop in its formative days. Herc came from Kingston, Jamaica, in 1967, when the toasting or DJ style of his own country was still fairly new. Giant speaker boxes were essential in the competitive world of Jamaican sound systems (sound-system battles were and still are central to the reggae scene) and Herc murdered the Bronx opposition with his volume and shattering frequency range.

Despite charismatic and influential figures like Flash or Zulu Nation leader DJ Afrika Bambaataa being meticulous in giving the lower-profile Herc a share of the limelight, the competitive spirit still flares among b boys (though seemingly less so among the b girls). For Bobby Robinson the contradiction is clear: 'Damn it, every group I meet is number one! Are there no number twos?'

Whatever the disagreements over lineage in the rap hall of fame or the history of hip hop, there is one thing on which all are agreed. 'Rap is nothing new', says Paul Winley. Rap's forebears stretch back through disco, street funk, radio DJs, Bo Diddley, the bebop singers, Cab Calloway, Pigmeat Markham, the tap dancers and comics, The Last Poets, Gil Scott-Heron, Muhammad Ali, acappella and doo-wop groups, ring games, skip-rope rhymes, prison and army songs, toasts, signifying and the dozens, all the way to the griots of Nigeria and the Gambia. No matter how far it penetrates into the twilight maze of Japanese video games and cool European electronics, its roots are still the deepest in all contemporary Afro-American music.

AFRIKA BAMBAATAA

JESSIE LOVE'S BOX

2. Doo-wop hip hop

Street culture has always been a good sales pitch for pushing vicarious thrills on the mass market. For a brief pause in all the phoney realism of *Flashdance*, the hyped-up dance movie of 1983, one of the sources for Jennifer Beal's overblown dance routines comes to life. Like a revisitation of Bill 'Bojangles' Robinson teaching Shirley Temple how to tap, the heroine takes in a few seconds of The Rock Steady Crew doing their robot routines in the park to the accompaniment of a huge portable tape box.

The music on the box is a hip-hop anthem – Jimmy Castor's 'It's Just Begun' – a hard dance track from 1972 which fuses one-chord riffing, a Sly Stone pop bridge, fuzz guitar, timbales breaks and an idealistic lyric applicable to any emergent movement, be it dance, music, politics or religion. It gives an impression of the breadth of Jimmy Castor's music and its reflection of the New York mix, encapsulating an involvement which dates back to the beginning of rock 'n' roll.

Hip hop is a peculiarly New York phenomenon in the same way that Jimmy Castor is a specifically New York musician. Born in 1943, he was an understudy for Frankie Lymon with The Teenagers by the age of 14, later developing an infectious dance music with a constant ear to the street and a capacity to absorb and introduce other influences. Early tracks like 'Block Party' are a link between the rent parties of the 1920s – functions at which Harlem stride pianists like Fats Waller, Willie the Lion Smith and James P. Johnson contested their skills – and the house parties and outdoor park gatherings which were the scene of hip-hop sound-system and rapping battles in the '70s. The break in 'Block Party' is a surprising eight-bar injection of Latin rhythm into the frantic 4/4 beat of the rest of the tune, a reminder that Jimmy was in the centre of the Latin Soul movement of the middle '60s. Other releases from the same period move from doo-wop and pop through to Motown-style stompers and

THE EVERYTHING MAN: JIMMY CASTOR

saxophone-guitar instrumentals with a pronounced white feel.

With songs like 'Hey Leroy, Your Mama's Callin' ' and later 'Say Leroy (The Creature From the Black Lagoon Is Your Father)', he introduced the insult contests known as the dozens as a dancefloor gimmick and threw yet another line back in time to the beginnings of Afro-American oral traditions and forward into the future to the embryonic rap scene.

It is hard to believe that the youthful Jimmy Castor's start in the music business came in an era notorious for its casualty rate, but he explains how a no-nonsense mother and a personal business sense have taken him from the streetcorner music of the '50s to hero status in the streetcorner music of the '70s and '80s:

Frankie Lymon, Leslie Uggams and myself went to the same elementary school – Public School 169 in Manhattan. It's upper Manhattan, Sugar Hill they call it. Washington Heights it's actually called. It was a primarily white school. It was really Polish and Irish up there then – it's all Spanish now, and black. Whenever there was an assembly or show they always called on us – I was the shyest. Leslie could always sing. I never understood what she was singing because she always sang legitimate songs when we were into doo-wop. Frankie was just a born – a natural – entertainer and I had to learn. I acquired it but I was a musician 'cos when I left that school I was chosen to attend the music classes in junior high school so Frankie went to that school and Mitch Miller picked Leslie up.

Frankie cut a record when he was 13 and I came running round to the grocery store. I said, 'You cut a *record*?' – that was a big thing. He had just cut 'Why Do Fools Fall In Love?' We would hang out together – Frankie was much more mature than I was. Frankie had ladies at the time that were 25 or 26 and he was 13. My mother was very strict – I had to be in at eight so I couldn't hang. I had a group called Jimmy Castor and the Juniors. I was writing a few songs and I wrote a song called 'I Promise To Remember' which Frankie heard and loved and took it to George Goldner and the rest is history.

With records like 'I Promise To Remember' and 'Why Do Fools Fall In Love?' on Goldner's Gee label, Frankie Lymon and the Teenagers were a huge influence on New York's aspiring young singers. If the money from their success encouraged Frankie into the high living which contributed to his premature death, Jimmy Castor used his composer royalties from 'I Promise To Remember' with some thoughts to the future:

That took me right out of the ghetto. I said, 'Mom, we're moving'. My first cheque was huge – it was a gold record. I eventually become Frankie's stand-in. Frankie was blossoming into a tremendous star — The Teenagers were the first supergroup. Herman [Santiago] and Jimmy [Merchant] still have the group. Sherman [Garnes] died. In fact we were gonna sit him up in the hospital bed – he wasn't dead – he was that sick – just to take the pictures. Joe Negroni died of a brain haemorrhage, and Frankie died, of course. I was very close with all of them 'cos we were going on the road together. I could only go weekends though – my mother made me stay in school.
     I went to music and art high school – that's where I learnt all my arranging but that's as far as it went. I was a stand-in. I wasn't on the same level because he had an ego and he wasn't easy to get along with. When he didn't show I was there. He had a better voice – what he did in

natural I did in falsetto. He tapped, then I took tap lessons from Cholly Atkins. Frankie got heavy into drugs – we had to lock him up a lot of times and keep him away from that. Once he got out he could get wasted.
     All through that period it was Richard Barrett who started everything. See, when you mention Bobby Robinson, Richard Barrett, Paul Winley – these people are the cornerstones of what we hear today.

Jimmy also sang with Lewis Lymon and the Teenchords, a group led by Frankie Lymon's brother and recorded by Bobby Robinson, and played saxophone with Dave 'Baby' Cortez (of 'Rinky Dink' fame). His own band worked at Paul Winley's Jazzland Ballroom on Harlem's 125th Street, playing tunes like 'Tequila' for social clubs, and later did the 99-cent dances run by Winley and disc jockey Jocko Henderson at the Audubon Ballroom. From watching or hearing records of Latin musicians like Tito Puente, Chano Pozo and Cal Tjader he learned to incorporate authentic Afro-Cuban rhythms and percussion, adding timbales to his vocal and multi-instrumental abilities.
     His music is fascinating, partly as a mini history of New York music and partly because of his tendency to recycle his own material in periodic updates. His witty use of jive talk in tracks like 'Dracula' from the 1976 *E Man Groovin'* album makes him a part of the rap music heritage, and in 1983 he recorded his own moralist rap, '(Tellin' On) The Devil', alongside a re-recording of

THE FORCE MDS: TRISCO, MERCURY, TCD AND JESSIE

'It's Just Begun', made in deference to its celebrity status on the hip-hop scene.

'It's Just Begun' is occasionally used by Staten Island group The Force MDs as entrance music for their show. Whatever should happen to this group in the future – fame, oblivion or any other of the limited choices available – their career up until their first record is an uncanny echo of Jimmy Castor's. With an average age of about 20, they are able to combine rapping and breakdancing with formation steps and vocal harmony which draws from doo-wop, acappella, '60s Motown, The Jackson Five, The Persuasions, television theme tunes and commercials. They can create an orchestrated human drum machine with their combined voices and do impressions ranging from Elvis Presley and Michael Jackson to the gravel-voiced Mr T. Like

Jimmy Castor before them, they encapsulate over 30 years of Afro-American music with a style that unconsciously includes elements from many decades further back. TCD, one of the most prolific talkers of the group, traces their saga:

> We started in Staten Island. We were called the LDs at first. This was around 1972 – little kids singing. We were imitating The Jackson Five like all the other groups but we sounded exactly like them. We just sung in the streets – songs to make people happy around the neighbourhood. Any time they wanted to be happy they'd come and knock on our doors and we'd come out singing! We started to do our own thing. One of our brothers became a Muslim. Another one moved away, so it was just us three left. We was working on harmony – getting everything right – going on Broadway and 42nd. So we bumped into Trisco and Mercury. Mercury was like a conjunction with Stevie D, my brother. They used to do a rap thing.

Stevie D and Mercury oblige with a high-powered rap that swaps back and forth between them and ends up with an inspired borrowing of the melody line from 'Santa Claus Is Coming To Town'. TCD continues the story:

> We used to entertain on the Staten Island ferry boat. People liked us a lot. What really got us known was rapping – we rapped in a lot of parts of New York, Jersey and Connecticut. People in Connecticut, when they hear these guys rap they'd make a tape and the tape would travel all the way down south – California, Florida. It just travels everywhere where that person goes. It goes in the army. The guys who used to listen to it recruit into the army and take the tapes with them.

From their classic acappella streetcorner origins The Force MDs expanded their repertoire by working with a DJ named Dr Rock who used all the scratching and cutting techniques developed in the south and west Bronx.

Scratching in its early form arose out of the normal technique of cueing a record: you move the record manually with the needle in the groove and listen for the right starting point on a headphone. One turntable is used for cueing while the other is playing a record through the main loudspeakers. DJs like Grandmaster Flash began experimenting by switching the mixer from the headphones to the speakers for isolated brass-section chords and drum slaps – augmenting the record that was already playing on the other turntable – and then learned how to use a record percussively by quickly moving it back and forth over the same chord or beat.

Both the showiness and gimmicky sound potential of this kind of creative mixing have supplemented The Force MDs' previously self-contained act. Scratching is used as a witty sound effect for the group's adaptation of TV themes from *The Brady Bunch*, *The Addams Family* and *F Troop*; it also extends into acrobatics and sleight-of-

THE FORCE MDs: TCD AND STEVIE D

hand trickery, as Mercury explains:

> He can cut up with his elbows, his chin, his feet, with handcuffs on, blindfolded. He can make beats with just one turntable. He's a mastermind on turntables. He can put the turntables on the floor and scratch with his feet . . . We have a back-up DJ. His name is Dr Shock – this guy, he goes crazy when it comes to scratching. He can take a record and put a cup underneath it – play the record backwards with the needle upside down and make scratching. He can scratch a record till it has a hole in it.

Much to the rest of the group's amusement, Mercury can reproduce most of Rock and Shock's sounds with his mouth; if the electricity gives out, then this group, along with many others like it, has the pedigree to carry on and hold the clientele.

In 1947, when the American folk-music collector Alan Lomax took a portable tape recorder (the first to appear on the market) into the horrific conditions of the Mississippi State Penitentiary, he recorded black acappella vocal music, which he claimed demonstrated 'that true African polyphony and poly-rhythm have somehow survived in the Southern US until our own epoch' (sleevenotes to *Negro Prison Songs*, Tradition Records reissue LP TLP 1020). The city can be a prison, too, and in many ways the formative neighbourhood vocalising of The Force MDs is part of a continuum that reaches back not just to the days when a 13-year-old Jimmy Castor was singing in school (hoping to make enough money to escape the ghetto) but even further to the group vocalising that made forced labour more bearable in prisons and plantations.

If the association seems far fetched, it's partly because the imagery has changed so dramatically – the mythological tricksters and heroes are replaced by electronic-age superheroes recruited from kung fu, karate, science fiction and blaxploitation movies, re-run television series, video games, comic books and advertising. The central heroes, of course, are the rappers themselves, aggressively claiming respect (as a means of finding self respect) with the same expertise in verbal improvisation as that wielded by streetcorner orators, stand-up comics, testifying preachers and vernacular poets for generations.

3. African jive

I float like a butterfly, sting like a bee,
There ain't no motherfucker than can rap
* like me*
                  'CC Crew Rap' by CC Crew
                  (Golden Flamingo Records)

In 1964 the white world was finding it hard to understand a young black boxer named Cassius Clay. Bill McDonald, the promoter of his first crack at Sonny Liston's world heavyweight title, and trainer Angelo Dundee, were failing to appreciate his reasons for associating with Elijah Muhammad and Malcolm X. The Nation of Islam was bad news in the white-run fight game. Those less close to the Clay camp were mystified by his seemingly hysterical behaviour and his rap poetry, the infuriating rhymes which predicted the demise of his opponents: 'Sonny Liston is great/But he'll fall in eight.'

The unfortunate Liston had a better idea of what was going on. An ex-badman, he was well aware that Clay (at the time secretly known as Cassius X but later known to the world as Muhammad Ali), along with his personal shaman, Drew Bundini Fastblack Brown, was engaged in a campaign to shame him into defeat before the first bell. Ali was prepared to take the campaign to Liston's home and remind his well-heeled white neighbours of their new resident's background in the black ghetto. History records that Liston was humiliated twice by Ali. Fight fans with a white complexion would have been less puzzled by the young braggard whipping the awesome monster if they had known something of black street culture.

The Clay versus Liston scenario has a storyline reminiscent of the famous black narrative poem called 'Signifying Monkey'. The monkey is a trickster who taunts the lion, despite its size and strength, and outwits it with verbal skill:

There hadn't been no shift for quite a bit
so the Monkey thought he'd start some of
* his signifying shit.*
It was one bright summer day
the Monkey told the Lion, 'There's a big
* bad burly motherfucker livin' down*
* your way.'*
He said, 'You know your mother that you
* love so dear?*
Said anybody can have her for a ten-cent
* glass a beer.'*

These kind of narrative poems are called toasts. They are rhyming stories, often lengthy, which are told mostly amongst men. Violent, scatalogical, obscene, misogynist, they have been used for decades to while away time in situations of enforced boredom, whether prison, armed service or streetcorner life. Bruce Jackson, who has made extensive studies of toasts and prison songs, has written:

There is much time to kill in county jails and little to do with that time, and a great portion of the population in county jails is lower-class black (they are the people without money to pay a bondsman for freedom before trial or who must serve jail time because they lack money to pay a fine).

Toasts, like most oral folk traditions, have become absorbed into commercial entertainment, albeit in a censored form. 'Stackolee', a badman figure familiar from many blues and ballads performed by both black and white musicians, was resurrected by Lloyd Price in 1958 as 'Stagger Lee' for a chart-topping hit and was revived for another shoot-out by The Isley Brothers in 1963. A year later, Rufus Thomas, a

remarkable man whose career stretched right back to the medicine-show era, released a tune called 'Jump Back' on Stax. Though the sound is typical of the bluesy soul of the time – uptempo and rough, with cutting saxophone and guitar breaks – the verses of the song date back at least as far as nineteenth-century minstrel shows; a children's line-game song, 'Mary Mack' quoted by Harold Courlander in his book *Negro Folk Music*, has almost identical words:

> *I went to the river, river, river,*
> *And I couldn't get across, across, across,*
> *And I paid five dollars, dollars, dollars,*
> *For the old grey horse, horse, horse.*

Thomas used another verse from 'Mary Mack' for his 'Walking the Dog', another revival, this time of a dance that was around in the early 1900s. Although parts of 'Jump Back' had also been collected as a work-song, they were first made famous by Thomas Rice, a white dancer who performed blackface and whose stage name was Daddy 'Jim Crow' Rice. The legend goes that Rice had the good fortune to see a black slave named after his owner, Jim Crow, doing a song and dance with a great potential for the stage. Rice stole the idea, added some verses and by the end of the 1820s had a craze going for himself, not only through America but also as far away as England and Ireland.

Rufus Thomas's reappropriation of 'Jump Jim Crow' was poetic justice. Working as a tapdancer, scat singer and all-round entertainer with the Rabbit Foot Minstrels in the 1930s, he felt the effects of racism both on and off stage.

For 'Jody's Got Your Girl and Gone', Johnny Taylor (a singer who, like Rufus Thomas, recorded for Stax) revived Jody, a character also known in toasts as Joe the Grinder. Jody's exploits, sung or narrated in prison or the army, symbolised the fear that somebody might be stealing your lover back home. Although the spoken toast fell into decline, the song version of the story – often about G.I. Joe returning from the war and finding Jody in bed with his wife – was still being sung in army camps in the 1970s, and Johnny Taylor's reworking is a testament to the longevity of the story's potency.

The cross talk between popular entertainment drawn back into folklore and mists-of-time traditions facelifted for contemporary styles can make it impossible to pinpoint origins. A toast collected by Bruce Jackson on Wynne Prison Farm in Texas in 1966 – 'Ups On the Farm' – and said by Jackson to be 'the only toast I've heard that expressly deals with black/white problems' was, in fact, part of Butterbeans and Susie's repertoire. Butterbeans and Susie were a husband and wife comedy singing/dancing act whose recordings spanned 40 years, from 1922 to 1962, and they formed part of a venerable tradition of comedy teams whose popularity was established on the TOBA (Theater Owner's Booking Association) black vaudeville circuit. A later team, Moke and Poke, were said by Marshall and Jean Stearns in *Jazz Dance* to 'conduct their dialogue in hip rhymes. "We're Moke and Poke, it ain't no joke, that's all she wrote, the pencil broke."'

Jazz Dance also notes the way in which the comedy dance teams developed a razor-sharp satirical humour aimed at and for black audiences, making the point that:

One of its sources was probably the West African song of allusion (where the subject pays the singer *not* to sing about him), reinterpreted in the West Indies as the political calypso, in New Orleans as the 'signifying' song, and in the South generally as 'the dozens'.

Although at least some of the origins of this rich material could be traced to the Bible or British folk songs, it had clear roots in West Africa. Ruth Finnegan, in her book *Oral Literature in Africa*, describes how poetry and music could function as a social weapon:

Lampoons are not only used between groups but can also be a means of communicating and expressing personal enmity between hostile individuals. We hear of Galla abusive poems, for instance, while among the Yoruba when two women have quarrelled they sometimes vent their enmity by singing at each other, especially in situations – like the laundry place – when other women will hear. Abusive songs against ordinary individuals are also sometimes directly used as a means of social pressure, enforcing the will of public opinion.

In the savannah belt of West Africa this social pressure is embodied by the caste of musicians known as griots. The griot is a professional singer, in the past often associated with a village but now an increasingly independent 'gun for hire', who combines the functions of living history book and newspaper with vocal and instrumental virtuosity. According to Paul Oliver in his book *Savannah Syncopators*,

> though he has to know many traditional songs without error, he must also have the ability to extemporise on current events, chance incidents and the passing scene. His wit can be devastating and his knowledge of local history formidable.

Although they are popularly known as praise singers, griots might combine appreciation of a rich employer with gossip and satire or turn their vocal expertise into an attack on the politically powerful or the financially stingy.

If the hip-hop message and protest rappers had an ancestry in the savannah griots, the Bronx braggers, boasters and verbal abusers are children of the black American word games known as signifying and the dozens. During the late 1950s and early '60s a folklore student named Roger D. Abrahams collected tape recordings of many toasts, jokes and verbal contests in the predominantly black area of Camingerly, Philadelphia, where he lived. In his book *Deep Down In the Jungle* he explains the importance of 'good talkers' in Afro-American society, and concentrates particularly on the crucial role of talking skills in male society:

> Verbal contest accounts for a large portion of the talk between members of this group. Proverbs, turns of phrases, jokes, almost any manner of discourse is used, not for purposes of discursive communication but as weapons in verbal battle. Any gathering of the men customarily turns into 'sounding', a teasing or boasting session.

Abrahams found this kind of teasing among children who used 'catches' to trick each other:

Say 'washing machine'.
'Washing machine.'

DESERT GRIOTS FROM SOKOTO, NORTHERN NIGERIA *Photo: Jeremy Marre*

DISCO FEVER

I'll bet you five dollars your drawers ain't clean.

As the participants got older so the contests got more serious – sounding or the dozens could lead to serious fights among adults. The dozens contests were generally between boys and men from the ages of 16 to 26 – a semi-ritualised battle of words which batted insults back and forth between the players until one or the other found the going too heavy. The insults could be a direct personal attack but were more frequently aimed at the opponent's family and in particular his mother. According to linguist William Labov, who studied these verbal shoot-outs in Harlem in the 1960s, 'In New York, "the dozens" seems to be even more specialised, referring to rhymed couplets of the form:

I don't play the dozens, the dozens ain't my game
But the way I fucked your mama is a god damn shame.'

Working with teenage clubs like the Jets and the Cobras, Labov came across poetic insults like, 'Your mother play dice with the midnight mice', and more elaborate exchanges which are like fully developed comedy routines:

Boot: Hey! I went up Money house and I walked in Money house, I say, I wanted to sit down, and then, you know a roach jumped up and said, 'Sorry, this seat is taken.'
Roger: I went in David house, I saw the roaches walking round in combat boots.

The distance between talking rough with the dozens on the streets and moving it inside a roots club like Disco Fever with some beats for dancing is very small. It leads to the contradictions of Melle Mel, lyricist for the Furious Five, onstage in his ultramacho metal warrior outfit trying to preach convincingly for an end to machismo and a beginning to peaceful co-existence.

Out among the grown-ups the dozens

TIMES SQUARE CLIFFHANGER

thrive in the 'dirty party' genre with a host of little-known comedians. You can also find Johnny Otis with Snatch and the Poontangs, the very funny Redd Foxx, the very unfunny Rudy Ray Moore whose record covers scale the greatest heights of porno-kitsch, and the notorious Blowfly. Blowfly, the unacceptable face of rap, is the pseudonym of Miami singer/producer Clarence Reid (the man who co-wrote 'Clean Up Woman' with Little Beaver for Betty Wright and released it on the Alston label).

One of the clearest links between present-day rappers and the rich vein of tall tales, tricksters, boasts and insults is Bo Diddley. Describing the type of rapping he was doing when he started out, Mr Biggs of Soul Sonic Force recollects that, 'we used to call it a Bo Diddley syndrome when we used to brag amongst ourselves'. Bo is the bragger *par excellence* – his street-talk boasts were originally combined with a unique Afro-Latin sound of maraccas, floor tom toms played by drummer Frank Kirkland and his own customised and distinctly weird guitar. His first single, recorded in 1955 for Chess Records in Chicago, was a double-sided punch on the nose for modesty – on the A side the ultimate macho anthem 'I'm a Man' and on the B side Diddley's personal plaudit called, aptly enough, 'Bo Diddley'.

Many of his later songs used material from toasts and the dozens: 'Who Do You Love', the story of a satanic badman who wears a cobra snake for a necktie, is like a toast in itself, using lines almost identical to Stackolee's 'I'm a bad motherfucker, that's why I don't mind dying'. Other songs use familiar themes – 'The Story of Bo Diddley' with its full-grown baby playing a gold guitar, 'Run Diddley Daddy' and its rumble-in-the-jungle tall tale and 'Say Man', a record which grew out of Bo and maracca player Jerome trading the dozens in the studio. Put down on tape with some judicious editing, it became one of Bo's biggest hits, striking back at the record company notion that too much black content keeps records out of the charts.

'Say Man' is the great-grandfather of the rap attack. The anonymous Ronnie Gee prepares the crowd for his 'Raptivity', a tall tale of microphone battles that run deep in the night leaving heart attacks in their wake: 'Warning – the surgeon general of chilltown New York has determined that the sounds you are about to hear can be devastating to your ear-ear-ear-ear-ear.'

SAY MAN: BO DIDDLEY, THE DUCHESS, AND JEROME
Photo: courtesy of Charlie Gillett

4. Beat bop

On a summer afternoon in 1979 at Columbia University in the middle of Harlem, Milford Graves is on stage drumming with his long-term associate, saxophonist Hugh Glover, and Japanese trumpeter Toshinori Kondo. The event is the Third Annual Children of the Sun concert with Baba Chief Bey, the Afrikan Poetry Theatre Ensemble and other guests. Strictly speaking, Milford is not on the stage; for a time he moves out into the audience with two long poles, speaking in strange tongues before getting back on the platform to launch into another whirlwind drum dialogue with Glover. His vocalising, an astonishing flow of percussive syllables, could be seen as one of the furthest outposts of the scat tradition – represented at the other pole by great jazz singers like Louis Armstrong, Ella Fitzgerald and Betty Carter.

For singers like these (including Milford Graves) scat is a way of using the voice as a pure instrument, but there is another tradition of scatting which, like rap, took street slang and transformed it into a musical style. Cabell 'Cab' Calloway is one of the cornerstones of jive scat, the author of a number of books including *The New Cab Calloway's Hepster's Dictionary*, and a bandleader in New York from 1930 to 1948. Cab appears in *Stormy Weather* (the 1943 equivalent of *Wildstyle* or *Beat Street*), a film loosely constructed around the great tapdancer Bill 'Bojangles' Robinson. Alongside Robinson was an all black cast – Lena Horne, Fats Waller, one of the original New York rappers with his hilarious jive disruptions of songs, and a host of eccentric dancers (rubber face antics), flash dancers and tapdancers. In the middle of this firework display of '40s black talent Cab Calloway is still a shock. Resplendent in a capacious zoot suit with chain and long greased hair, he glides across the stage in a move that pre-dates moonwalking by 40 years.

Cab was one of the out-front bandleaders, a conductor who sang, danced and provided a focal point for the audience. Working at the famous Cotton Club on 142nd and Lennox Avenue, the nightspot where rich whites came to indulge their fantasies about the noble savage, Calloway mixed up call-and-response scatting (on 'Zah Zuh Zah' Cab sings variants on the title and the audience and orchestra repeat whatever new outrage he comes up with), jive lyrics with coded references to drugs ('Kicking the Gong Around' or 'Viper's Drag'), or chat and scat talkovers like 'Harlem Camp Meeting' with the immortal lines, 'That's it, son, your credit for this sermon I'm gonna give you here. Look out now – skipndigipipndibobopakoodoot', as the clarinet player finishes his solo.

This type of commentary could work both ways. There was also a strong tradition of the instrumentalists trying to discourage the singer with half-concealed sarcasm sent out at just enough volume to cross the footlights. Bandleaders like Cab Calloway occupied a role somewhere between the piano-playing leaders like Duke Ellington and Count Basie and the masters of ceremonies who used jive talk and rhyming couplets to introduce the acts – one of the strongest links with hip hop, which started out with rappers talking on the microphone about the skill of the disc jockey. MCs developed their own line of patter to keep a show rolling. Ernie 'Bubbles' Whitman, also known as 'the stomach that walked like a man', was an MC who worked for Billy Eckstine. He was given to flights of fancy on the lines of:

Yessirree, send me that ballad from Dallas. I'm floating on a swoonbeam. And now to keep the downbeat bouncing right along, here's a zootful snootful called 'Mr Chips', as it is fleeced and released by Billy Eckstine and his trilly tune-tossers. Toss it, Billy, toss it!

Another man with a sharp line in introductions was Slim Gaillard who could be heard from the late 1930s right up until the present prefacing songs with lead-ins in the fashion of: 'We'd like to get together and play a little special arrangement on this new opus, a little number titled "Minuet oh vouty laho reetie o dingo reenie mo in oh vouty sow routie mo oh scoodly reenie mo".' Slim began as a tapdancing guitarist and progressed from that semi-impossibility to playing piano with the backs of his hands and reinterpreting standards with a language and logic all his own. The language was called vout and it made Gaillard into one of the key figures of 1940s jive hipsterism. His musical style would cause Afrika Bambaataa to double take – the easy-going bebop with its fractured vout lyrics could be quick-cut at the drop of a bagel into a few bars of Latin with some Spanish commercials or a sudden skid on the tempo for a dash of Billy Eckstine. The high priest of vout can be seen in the 1942 movie *Hellzapoppin* playing accompaniment for the wildest breakdancing ever seen on film. Slim, along with other hepcats like Harry 'The Hipster' Gibson and Leo Watson, was turning language inside out on the fringes of bebop.

Eddie Jefferson was probably the first of the bebop-era jazz singers to take jazz solos or tunes like Coleman Hawkins's 'Body and Soul' and turn them into vocal improvisations. Jefferson was inspired by the apparently bottomless well of source material in jazz dance and evolved his style by singing over records in the late '30s. His versions of Charlie Parker tunes like 'Parker's Mood' were languid excursions into hip phrasing and phraseology, following up lines of more pauses than words with triple-time tongue-twisters. Jefferson's initiative was taken up by a singer named Clarence Beeks, better known as King Pleasure. Pleasure's vocalmentals versioned jazz solos, taking all the slurs, smears and surges of saxophonists Charlie Parker and Lester Young with their tunes 'Jumping With Symphony Sid' or 'Parker's Mood'.

Another Parker tune, 'Ornithology', based on the chords of 'How High the Moon', was the starting-off point for two of the hippest of hepster anthems – the great

Babs Gonzalez's 'Ornithology' and 'Sugar Ray' (a song about one of the most popular black boxers of all time – Sugar Ray Robinson). Babs was among the cleverest at fitting strings of words around the convoluted Parker melodies while still sounding cool.

In his autobiography *To Be Or Not To Bop*, Dizzy Gillespie writes:

> We added some colorful and creative concepts to the English language, but I can't think of any word besides bebop that I actually invented. Daddy-O Daylie, a disc jockey in Chicago, originated much more of the hip language during our era than I did.

Daddy-O Daylie was one of a number of black radio DJs who from the 1940s until the 1960s lit up the airwaves of America with their hepcat jive – bringing back the live feel to recorded music. One of the first black radio jocks, Dr Hep Cat, shook up listeners to KVET in Austin, Texas, with his crazy couplets:

> *If you want to hip to the tip and bop to the top*
> *You get some mad threads that just won't stop*

Dr Hep Cat's real name was Lavada Durst. He also played piano and sang – recording songs such as 'Hepcat's Boogie' – and in 1953 he published his own hepcat's dictionary, *The Jives of Dr Hep Cat*. In New Orleans, the first black disc jockey was Vernon Winslow, known as Dr Daddy-O, broadcasting for WWEZ in 1949 with his show 'Jivin' with Jax'. Dr Daddy-O's story is a case history in racism. Refused a broadcasting job because of his colour, he was offered the task of training a white announcer to talk black. Winslow organised the whole show for WJMR, writing the script, choosing the records, teaching the DJ how to talk and even selecting a name for him – Poppa Stoppa. In an interview in *Wavelength* magazine, he talks about the origin of the name.

> Poppa Stoppa came out of that rhyme-rap that the people in the street were using. That's what the ghetto produced. The people were trying to mystify outsiders. It became a unique identity and they were proud of it. So I began writing my script in that language. 'Look at your gold tooth in a telephone booth, Ruth – wham bam, thank you, man.' I had a penchant for alliteration.

Eventually, with the 'Jam, Jive and Gumbo' show becoming the most popular shown on WJMR, Winslow grabbed the opportunity to read his own script over the air. He was fired immediately. Six months later he was offered a job by the Jackson Brewing Company as a disc jockey and advertising consultant for Jax beer. Recording his shows in Cosimo Matassa's studio to avoid having to ride the freight elevator at the New Orleans Hotel where the shows were broadcast (another of the destructive humiliations of racism at the time), his show created havoc in radio. Soon everybody had their own jive-talking jock, each with an imitative name like Jack the Cat, Okey

Dokey, Momma Stoppa and Ernie the Whip.

Dr Daddy-O started by playing jazz but was soon playing the new R&B sound of Professor Longhair and Roy Brown. With the coming of hard rhythm and blues and rock 'n' roll, the jiving jocks found a new power: machine-gun poets like Georgie Woods (the guy with the goods), Maurice 'Hotrod' Hulbert from Baltimore, Sonny Hopson on WDAS, Clarence Heyman who took over the Poppa Stoppa title in New Orleans, Dr Jive (Tommy Smalls) and one of the best-known of them all – Douglas 'Jocko' Henderson, the ace from space with his '1280 Rocket' show. Roger Abrahams quotes one of his raps in *Deep Down in the Jungle*:

> *Be, bebop*
> *This is your Jock*
> *Back on the scene*
> *With a record machine*
> *Saying 'Hoo-popsie-doo,*
> *How do you do?'*
> *When you up, you up,*
> *And when you down, you down,*
> *And when you mess with Jock*
> *You upside down*

One of Jocko's favourite expressions was 'great gugga mugga shooga booga', a catchy phrase familiar to collectors of Jamaican ska records. 'The Great Wuga Wuga' by Sir Lord Comic is a fine example of the way in which radio jive was adapted for Jamaican sound-system music. On collecting trips to the States, searching out R&B records for his sound systems back home, Jamaican producer Coxsone Dodd was impressed enough with radio DJs like Jocko to encourage his own top DJ, Count Machouki, to try out the same techniques. In the hot-house competition of the sound systems the idea was rapidly picked up by rivals, eventually to appear on records like Sir Lord Comic's 'Ska-ing West' from 1965: 'Come on you cats, get hep, we're going west'. Machouki and Sir Lord Comic, along with U Roy who recorded a DJ record called 'Your Ace From Space', King Stitt and other lesser-known DJs, developed the Jamaican style of toasting – at first in a similar fashion to the American radio DJs but rapidly transforming it into the form taken on by toasters like Big Youth and Dennis Alcapone through to Eek A Mouse and Yellowman. With his MC crew the Herculoids, the Jamaican-born hip-hop break mixer Kool DJ Herc started a movement which recycled the creativity of black American jive jocks back into the USA – a circle which closed with the recording studio collaboration of Yellowman with Afrika Bambaataa.

Although DJs like Jocko and Dr Jive had many white listeners and imitators (it was white jive jocks like Alan Freed who were crucial in crossing black R&B and doo-wop over to a white audience, and another self-confessed imitator of the black DJ style, Wolfman Jack, is still going strong with his syndicated shows), it was in the black community that their position was strongest. Jocko, Dr Jive and Rocky G began headlining the rhythm and blues shows at The Apollo Theatre (Jocko was first introduced to Apollo owner Bobby Schiffman by

THE APOLLO THEATRE, 125TH STREET

Bobby Robinson) along with jocks like Frankie Crocker and Eddie O'Jay, the man who gave The O'Jays their name. At other times it was the comedians who were required to introduce the shows.

'The first person I really heard do it was Pigmeat Markham. That was the first rap record I ever heard – on a record my father had.' A surprising statement from someone as young as The Fearless Four's Mike C, considering that Pigmeat introduced the routine that Mike is talking about, 'Heah Come De Judge', to the Alhambra Theatre in New York in 1929. He was still turning up new angles on the 'Judge' routine in the '60s, with hip soul versions on Chess Records like 'Sock It To 'Em Judge' (by

then aged around 60) and, as the Mighty Mike C says, they are rap records before rap records existed.

Jackie 'Moms' Mabley with her folksy monologues, Timmie 'Clark Dark' Rogers (the man who made a stand against black-face for black comedians), Scoey Mitchlll, Flip Wilson, Nipsey Russell, the very hip Redd Foxx, Richard Pryor and latterly Eddie Murphy are a small selection of the black comedians whose routines are part of the background to rap. In an extraordinary forerunner of the message rap of the 1980s, Ray Scott recorded a mock sermon monologue set to music which was based on a Redd Foxx routine – probably one of the most vitriolic diatribes ever put on a disc. Called 'The Prayer', it was a savagely, lovingly detailed wish-fulfilment fantasy about all the gruesome deaths that might befall the racist governor George Wallace. After Wallace's death, Scott hopes that 14 possums suffering from hydrophobia will break into his casket and eat enough of him to make him look like a gorilla sucking hot Chinese mustard. If all that isn't enough, then the worst fate would be to wake up black.

It was like a political version of the finely detailed voodoo madness of another performer who worked a thin line between comedy and deadly serious rhythm and blues – Screamin' Jay Hawkins. A crazed monologue like 'Alligator Wine' could still give the hip hoppers a run for their money.

Screamin' Jay Hawkins was at the apex of the kind of music that struck terror into the hearts of white American parents in the 1950s – the idea of their children pressing

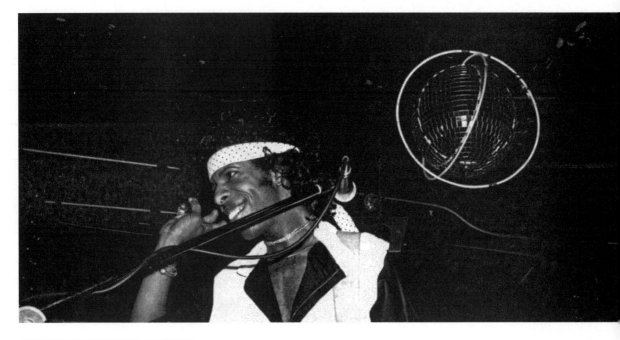

YOU CAUGHT ME SMILING: SLY STONE

pink ears to the loudspeaker of a radio that was blasting out this blatantly sexual and demonic delirium was too much to bear. The federal payola investigations of 1959–60 helped put paid to it all. One of the job opportunities for ex-radio jocks in the '60s was dance instruction discs – another of the sources of rap's 'throw your hands in the air' formulae. Radio DJs were expert in telling people what to do, so the dance instruction genre came easily to them. Rodney Jones had 'R&B Time' ('hit it to the left – back to the right'); Rufus Thomas, who was a DJ on WDIA in Memphis, was the doyen of dance crazies with his Dogs, Penguins, Robots and Chickens; Sly Stone worked as a DJ on San Francisco radio as well as producing

and writing dance discs for Bobby Freeman ('C'mon and Swim'), and Frankie Crocker, whose chequered career rejoiced under names like 'Loveman', 'Black Satin' and 'Hollywood', took a credit on Turbo Records's dance tune 'Ton of Dynamite' – a slight reworking of Willie and the Mighty Magnificents' 'Funky 8 Corners', originally released on All Platinum. After being indicted on payola charges in 1976, Crocker used his enforced sabbatical from New York radio to produce records like 'Love In C Minor' for Casablanca Records. Strictly speaking, they weren't dance instruction discs (more Barry White groaners) but they were hardcore disco records (and absolutely unlistenable now).

Plenty of far superior funk and disco records kept alive a tradition of street slang, radio jive and dance calling with party vocals, dancefloor chants and talkovers – 'Black Water Gold (Pearl)' by African Music Machine, 'Jungle Fever' by Chakachas, 'Get On Down' by East Harlem Bus Stop, 'Fruitman' and 'Spirit of the Boogie' by Kool and the Gang, 'Mango Meat' and 'Ali Bom-Ba-Ye' by Mandrill (the rope-a-dope song), 'Do It 'Til You're Satisifed' by B.T. Express, 'O-Wa' by Babatunde Olatunji, 'Rap On Mr D.J.' by Hamilton Bohannon, 'Ali Shuffle' by Alvin Cash and literally hundreds more from the JBs, The Meters, The Ohio Players, War, Fatback, the George Clinton funk empire and Bootsy's Rubber Band all the way to the present with Washington Go-Go groups like Chuck Brown and the Soul Searchers and Trouble Funk or the New York hip hop meets electro-Afro funk of Shango.

George Clinton, in particular, connects strongly with the radio jive DJs – tracks like 'Chocolate City', 'P. Funk (Wants to get funked up)', 'You Shouldn't-Nuf Bit Fish', 'Atomic Dog', 'Loopzilla' and 'Mr Wiggles' are all inspired by radio jocks; 'Mr Wiggles' from *Motor Booty Affair* was rapped by Clinton in the guise of an underwater disc jockey called Mr Wiggles the Worm who quotes freely from Jocko Henderson. It was a natural for George to make his own hip-hop rap records, and 'Dog Talk' by K-9 Corps (based on the rhythm of 'Atomic Dog') and 'Nubian Nut' were both funny

GEORGE CLINTON P FUNKS THE RITZ

42

and funky, spanning three and a half decades of Afro-American music creativity with the essence of R&B radio, '80s electronics and an update of the cosmic orchestra concept of Sun Ra. The Afro-Saturnian swing of Ra and his Arkestra with its chants of 'sign up for Outer Spaceways Incorporated' is not *so* very far from 'one nation under a groove'. The Jonzun Crew certainly saw the connection when they recorded 'Space Is the Place' (the title of a 1973 Sun Ra album on Blue Thumb) and thanked Mr Ra on the sleeve of their *Lost In Space* LP.

Also cruising the ether was Captain Sky, an ex-radio jock from Chicago heavily inspired by the P. Funk Nation. The Captain underlined the radio rap connection with his 'Don't Touch That Dial' (a phrase from a thousand and one Clinton songs) and 'Station Brake', a rap broadcast directly from Station WSKY on a day when nothing really happened. Captain Sky was just one of the mothership commanders and space wanderers whose mission lay in taking *Star Trek* to the stage. Beaming down on New York was Captain Rock, the figurehead of a rap project put together by The Fantastic Aleems (who recorded their own mystic disco album on Prelude in 1977 as Prana People) and Dr Jeckyl and Mr Hyde. Captain Rock was obviously able to buy George Clinton albums in deep space because his 'Cosmic Glide' on Nia Records had all the signs of the Mothership Connection.

Station WSKY may not have much happening but on Gary Byrd's phone-in/chat show on WLIB there's plenty going on. When it comes to black culture and politics, there is so much hidden from view or swept

DON'T TOUCH THAT DIAL: CAPTAIN SKY

GARY BYRD AT W.L.I.B.

under history's carpet that 24-hour chat shows would be a mere scratch on the surface. Gary began his career in the middle '60s at the age of 17, broadcasting on station WUFO in his home town of Buffalo. Fascinated by the raps of Jocko and 'Hotrod' Hulbert, he tried out one of his own, only to be told that he would lose his job if he did it again. Raps were a dirty word by that time in American radio history. Moving to New York, he was the youngest DJ in the city, and by the early '70s he was creating social protest mastermixes from tracks by War and The Temptations combined with sound effects. He also moved into music-making with his group The Gary Byrd Experience (named after The Jimi Hendrix Experience) and made records produced by the everywhere/everything man, Jimmy Castor. His radio rapping experience became useful when he developed a social programme researching literacy and taking presentations into schools in New York and New Jersey:

We found that the kids were processing information faster than the school system was able to project it. What was actually happening was that the kids were bored because they were so electronically conditioned by radio and television to get their information that when the teacher walked into the classroom the teacher was completely unaware that what they were in fact giving was a performance. At the end of 10 minutes the kids' attention would wane and the teacher would wonder what happened. The 10-minute wane was having been conditioned by

television for the commercial interruption.

We were knee deep in heavy-duty disco fever and I was trying to figure out some way to do something to work with the schools to improve reading levels. My not being an 'educator' but more like a motivator I figured that if you could at least motivate kids to be interested enough in reading that's the first step.

What we did was hook up this programme, which I was doing in rap – which is the way I always perform – and we hooked it into recording artists, the people they admired most. The Jacksons and Muhammad Ali, who, most of them, because they see them in highly verbal but usually memorised improvisational circumstances, don't really see anything around them that indicates that there is any need to read anything.

We had shots of all the different artists and I'd do raps and show them inside of the raps what has happening with each individual on the outside of what they saw. So, in other words, you had to understand that Michael Jackson didn't just walk into the studio and start singing the tune! 'So they write those songs?' You get that kind of reaction. 'Oh, so Michael reads it, then he learns it. Oh. Ahh.' A lot of surprise there.

Through his work in schools Gary also found that many American blacks were unaware that the Nile civilisation was a part of black history. His raps had already surfaced to a small extent on Stevie Wonder's 'Black Man' from the *Songs In the Key of Life* album. The last part of the song is a question and answer, call and response session from the Al Fann Theatrical Ensemble in Harlem with Gary Byrd as one of the teachers. In 1979 he started work on a rap called 'The Crown', about the black heritage from Egypt to West Africa to Malcolm X, Langston Hughes, Ali, Ella and Joe Louis. With music by Stevie Wonder, it was a tremendously effective use of rap which brought together much of its roots tradition and its potential.

Rap, hip-hop style, came onto the radio courtesy of Mr Magic, whose first show – 'Mr Magic's Rap Attack' – went on the air in 1979 on station WHBI, a small station in New Jersey on which you buy your own time and then sell your own commercials. This was the same station on which The World's Famous Supreme Team, the duo that can be heard on Malcolm McLaren's *Duck Rock* album (phone-in rapping over T-Ski Valley's 'Catch The Beat'), hosted their own show. With their single, 'Hey D.J.', The Supreme Team joined the long line of radio jocks and rappers who have graduated from playing other people's records to making their own. There is also a tradition of recording homages to disc jockeys. In the same spirit as Bobby Day's 'Rockin' Robin' (a 1958 tribute to a radio jock) the Brooklyn group Whodini released 'Magic's Wand' to salute Mr Magic, the jock from their own borough whose Rap Attack show had progressed from WHBI onto WBLS, the station programmed by Frankie Crocker and said to be the most listened to in America. Rap was back on the radio.

5. Sister brother rapp

The Reverend J. D. Montgomery is beginning to build his sermon at Mt Carmel Baptist Church on Detroit's east side. His theme is 'God's Newspaper' and as the pace begins to quicken he develops his striking image. The congregation, whom he describes as 'God's paperboys', are responding to every phrase with a chorus of 'yeahs' as the pastor weaves in a counterattack on young blacks who reject the Bible as a white people's book. It seems doubtful that a paper edited by the Holy Spirit with a sport section headlining Jacob wrestling an angel could displace heroes like Sugar Ray Leonard, but the power of sermons like 'God's Newspaper' is undeniable. By the time the organ and drums have joined in, the Reverend is roaring and tearing up and the people are shouting.

In another recorded sermon, the Reverend Willie T. Sneed begins his metaphor of the dead-end street haltingly, his voice pious and the congregation murmuring their responses. Again, as the song begins to form, Willie is hoarse and the flock are screaming. In his book *Black Music of Two Worlds*, John Storm Roberts writes: 'The "spiritual" sermon normally begins in a conversational tone, differentiated from white sermons only by the responses of the congregation, reminiscent of the old African belief that it is discourteous to listen dumbly, without response, or of the interjections made during the griot's telling of traditional tales.'

The power of oratory in Afro-American religion has been the foundation of the soul rap, a style of spoken song which should be seen as one of the forerunners of hip-hop rapping. The preachers like Aretha Franklin's father, the Reverend C. L. Franklin; the gospel storytellers like Dorothy Norwood with her spoken tales such as 'The Denied Mother', described by Tony Heilbut in *The Gospel Sound* as part of a 'long line of gospel records about ungrateful children and put-upon mothers'; the songs of Edna Gallman Cooke with their brief sermonettes – 'Somebody Touched Me' and 'Walk Through the Valley' – are all links in a chain which joins Marion Williams's 'The Moan That Keeps Homes Together' to Millie Jackson, Isaac Hayes, James Brown and Melle Mel's religious rap in The Furious Five's 'You Are'.

Soul rapping became such a fad in the early 1970s that one preacher, Richard 'Mr Clean' White, an ex-street gang member from New Orleans, felt compelled to claim back some lost ground, albeit 10 years too late. His sermon called 'You Got To Believe' on Savoy namechecks Isaac Hayes, Barry White, James Brown and Lou Rawls but, in a clear case of slamming the stable door after the horse had bolted, claims that 'somebody ought to rap about Jesus'.

Soul raps existed long before they became a money spinner, of course, for the simple reason that many soul singers had come out of the church. Johnnie Taylor, for instance, a singer with a half-rapped preacher-style delivery, sang lead as a replacement for

Sam Cooke in the renowned gospel group The Soul Stirrers. Songs like 'It's Cheaper To Keep Her' and 'I'd Rather Drink Muddy Water' use a conversational rap to introduce the song, and in one of his best recordings, 'I've Been Born Again', the idea is extended into a street rap complete with traffic noise as Johnnie turns down yet another night out with the boys in favour of his new love affair.

Soul raps are effective because they give the illusion of a direct and intimate communion between the singer and each individual listener. Different singers use the confessional in different ways. The grainy-voiced Laura Lee, one of the pioneers of soul rapping, used raps partly to heighten drama – in songs like 'Guess Who I Saw Today' (from her second Hot Wax album *Two Sides of Laura Lee*) dropping into speech to instil extra emotion into a line or to portray her half of a conversation. Laura

Lee was also important for suggesting raps as a means by which women could voice a new independence (or at least the struggle to attain it). Songs like 'Dirty Man' and 'Uptight Good Man' suggested that the powerful female voices of black music were asking to be recognised as the voices of human beings with complex needs and qualities – not just as sets of vocal chords, lust objects or mother surrogates.

Laura Lee's precedent was followed up by a number of women. Irma Thomas, a Louisiana-born singer, recorded a stunning world-weary, men-weary rap called 'Coming From Behind (Monologue)' on the Fungus label, produced by Jerry 'Swamp Dogg' Williams. One of the clearest examples of the way in which the sermon format had been absorbed into soul music, 'Coming From Behind', released in 1973, begins with an extended rap about men, their incapacity to love and their sexual in-

I'VE BEEN BORN AGAIN: JOHNNIE TAYLOR
Photo: courtesy of Charlie Gillett

WOMEN'S LOVE RIGHTS: LAURA LEE
Photo: courtesy of Charlie Gillett

feriority, then slips into the song and ends with Irma screaming over the hypnotic backing.

Joe Tex touched on some of the same subject matter, albeit with a witty cynicism, in a rapped extension of Burt Bacharach and Hal David's 'I'll Never Fall In Love Again', included on his 1972 album *From the Roots Came the Rapper*. Tex, who died in 1982, was one of the philosophers of rap. His 'I Had a Good Home, Part Two' switches from rap to singing and back, warning you to hold on to what you've got and learn from your mistakes. As Cliff White so aptly put it in his *New Musical Express* obituary: 'Joe's quirky delivery, couched midway between benevolent preacher and lecherous uncle, gave the performance an ambiguous quality.' Starting out his career by winning a talent show with a comedy sketch, his raps also hovered on the edge of being stand-up comic routines.

The same ambivalence can be found in many soul raps – in most instances they exist in the context of songs, drawing on preaching, comedy and soap-opera drama.

Lou Rawls's 'Dead End Street' is a case in point. Lou pushes home the moral of a serious story by throwing in jokes about Chicago's razor-sharp wind, the Hawk. Rawls was another gospel graduate, having started out in The Pilgrim Travellers, and he was among the first to popularise monologues with his *Live* album back in the middle '60s. The raps served to show that soul was a new kind of music with one shiny shoe in a shouting heaven and the other striding out into the material (and sexual) world.

A contemporary of Joe Tex and Lou Rawls who embodied the age-old split between the Devil and Christ was Solomon Burke. He even recorded a song called 'I Feel A Sin Coming On' as if sex was like

I'LL NEVER FALL IN LOVE AGAIN: JOE TEX
Photo: courtesy of Charlie Gillett

I FEEL A SIN COMING ON: SOLOMON BURKE
Photo: courtesy of Charlie Gillett

catching the flu. Solomon's powerful, smokey delivery is heard at its best testifying effect on a song like 'The Price', with its rapped intro stringing together the titles of his earlier recordings. In a story of such despair as 'The Price' the effect is perilously close to gimmickry, and raps can certainly skate close to bathos at times. The most risky but often the most affecting and genuinely moving are conversation raps. The implied voyeurism of overhearing somebody else's domestic squabbles is enough in itself to cause a nervous laugh – not to mention the theatricality of the whole device. A long heart-to-heart rap like Harold Melvin and the Blue Notes's 'Be For Real' completely washes out any doubts through the intensity of lead vocalist Teddy Pendergrass's searing performance. The same is true of The Soul Children's 'What's Happening Baby': John Blackfoot Colbert's voice is so full of hurt and confusion that it becomes almost painful to listen to. When it comes, his singing voice is a relief – the spoken voice cuts too close to the bone.

The moral message of 'Be For Real' – semi-religious, remember your roots, stay humble – is at the heart of many spellbinding recordings by Bobby Womack. Bobby began singing gospel with his brothers, who came to record secular material as The Valentinos, and eventually launched out on a solo career. With a singing style that could move from conversational to a hoarse shout in the space of a word, Bobby Womack has made a monologue style all his own. Maybe tracks like 'Monologue/They Long To Be Close To You' from his 1971 *Communication* album walk a thin line with their down-

home wisdom, but they avoid mawkishness and manage to convince through the sheer force of personality in his voice. In another long rap medley, 'Facts of Life/He'll Be There When the Sun Goes Down', the title track from a 1973 album, he even raises the question of why he talks before he sings. It doesn't really get answered but the general conclusion – that in the midst of the entertainment circus 'it's all about feelings' – seems to sum up his music.

Despite Lou Rawls, Irma Thomas and Bobby Womack using the word *monologue* to describe their raps they were more like conversational style mixed in with songs. Monologues do exist in black music but they are far more prevalent in country music, with narrators like Red Sovine and Tex Ritter. Two black music monologues that stand out are 'Jack, That Cat Was Clean' by the mysterious Dr Horse, a story of sharp-dressing Bobo which draws heavily on the storytelling heritage of toasts, and 'King Heroin', a trenchantly eerie anti-drug rap by James Brown.

These were exceptions, though, and in the main, raps and monologues were an essential, if peripheral, aspect of deep soul. Records like Jimmy Lewis's 'Stop Half Loving These Women', Mattie Moultrie's 'The Saddest Story Ever Told', The Sons of Truth's 'Give It Up', Gwen McCrae's 'Starting All Over Again', George Kerr's 'Hey George (the masquerade is over)', Little Johnny Taylor's 'All I Want Is You' and Tami Lynn's 'Wings Upon Your Horns' are all excellent examples of the ways in which raps fit into soul.

It was three singers in the 1970s who

raided deep soul for its rapping and crossed it over to a broad international audience, making themselves stars in the process. Barry White, Isaac Hayes and Millie Jackson all had fairly established careers before they turned to the raps and monologues that gave them their notoriety. With Barry White, a west coast arranger and producer gone solo, it was a case of making the most of a limited vocal range. White growled and rumbled his way through romantic epics like 'Love Serenade' in a visionary haze of satin sheets. With a passion that threatened to rend his monstrous frame, his appeal was limitless as a focus for unexpressed sexual fantasies.

White's music appeared to be influenced by Isaac Hayes, a masterful writer and studio musician who found himself with a runaway success in *Hot Buttered Soul*, an album recorded in 1969 for Stax. It was a radical departure for soul music, obviously created by a musician accustomed to the studio and arranging. Its extended rap on 'By The Time I Get to Phoenix' – all 18 minutes of it – was a hypnotic and compelling story that built with a cinematic scope and perspective more familiar from white producers like Phil Spector and Brian Wilson. Other Ike Hayes raps like 'Monologue: Ike's Rap 1' from the *To Be Continued* album explored this compulsive area of bitter-sweet romantic tragedy further, and a whole new audience of soft-centred symphonic soul fans was created.

The singer who has developed monologues most consistently over a long period is Millie Jackson. With the ubiquitous church upbringing and a tremendously

THE ROYAL RAPPERS: ISAAC HAYES AND MILLIE JACKSON
Photo: courtesy of Stuart Cosgrove

strong and expressive voice, Millie gave every impression of following in the footsteps of Aretha Franklin or Carla Thomas, but with *Caught Up*, her fourth album, she embarked on a vinyl soap opera which was so massively popular that she has pursued ideas from it ever since. The central song on *Caught Up* was a lengthy rap framed by one of the great soul ballads, '(If Loving You Is Wrong) I Don't Want To Be Right', previously recorded by Luther Ingram. The rap was a *tour de force* – a breakdown of the pros and cons of having an affair with a married man – and on the next track, 'All I Want Is a Fighting Chance', Millie confronted the wife in a playlet which continued on the follow-up album. *Still Caught Up* used rapping on almost every track and repeated the mini-dramas of its predecessor but with the complete 'love triangle' battling it out. By the end, Millie is being carried out screaming in a straitjacket.

It was an ominous sign in more ways than one and though she returned to more conventional (if less powerful) albums subsequently, the extended raps became the focus of her stage shows. As they gradually introduced more supposedly taboo material – much of it taking the lead from Laura Lee's 'Women's Love Rights' – they also slipped into formula and self-parody. As Millie Jackson herself admitted, the monologues had become a trap which prevented her from fulfilling her potential as a singer.

Another singer who believed in confrontation tactics when approaching love triangles was Shirley Brown, who got straight on the phone to her old man's friend Barbara in 'Woman to Woman'. One of the most effective 'telephone' raps, 'Woman to Woman' was a gorgeous performance which raised the question of who-owns-who in a marriage, also pursued in Richard 'Dimples' Fields's and Betty Wright's bitter row in 'She's Got Papers On Me' and Barbara Mason's response, 'She's Got the Papers But I've Got the Man'. Betty Wright's outburst in 'She's Got Papers On Me' – 'use my life up, use my body up' – showed that there were areas in which speech could say what singing couldn't.

With raps growing out of the gospel-drenched melodramas of deep soul it was no surprise that disco was too awkward a medium for monologues to flourish. Its tempos were too fast and its mood was too

optimistic. Lolleata Holloway kept the faith, though, with her scorching voice as strong on fast raps like 'All About the Paper' as it was on ecstatic shouters like 'Catch Me On the Rebound'.

In 1983–84, with the revival of interest in traditional soul, raps became fashionable again, appearing on Barbara Mason's 'Another Man', its answer – 'Another Man Is Twice As Nice' – by Tout Sweet, Fatback's 'Is This the Future', Cameo's 'She's Strange', Rich Cason's 'Street Symphony' and a host of others.

The older monologue style nearly always used speech rhythms which, though they might have more cadence to them than a lot of white speech, were not strictly related to the beat of the underlying music. In contrast, the new soul raps showed the influence of hip hop in sticking close to the drums. Some of the old-style rappers had shown an awareness of hip hop and recorded one-off singles which were premonitions of

this new hybrid – Millie Jackson released an embarrassing attack on rap, welfare scroungers and white women who go with black men. It would have been better left in the tape vaults.

James Brown, on the other hand, put together a glorious rap, 'Rapp Payback (Where Iz Moses)', that was a welcome return to records like 'Brother Rapp' and 'I Don't Want Nobody To Give Me Nothing'. It was a forceful jog to the memory. Brown was the most direct connection between soulful testifying and Bronx poetry. Though he could sing the pants off the average vocalist (as he frequently chose to prove with renditions of songs like 'If I Ruled the World'), many of his best performances existed in a unique vocal space somewhere between speech and scream. His position as spokesman for black consciousness and minister of super-heavy funk might have been on the wane by the '70s, but for the b boys he was still Soul Brother Number One.

ROXY SIDEWALK

6. Uptown throwdown

Saturday night at The Roxy on West 18th. Trouble Funk, the heaviest of heavy funk 'n' rap groups from the Washington go-go scene, are just finishing a marathon set which runs the gamut of modern black music. Each number lasts around 30 minutes – segues of their own releases, 'Pump Me Up', 'Drop the Bomb', 'Trouble Funk Express', intercut with quotes from 'Alexander's Ragtime Band', 'Atomic Dog', 'Work That Sucker To Death', *The Munsters* theme, Taana Gardner's 'Heartbeat', Kraftwerk's 'Trans-Europe Express', all powered by the rock-hard drumming of Mack Carey. The dancers are going crazy as the group chant 'drop the bomb on the white boy too', forming a circle and challenging one another's moves. The last note dies and they file off the stage. Afrika Bambaataa, the imposing presence on the DJ platform, drops the needle onto Michael Jackson's 'P.Y.T.', the sweetest dance tune from *Thriller*.

Bambaataa may look mean when he's at the turntables but he also looks comfortable. A large man, dressed casually in sweatshirt and trainers, his image could be described as homely – certainly a million miles from the sci-fi warrior of his publicity pictures. He has a reputation for being iconoclastic in his record choices and there is no doubt that 'P.Y.T.' is a shock to the system after 90 minutes of Trouble Funk's intense bombardment of comic-strip and electronic images. The atmosphere lightens up and Bam gets to work with Soul Sonic's scratch DJ, Jazzy Jay.

Two days later, in Arthur Baker's new studio, Shakedown Sound, Bambaataa is being uncharacteristically vehement about Tommy Boy Records boss Tom Silverman's reluctance to have Soul Sonic Force and Shango sharing the same stage in the in-production movie *Beat Street*. His more usual soft-spoken manner and apparent awkwardness belie his importance as a figurehead for many black youths in the Bronx and a pioneer in the roots development and eventual international success of hip hop. His name is taken from a nineteenth-century Zulu chief (it means Chief Affection) and, ironically enough, it was

TROUBLE FUNK AT THE ROXY

RENEGADES OF FUNK: JAZZY JAY AND AFRIKA BAMBAATAA

the British film *Zulu* which gave him the idea in the early 1960s to form the Zulu Nation, a loose organisation dedicated to peace and survival which has since spread outwards from the Bronx to other parts of America. Bambaataa outlines the development:

> The Zulu Nation. I got the idea when I seen this movie called *Zulu* which featured Michael Caine. It was showing how when the British came to take over the land of the Zulus how the Zulus fought to uphold their land. They were proud warriors and they was fighting very well against bullets, cannons and stuff.

They fought like warriors for a land which was theirs. When the British thought they'd won the next thing you see is the whole mountain full with thousands of Zulus and the British knew they was gonna die then. But the Zulus chanted – praised them as warriors and let them live. So from there that's when I decided one of these days I hope to have a Zulu Nation too.

And then, as the years went by, through all the civil rights movement, human rights, Vietnam war and all the folk and rock that was happening – all the change of the '60s that was happening to the whole world – it just stayed with me to have some type of group like that.

Bambaataa was once a member of The Black Spades, the largest black gang in New York. Although he concedes that the gang era was tough he determinedly looks on the positive side:

> To me, the gangs was educational – it got me to learn about the streets, and The Black Spades they had a unity that I couldn't find elsewhere. I've been in a lot of different gang groups but The Black Spades had a unity among each other. The gang was like your family. You learned about how to travel around the New York streets. A lot of times when there were no jobs for youths, no trips happening in the Community Centres so the gangs got them there. If the gangs, 'scuse the expression, tore shit up, the government would start sending people to speak to you, throwing in money to

calm the gangs down. America is raised on violence. Only time America really listens is when somebody starts getting violent back.

His downplaying of gang warfare is a response to what he sees as the media's thirst for negative stories and sensationalism. That notwithstanding, the gangs escalated their rivalry to a frightening level of violence between 1968 and 1973. This internal destructiveness can only have contributed to their demise in 1974. Bambaataa puts it down to pressures from the City, drugs and the reaction of women against the fighting among the men.

In his classic study of a black Chicago gang of the '60s, the Vice Lord Nation, R. Lincoln Keiser documents the changes that caused the gang to evolve from a social group into an organised fighting gang and latterly, under the influence of Black Nationalism, into a community group:

> The club was now legally incorporated, and had received a substantial grant from government sources to undertake self-help projects. The group had started a restaurant called 'Teen Town', begun an employment service, and opened a recreation centre called 'House of Lords'. They had entered into agreements with both the Cobras and the Roman Saints, and all three of the clubs had co-operated in community help projects. The Vice Lords were strongly involved in Black pride and Black consciousness programs. A staff of both Whites and Blacks was working in the Vice Lord office on legal

problems faced by members of the Lawndale community.

To outsiders the gangs may have seemed like uncontrolled mayhem but each gang had its own structure, method of operation and recognised leaders. Bambaataa joined a division of The Black Spades formed at Bronx River Project in 1969. Through the influence of his mother his main interest was music, but he was also aware of politics within the black community:

> In the '60s, that's when I was young and I was seeing a lot of things that was happening around the world. What got me excited first was when James Brown came out with 'Say It Loud, I'm Black and I'm Proud'. That's when we transcend from negro to black. Negro to us was somebody who needed to grow into a knowledge of themself. There was no land called negroland. Everbody in America – when they came here they knew what country they was from. If you were Italian you called yourself Italian-American, but the blacks didn't know which way they was going. They was brainwashed – all this stuff was put into our mentality. Black was evil, turn the other cheek, believe all the stuff that the Bible is telling you. The Bible contradicts itself. So Martin Luther King was the thing that was happening because he was fighting for civil rights, but Malcolm X was more on the aggressive side. Myself, I was more on the Malcolm X way of thinking. I respect Martin Luther King for what he was doing.

The '60s was a beautiful time because that's when you saw change – not just in America but happening all around the world. I was watching all of that and then later when gangs was fading out I decided to get into the Nation of Islam. It put a big change on me. It got me to respect people even though they might not like us because we was Muslims. The Nation of Islam was doing things that America had been trying to for a while – taking people from the streets like junkies and prostitutes and cleaning them up. Rehabilitating them like the jail system wasn't doing.

Bambaataa's dream of having his own Zulu Nation had to wait until the gang scene had faded. While still in high school he started a group called The Organisation which lasted for two years, and with the emergence of the hip-hop scene he changed the name to the Zulu Nation:

There were five members and we used to call them Zulu Kings. They were breakdancers. They were taking out a lot of talent that was happening in high schools and clubs and winning trophies and then more people wanted to join. As we kept playing from place to place more people came and joined and it got large like that. It started stretching from the Bronx to Manhattan, Yonkers, upstate New York to Connecticut to a lot of other places. When people used to leave and go to other states they'd build Zulu Nations according to their own way of thinking.

MR BIGGS

Mr Biggs, one of the rappers in Soul Sonic Force, the group who hit big with 'Planet Rock', backtracks to their beginnings in hip hop:

> I was rapping before the Zulu Nation even started. I started rapping back in about 1974 – just me and Bambaataa and a guy by the name of Cowboy (not the one that's with Grandmaster Flash), and this girl called Queen Kenya. Bam had just been given a new DJ set for a graduation present when he got out of high school and he started spinning records. I just picked up a mike one time, just playing around rapping, and I just kept rapping from there.

In those early days each DJ was strong in his own district and was supported by local followers. Few had access to the big clubs so the venues were block parties and schools or, in the summer, the parks. A party in the park would entail wiring the sound system to a lamp post or going to the house nearest the park, paying the owner and running a cable to their electricity. Then the party could go on until the police broke it up. DJs like Kool Dee, Flowers, Pete DJ Jones, Maboya and Smokey were all popular at the time, but for many partygoers the attention shifted to a Jamaican jock called Kool DJ Herc.

Initially, Herc was trying out his reggae records but since they failed to cut ice he switched to Latin-tinged funk, just playing the fragments that were popular with the dancers and ignoring the rest of the track. The most popular part was usually the per-cussion break. In Bambaataa's words: 'Now he took the music of like Mandrill, like 'Fencewalk', certain disco records that had funky percussion breaks like The Incredible Bongo Band when they came out with 'Apache' and he just kept that beat *going*. It might be that certain part of the record that everybody waits for – they just let their inner self go and get wild. The next thing you know the singer comes back in and you'd be mad'.

A conga or bongo solo, a timbales break or simply the drummer hammering out the beat – these could be isolated by using two copies of the record on twin turntables and playing the one section over and over, flipping the needle back to the start on one while the other played through. The music made in this way came to be known as beats or break beats.

Break-beat music and the hip-hop culture were happening at the same time as the emergence of disco (in 1974 known as *party music*). Disco was also created by DJs in its initial phase, though these tended to be club jocks rather than mobile party jocks – records by Barry White, Eddie Kendricks and others became dancefloor hits in New York clubs like Tamberlane and Sanctuary and were crossed over onto radio by Frankie Crocker at station WBLS. There were many parallels in the techniques used by Kool DJ Herc and a pioneering disco DJ like Francis Grasso, who worked at Sanctuary, as they used similar mixtures and superimpositions of drumbeats, rock music, funk and African records. For less creative disco DJs, however, the ideal was to slip-cue smoothly from the end of one

record into the beginning of the next. They also created a context for the breaks rather than foregrounding them, and the disco records which emerged out of the influence of this type of mixing tended to feature long introductions, anthemic choruses and extended vamp sections, all creating a tension which was released by the break. Breakbeat music simply ate the cherry off the top of the cake and threw the rest away.

In the words of DJ Grandmaster Flash:

> Disco was brand new then and there were a few jocks that had monstrous sound systems but they wouldn't dare play this kind of music. They would never play a record where only two minutes of the song was all it was worth. They wouldn't buy those type of records. The type of mixing that was out then was blending from one record to the next or waiting for the record to go off and wait for the jock to put the needle back on.

Flash has become world famous through Sugarhill releases like 'The Message', yet Herc faded from view despite his innovations in both mixing and rapping. Part of the reason for his demise was a fight at the Executive Playhouse in which he intervened and was stabbed, yet Flash also claims he had limitations as a mixer:

> Herc really slipped up. With the monstrous power he had he couldn't mix too well. He was playing little breaks but it would sound so sloppy. I noticed that the mixer he was using was a GLI 3800. It was a very popular mixer at that time. It's a scarcity today but it's still one of the best mixers GLI ever made. At the time

he wasn't using no cueing. In other words, the hole was there for a headphone to go in but I remember he never had headphones over his ears. All of a sudden, Herc had headphones but I guess he was so used to dropping the needle down by eyesight and trying to mix it that from the audio part of it he couldn't get into it too well.

Herc's sound system was so powerful that when he held a block party nobody tried to compete. He would even occasionally shame Flash in public, demonstrating the superiority of his set-up over Flash's homemade rig. Grandmaster Flash's entry into mixing stemmed both from his fascination for his father's record collection and his mother's desire for him to study electronics:

> My father – he was a record collector. I think what really made me interested into wanting to get into records was because I used to get scolded for touching his records. When I was living in this town up in the Bronx called Throgs Neck he used to have this closet and in this closet were some of the classics. I mean like Benny Goodman, Artie Shaw, all the popular stuff of the time. He would close it but sometimes he would forget to lock it. He would always tell my mother, 'Don't let Joseph go in there and touch the records'. So what I would do – when my mother's back was turned or she was in the kitchen I would tiptoe up to the closet, turn the knob, go inside the closet and take a record. I would attempt to turn the stereo on. The stereo had a little red light at the bottom of the speaker and

that red light really intrigued me. Every time I'd get caught I'd get scolded or I'd get beat. Think I learned my lesson? Hell no!

I was in this place called Grier School, Hope Farm, New York upstate, where I had to stay when my mother had gotten sick. Up there they wanted parental advice on what you wanted your son or daughter to be into, so my mother chose electronics because I always had a knack of tinkering with things and taking things apart.

From there, I came out of Grier School and my mother put me into Samuel Gompers vocational high school in the Bronx there, 147th Street and Southern Boulevard. From there I caught the knack of dealing with televisions, hi-fi stereo and stuff, and that's where I really started to get a love for *sound*. We grew up underprivileged so we didn't really have the money for me to get a really nice sound system for my room. I'd get stuff that was half-disabled and put it back the best way I possibly can.

Flash was one of the first to pick upon Herc's break-beat music which, after less than a year, was becoming the dominant style in the Bronx. He began by playing records for small parties on Fox Street or Hoe Avenue, Faile Street, where there were a few empty apartments. The music was Jimmy Castor, Barry White, James Brown, Sly and the Family Stone and The Jackson Five. As his popularity grew he became aware of his own inability to synchronise beats:

I was in the experimentation phase of trying to lock the beat together. I had to be able to hear the other turntable before I mixed it over. This is when I met Pete DJ Jones. He was a big tall guy, six and some change – he was a sit-down DJ but his knees was like HUGE. I'm saying to myself, wow, how can he take these records and blend them on time, keep this music going without missing a beat? So, I finally got the heart to ask him if I could play on his system. I think he told me no twice. Then after a while he'd heard about me playing for the kids and he gave me permission to play on his system. He told me what to do and to my amazement, wow, you can actually hear the other turntable before you play it out to the people.

I knew what it was because I was going to the technical school for electronics. I knew that inside the unit it was a single pole, double throw switch, meaning that when it's in the centre it's off. When it's to the left you're listening to the left turntable and when it's to the right you're listening to the right turntable. I had to go to the raw parts shop downtown to find me a single pole double throw switch, some crazy glue to glue this part to my mixer, an external amplifier and a headphone. What I did when I had all this soldered together, I jumped for joy – I've got it, I've got it, I've got it!

I knew how to blend. Right away, when I got on Pete's set, I know how to blend. That just came naturally. My main objective was to take small parts of records and, at first, keep it on time, no

tricks, keep it on time. I'm talking about very short beats, maybe 40 seconds, keeping it going for about five minutes, depending on how popular that particular record was.

After that, I mastered punch phasing – taking certain parts of a record where there's a vocal or drum slap or a horn. I would throw it out and bring it back, keeping the other turntable playing. If this record had a horn in it before the break came down I would go – BAM, BAM, BAM-BAM – just to try this on the crowd.

The crowd, they didn't understand it at first but after a while it became a thing. After I became popular with it I wanted to get more popular, but a lot of places where they heard *of* me I would ask them if I could get on their turntables. A few clubs I used to go to, even Disco Fever, they'd say, 'No man, I heard you be scratching up people's records, man. I heard you get a wild crowd too, man. You ain't playing on my set.'

A scratch is *nothing* but the back-cueing that you hear in your ear before you push it out to the crowd. All you have to know is mathematically how many times to scratch it and when to let it go – when certain things will enhance the record you're listening to. For instance, if you're playing a record with drums – horns would sound nice to enhance it so you get a record with horns and slip it in at certain times.

A large part of the disc jockeys' mystique and power is their resourcefulness in find-ing unknown or obscure records that can move a crowd. These can be rarities, white-label pre-releases, acetates, unreleased tapes or simply good songs which slipped through the net at the time they were released. Given the obvious difficulty of identifying tunes in the non-stop collages of the b boy style, the most creative DJs in the Bronx were able to build up strong local reputations as 'masters of records' – the librarians of arcane and unpredictable sounds that few could match. In time-honoured fashion their secrecy extended to soaking records in the bath to peel off the centre labels or giving records new names. Previously jealously guarded lists, emerging gradually at the beginning of 1984, make bizarre reading. Bambaataa was one of the most outrageous:

The Bronx wasn't really into radio music no more. It was an anti-disco movement. Like you had a lot of new wavers and other people coming out and saying, 'Disco sucks'. Well, the same thing with hip hop, 'cos they was against the disco that was being played on the radio. Everybody wanted the funky style that Kool Herc was playing. Myself, I was always a record collector and when I heard this DJ, I said, 'Oh, I got records like that.' I started digging in my collection.

When I came on the scene after him I built in other types of records and I started getting a name for master of records. I started playing all forms of music. Myself, I used to play the weirdest stuff at a party. Everybody just thought I was crazy. When everybody was going crazy I would throw a commercial on to cool them out – I'd throw on *The Pink Panther* theme for everybody who thought they was cool like the Pink Panther, and then I would play 'Honky Tonk Woman' by The Rolling Stones and just keep that beat going. I'd play something from metal rock records like Grand Funk Railroad. 'Inside Looking Out' is just the bass and drumming . . . rrrrrmmmmmmmm . . . and everybody starts freaking out.

I used to like to catch the people who'd say, 'I don't like rock. I don't like Latin.' I'd throw on Mick Jagger – you'd see the blacks and the Spanish just *throwing* down, dancing crazy. I'd say, 'I thought you said you didn't like rock.' They'd say, 'Get out of here.' I'd say, 'Well, you just danced to The Rolling Stones.' 'You're kidding!'

I'd throw on 'Sergeant Pepper's Lonely Hearts Club Band' – just that drum part. One, two, three, BAM – and they'd be screaming and partying. I'd throw on The Monkees, 'Mary Mary' – just the beat part where they'd go 'Mary, Mary, where are you going?' – and they'd start going crazy. I'd say, 'You just danced to The Monkees'. They'd say, 'You liar. I didn't dance to no Monkees'. I'd like to catch people who categorise records.

Through listening to the type of records that were popular in the beginnings of hip hop (and have remained popular) it becomes easier to understand how the better-known aspects of the culture – rapping, scratching, beat-box music – came to evolve. A b boy classic like James Brown's 'Get Up, Get Into It, Get Involved', released in late 1970, is an up-tempo call and answer routine between Brown and singer Bobby Byrd. For most whites at the time, this was the most meaningless type of James Brown release, but for those young blacks still living in areas like the Bronx and Harlem every phrase had a message.

The record is a single, harsh, see-sawing guitar riff with the bass rumbling upfront in the mix and the drummer playing loose funk with the hi-hat cymbal opened then choked shut on the fourth beat of the bar. There is no bridge: the only change in the structure comes half-way through, with a drum break where James shouts, 'Fellers, I want you to hit me.' the band shout back 'Yeah' and the horns hit, 'Hit me' . . . BAM . . . 'Alright, hit me' . . . BAM . . . 'Hey' . . . BAM.

The effect is identical to the kind of punch phasing using horns over drum tracks that can be heard on bootlegs of b boy parties. The break is followed by a tortured rock guitar solo and at the end Brown shouts the prophetic, 'You can be like a tape deck, you know . . . they can plug you in . . . say what they want you to say . . . don't let 'em do it'. The last phrase is repeated four times, with Bobby Byrd shouting back a resist and survive NO each time.

Most of the words – phrases like 'get an education' and 'do it one time . . . get it right' – are shouted or rapped over the music, with Brown's voice rising to a scream towards the close. The general message – a positive exhortation not to waste your life or be manipulated by others – was part of a series of records which encouraged black youth to stay in school, avoid succumbing to hard drugs and be proud of the colour of their skin.

The other important break-beat records had some or all of the same ingredients – a funky beat, a positive message, a drum break and some rock guitar: Jimmy Castor's 'It's Just Begun', Rufus Thomas's 'Do the Funky Penguin' and 'The Breakdown', Baby Huey and the Babysitters' 'Listen To Me', The Isley Brothers' 'Get Into Something' and Dyke and the Blazers' 'Let a Woman Be a Woman – Let a Man Be a Man'. Other records with drum breaks that could be used to construct new tunes were 'Johnny The Fox Meets Jimmy the Weed' by Thin Lizzy (released as a bootleg mix on Dirt Bag Records and called 'Johnny the Fox' by Skinny Lizzy); 'The Big Beat' by heavy-metal guitarist Billy Squire (also released as a bootleg record featuring just the opening bars of the song) and 'Scorpio' by Dennis Coffey, a white session guitarist. 'Scorpio' (an inspiration in name if nothing else to the 1982 electro track by Grandmaster Flash and the Furious Five) was included on one of Paul Winley's *Super Disco Brakes* anthologies. The first volume of *Super Disco Brakes* includes New Birth's peculiar Sly Stone-meets-psychedelia fusion, 'Gotta Get a Knutt', which can be heard on another bootleg, *Live Convention '82* (volume two), recorded at T Connection.

Live Connection '82 (Disco Wax Records) begins with an extract from 'Academy Awards', a track from Masterfleet's 1973 album *High On The Seas* featuring Star Trek actress Nichelle Nichols. After fragments of the 'Good Times' bass riff, some Sly Stone, 'Gangster Boogie' and a litany of guest DJs and MCs who are 'in the house', there is a five-minute 27-second rap which uses the first six bars (13 seconds in total) of 'Do the Funky Penguin' cut together by the Grand Wizard Theodore:

It's like a one for the treble and two for the bass
Theodore – let's dog the place
You don't stop, you don't stop, that body rock
Just clap your hands, it's the sure shot sound
Brace yourself – for the one that goes down
Got a little news that you all can tell
Theodore – he got the clientele
All night, y'all, if it's alright
All night, y'all, if it's alright
Porto Rico, Porto Rico
Make money, make money, make money into the Patty Duke
Throw your hands in the air
Wave 'em like you just don't care
Getting down with these sure-shot sounds your body say oh yeah
Yeah, a little louder, little louder
You don't stop, you don't, you won't don't don't
You won't don't don't, you don't don't stop the body rock
Because the people in the back – you ain't the wack
But – don't stop the body rock

B BOY GLOVE, THE ROXY

The people in the middle, let me see you
   wiggle
(but don't stop that body rock)
The people on the side − let's ride
(but don't you stop that body rock)
The girls in the rear, you come up here
(but don't you stop that body rock)
Young lady in the blue, I'm talking to you
(but don't you stop that body rock)
Young lady in the brown, you know
   you're down
(don't stop that body rock)
Young lady in the green, you're looking
   real clean
(don't you stop that body rock)
Young lady in the black, you ain't the
   wack
(you ain't thinking 'bout stopping that

body rock)
Young lady in the white, she'll bite all
   night
(but don't you stop that body rock)
Young lady in the yellow got a faggot for a
   fellow
(but don't you stop that body rock)
'Cos the body rock is sho nuff the shot
(but you won't stop, you don't stop)
Ain't thinking 'bout stopping that body
   rock
Punk rock, rock the house
Patty Duke, y'all, get cute y'all
Patty Duke, y'all, get cute y'all
Gonna tell you little something, I'm one
   of a kind
But now I'm gonna rock − the zodiac
   signs

Pisces − rock the house
Aquarius − rock the house
And Gemini − said get on high
Scorpio − you're the go
Pisces − the higher degree
Just the beat beat beat, the beat beat the
  beat
Patty Dukeing to the rhythm, get up out
  your seat
Young ladies − are you with me?
Young ladies − are you with me?
Young ladies in the house say OWW
Say OWW − to the beat, y'all
You don't quit, you don't quit
You don't you don't quit quit
The sure-shot shit
It's like superstition with a bag of tricks
I say this is the way we harmonise
This is the way we turn it up
This is the way we turn it up

And the beat goes on. Raps like these, with their eulogies to the young ladies in blue, red, etc., are reminiscent of black dance music from all eras − country blues and jug bands, piano blues like 'Pinetop's Boogie Woogie', the shouters like Big Joe Turner, the electric blues of John Lee Hooker and Junior Wells, the rock 'n roll of Larry Williams and Little Richard − not great poetry but dancehall rhymes.

As has already been shown, rapping has roots in a variety of sources, but for the hip-hop purists it is again Kool DJ Herc who was the first to come up with a Bronx MC style. Bambaataa remembers:

There's a lot of people trying to take credit like Cheeba and DJ Hollywood − the disco type of DJs that was out there −

but I challenge any of these people to sit down and base their facts on when they started to do what we was doing in the street. A lot of these people who claim to be the start of it was doing rapping something like Frankie Crocker or talk like disco-style radio-type rapping. Herc took phrases, like what was happening in the streets, what was the new saying going round the high school like 'rock on my mellow', 'to the beat y'all', 'you don't stop', and just elaborated on that.

Bambaataa sees a connection between Herc's Jamaican origins and his rapping: 'He knew that a lot of American blacks were not getting into the reggae of his country. He took the same thing that they was doing − toasting − and did it with American records, Latin or records with beats.'

Rappers like Mr Biggs are more inclined to give some credit to Eddie Cheeba and DJ Hollywood for their part in the general development of rap, even though their sources were the radio rather than the schoolyard. DJ Hollywood was in fact rapping over disco records between acts at Harlem's Apollo Theatre. Kurtis Blow, whose smooth style is closer to this kind of combined DJ/MC, remembers Hollywood as the rap innovator, although the Hollywood rhyme he recites from memory is word-for-word Isaac Hayes's badman rap 'Good Love 6-9969' from his 1975 album *Use Me*. Ike's career may have been on the wane by that time, but his influence was obviously still alive in the streets.

Flash also gives Hollywood credit: 'He

was one of the greatest solo rappers that ever there was. That boy could blaze a crowd – the rhymes he says. I expected him to shoot right to the top – he had a chance before we did.' Hollywood also played at Club 371 and his style was capable of appealing to the older fans as well as the b boys.

Lil Rodney Cee, now with Double Trouble, recalls the formative years of MCs in the middle 1970s:

The way rap is *now* – it isn't the way it was *then*. Whereas then it was just phrases; the MC would say little phrases like, 'To the Eastside, make money. To the West-side, make money', or 'To the rock, rock, rock, to the rock, rock, rock'. In '77–'78 I was with The Magnificent Seven. We was playing in the streets.

Rap, then, was only a street thing. At that time, everything was happening at once. B boying was happening at the same time as DJing and rapping came out. Everything was strictly competitive.

The groups that came out was in strict competition, so when we did play in the wintertime we rented small clubs, disco-theques, recs, boys' clubs, PALs. We charged little bits of money and people came and that's what we did in the wintertime. With the money that we made we invested in our sound system for the summertime. That was the basic foundation of what every group did to start off and get into the rap industry.

At the time it wasn't groups rapping – it was solo MCs and they would have a DJ. It would be one DJ and one MC. They would just come out and the people

DOUBLE TROUBLE AT DANCETERIA

liked it. The more they did the more it got into a unified stage. We said, 'Hey, we should get more MCs'.

Along with his partner in Double Trouble, KK Rockwell, Rodney was in one of the very first rap groups, Funky Four Plus One More. He recalls the emergence of rap styles and the competitiveness:

The first MC that I know of is Cowboy, from Grandmaster Flash and the Furious Five. He was the first MC to talk about the DJ. He would talk for Grandmaster Flash and say how great Flash is – you know, 'the pulsating, inflating, disco shaking, heartbreaking, the man on the turntable' and that's all it was. And then, to have fun, it got into – okay, everybody came from all different places to hear the music so when they came they all were into whatever they were into whether it was graffiti, dancing, b boying – the b boys were strictly in competition, too.

An uptown group would battle a downtown group. What I mean by battle is that they could come and they would say, 'Okay. Us four are better than your four', and we would go at it. We would pick one and we would dance against each other. We'd do one move and they'd do a move and the crowd liked it. That's where the competition came in. This is before any records, before any money was made. This was from our hearts.

Grandmaster Flash and the Furious Five embody the gradual move from under-ground to overground. Dressed in red leathers (old-style DC Comics Flash) and working his way through a pack of Lucky Spike bubblegum, Flash waxes nostalgic over the good old days. The contradictions of roots culture in the marketplace have hit very hard; five years after the first rap records and 10 years since hip hop began to stir, most groups and soloists are gathering themselves to launch out on the second phase in the music business, often with a sobering hindsight wisdom that show business can be no business at all. As a 17-year-old the chances of having good financial and legal advice are very slim. Flash is very conscious that pioneer rappers like DJ Hollywood and Busy Bee Starski have not had the breaks of other, lesser talents, and he is also depressed by the changes that have inevitably wrung the verve out of the scene as a whole. His career shows the process in microcosm:

I had to prove to myself that I could rock a crowd, so as opposed to making them pay I tried it for free. Meaning that I would go in the park and play – St Marys, 23 Park, 63 Park – these are various parks I used to play at and just do this new thing called scratching and called phasing and see if they would like it. And it just so happened that they did like it. Not knowing, all the time I was doing this, that there were people following me – older men following me. They made a proposal to me: 'Flash, let's take it on the inside for a dollar or two and see how this works.'

At that time, with my mixing ability,

once I warmed up and really got into it, the crowd would stop dancing and just gather round as if it was a seminar. This was what I didn't want. This wasn't school – it was time to shake your ass. From there I knew it was important to have vocal entertainment. There were quite a few MCs, as we called it before the industry called it rap, that tried out for the job to rap with me and the first member of the crew to really pass the test was Keith Wiggins, known as Cowboy.

He had a Simon Says-ish type of style. The particular MC I was looking for was somebody who could complement scratching. This person had to be able to talk with all the obscure scratching I was doing. I'm doing all this but I'm doing it all on time so you have to have the ear to really know. Even now, I might walk into a club and if I'm cutting and keeping it going they rap, but if I stop on time to the beat they get lost. There's some that can't really catch on to it when the music's being phased in and out to the beat. Cowboy, he was superb at it. As far as that 'Ho', 'Clap your hands to the beat' and 'Say oh yeah', I'd have to give him credit for being one of the creators of that.

From there I had gotten Melvin Glover who had almost like a scholastic type of style. From there I had got Danny – he could say rhymes from now to dooms-day. He was a person who run his mouth but he could also talk with the sort of obscure scratching I was doing. So it was like Grandmaster Flash and the Three MCs. It worked pretty good. From there

I was ready to take it to the inside.

We tried in this club called the Back Door at 169th Street and Boston Road for a dollar. We would party from like 10 at night till 7 in the morning. When we were playing at the Back Door we had diehard fans – it was to a point where kids were sneaking out the house. I try to keep a rapport with some of my close fans and with their parents. I'd even give them the cab fare to get home after the party. I would sit down with some of the mothers and like, 'Flash, they won't go to school. They won't go to church but let them hear about you playing at the Back Door – boy, they'll get up, get dressed and they'll definitely be there'.

It was like an omen. If you don't come to a Flash party it's something you missed. If you weren't there you felt like an onion – you had to be there, even against your mother's and father's wishes. Then after a while there were crews being created – this was when crews were *really* being created seven or eight years ago. The Malachi Crew, oh, there were so many crews.

Flash's number-one fan, his minder Kevin, has a good memory for crews: 'The Casanovas, The Potheads, The Cheeba Crew, there was a crew for every block.' He also remembers some of the wilder turntable trickery of the time:

He did this shit one day that fascinated me. See, I was a devoted fan. I wasn't down with the crew – now I am. It was at Roosevelt High School or Bronx River, one of those two. Him and Mike and Disco B were doing their Terrible Trio thing. Flash would cut the record and move out of the way, then Disco B would do it then Flash would do it then Mike would do it. Then they had this other thing they did where they would pop up out of nowhere – from this angle you couldn't see them. It was a different DJ every second – 'Good times . . . good times . . . good times'. The most phenomenal was at Roosevelt. This nigger did this shit. He drop back. He fell back – I thought he'd bust his *ass*. What it was, he had kicked off his shoe and *kicked* the fader. It was perfectly on time. The crowd went *wild* – I mean, niggers was pushing and falling and shit!

Taking this kind of DJ style from community venues into the commercial world of the clubs (no matter how small) involved an inevitable growth in following. Flash recalls the nights at the Back Door:

It was a big success but it was a small place. We would open the doors at 11 o'clock, and 12 o'clock the doors would be *closed*. It was a thing where I would have to pace it. Eleven to 12.30 I would play cool-out hustle music for the calm people, the sophisticated b boy people in the place that wanted to do the hustle or dance proper. But from 1 to 2.30, that's like grab your partner 'cos I'm playing the hottest shit in the crates. My assistant pulls out the *powerful* shit – I'd set up the order according to beats-per-minute,

tempo and I'd say, 'Hand it to me, man, just like that', and once I'd start playing that shit the crowd would just go. The Incredible Bongo Band, 'Bongo Rock', 'Johnny the Fox', 'The Bells' – Bob James – 'Mardi Gras'. Me watching them enjoy themselves so much I would really like 'pop pop pop pop poppoppop u u u'. I would like break the shit down to eighth, sixteenth notes. It amazed me sometimes.

Bob James was like 102 beats-per-minute and I would go from 102 beats-per-minute to 118 so from there it was like Bob James, James Brown, Donald Byrd, Roy Ayers to John Davis and the Monster Orchestra, 'I Can't Stop', and that's like the ultimate, you know. From there I would keep it going but I would give myself a break because for about 50 minutes I'm bending down uncomfortably. I'd put on 'Dance to the Drummer's Beat', which is a fairly long break, about four minutes, let it play for a while and then play the slow jams, the real oldies. After you sweat and you're tired you appreciate it: 'Oh, he finally slowed it down.' The Delfonics, The Moments, The Five Stairsteps – the real slow, out-of-date stuff that was really love songs. I had all that stuff in my crates. I had something like 45 crates behind me.

Flash and Kevin reminisce by singing the chorus of The Delfonics' 'For the Love I Gave To You' and recalling how Flash would cut mix the same line over and over, keeping the romantic dancers going for over a minute on the same spot. Eventually,

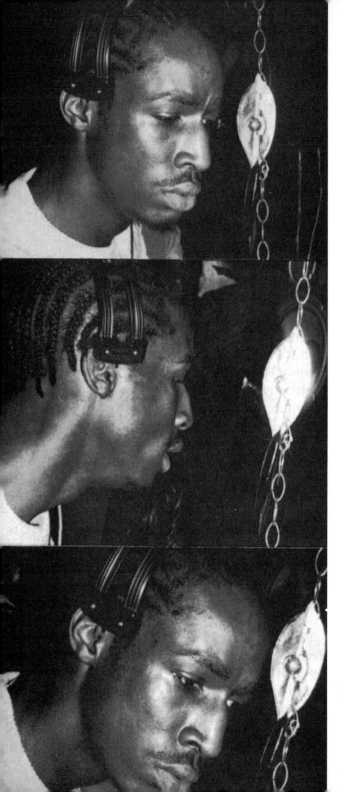

the crowd at the Back Door swelled beyond capacity to the point of discomfort:

So it was to a point where we had to move the corporation down the block to Freeman Street. It was this place called the Dixie Club. That became our new home. The crowd got monstrous and the high school students, who had heard of me and really used to down me, they came to the parties a few times – got a taste of it – they really enjoyed that. We gave them a good time. So they would go to their school organisations and say, 'You want Flash.' After a while we started knocking all the schools off – Roosevelt, Taft, Monroe, Bronx River. It wasn't so much a party – it was a commercial thing where we were getting hired on a professional basis. By that time we had built up a pretty decent sound system.

A year and a half, two years later, the pinnacle of a DJ's group's career, before it was recording, was who can make it to The Audubon. Once you've played there you are famous throughout the five boroughs. The place held 3,000 people so you're bound to get people from all over the place. It was real strange. The people who were working with me, they said, 'Flash, we've played all the schools. We're growing out of the Dixie Club. We've grown out of most gymnasiums we've played in. I want to take you to this place, Flash. I've already rated it and I'm setting it up for the next month.'

ADVENTURES ON THE WHEELS OF STEEL: GRANDMASTER FLASH AT BROADWAY INTERNATIONAL

He takes me to this building – this place is like a block and a half *long*. I said, 'No, please. Let's not try *this* step.' He says, 'Flash, there's no other place that you can try. Anything smaller than this would be a step down. Give me a month to publicise it.' After that day he showed me, I would go down there by myself for about four or five days and think, 'I'm not ready for this place. This is too big.' The Fire Department sign says '3,000 people. No More.' I said to myself, 'I'll be lucky to get 400 in this motherfucker, talk about *3,000!*'

So the night came. After a month publicising me everyone who was interested knew about this big affair. So I bring my sound system in there. It's not really powerful enough to rock this whole place but I put it up high. Strategically, if you put it up high the sound might not be strong but you can at least hear it. The night before I had come up with a way to cut without cueing and I showed it to this guy named Georgie George and Melvin. And Melvin – Melle Mel – as soon as he had seen it he made up a routine. I said, 'I'm not ready to do this shit', but it was too late. I didn't want to back out.

So the Audubon comes. Open the doors 11 o'clock. It was like 200 or 300 people. I left out 'cos I was kind of embarrassed, you know, and came back about 12.30, 1 o'clock. This place was JAM PACKED FULL! I said, 'Oh shit!' Kool DJ AJ was playing with us. He was pumping the crowd. Everybody was there – the gangsters, the scramblers, the little kids. I went downstairs – the line

was around the corner. The shit is jumping off.

We played. Melvin says, 'Stop the music' and introduces me – 'The world's greatest DJ – Grandmaster Flash'. Everybody thought I was going to do regular stuff. I went into my spinning back, turning backwards. The crowd was screaming. I said, 'I'm not gonna get nervous. If I let my emotions get to me I'm going to fuck up and it's gonna jump out of the grooves.' I'm trying to stay steady. After a while, I had to do the other thing, which is taking the needle and dropping it with no cueing at all – keeping the beat on time. It was taking one beat – dropping it and counting. This is blind – BAM – BAM – I kept it on time. I did it about 10 times. Backed off and the crowd went berserk. The fucking floor was like about to cave in. After that night I felt so good. That was September 2nd 1976.

I was ready to try that shit again. Two months later we tried it and after a while what had happened was other corporations, other b boy groups, were going in there and tearing the place up, breaking out the windows and then the news media and the cops started talking bad about it . . . 'These groups, they call themselves b boys, they're coming down to rent the place and bringing all these wild people. People are getting shot and windows are getting broken out.' So the Audubon was out. There was no super-large place that you could play in.

We was doing it with just us and one other DJ. Other groups that didn't have the heart to go in by themselves were going in there with six or seven DJ groups. Seven or eight different sound systems – it was too confusing. This person was taking too long to turn on or this person's system was fucking up and once you've got that big mass of people you have to keep them entertained. So after a while motherfuckers was getting shot and this and that, so by the time we went back after the third time our clientele was getting kind of scared so we gave it up. Then we started knocking off schools – older places, the Savoy Manor Ballroom, the Renaissance Ballroom – all the posh clubs. For three years things were going great, then all of a sudden you hear on the radio, 'To the hip hop, hippedy hop, you don't stop'. I'm saying to myself, 'I know of anybody else from here to Queens or Long Island that's doing this. Why don't I know of this group called The Sugarhill who? The Sugarhill Gang. They don't know of me and I don't know them. Who are these people?'

They got a record on the radio and that shit was haunting me because I felt we should have been the first to do it. We were the first *group* to really do this – someone took our shot. Every night I would hear this fucking record on the radio, 92KTU, 98, BLS, rock stations. I was hearing this shit in my dreams.

7. Raptivity in captivity

Until 1979 the sole documentation of Bronx hip hop was cassette tapes – either clandestine tapes made by would-be bootleggers at parties and clubs, or tapes made by the groups themselves and given out to friends, to cab drivers or to kids with giant tape boxes just to get the music out. Some, like Flash, are reputed to have sold their tapes for 'a buck a minute'.

The lack of industry connections in the Bronx, the young age group involved in hip hop and the radical primitivism of the music itself conspired to produce an island of relatively undisturbed invention in a sea of go-getter commerce. Although hip hop was an idealistic movement it was based in self-determination – a positive and realist attitude. This was very different from the romanticism central to disco which, although uplifting, was more likely to be fixed on an upwardly mobile good life. Hip hop was raw and its environment was seen as being uniformly tough and rough, even if some of it wasn't. The young MCs who chanted about their expensive clothes, champagne, cars and apartments lived with the most minimal hope of ever possessing them; for a group like Chic, on the other hand, whose name, image and subject matter exclusively suggested a moneyed party set hard at play, the fantasy was, in a material sense at least, close to being real. Chic made an awful lot of money and though *they* might spend their time hard at

work in recording studios their fans were inspired by the buoyancy and crazy optimism embodied in their dance tunes. Some of them might even have owned a car to get them home from the disco.

One of the last great records of the disco era (an era in many ways defined by a marketing concept as much as a musical form) was Chic's 'Good Times', a release which gave them twelfth place in the Cashbox top singles for 1979. Logic suggested that if these were the good times then bad times must be just around the corner. They were, of course, and the record captured that sunset feeling.

It was a studio remake of the 'Good Times' rhythm which provided the backing track for the record that came to haunt the dreams of Grandmaster Flash. 'Rapper's Delight' by The Sugarhill Gang was the first release on a new label called Sugarhill, operating out of West Street, Englewood, New Jersey. Reportedly bankrolled with a third share from the legendary Morris Levy of Roulette Records, it was the newest incarnation of a group of companies run by Sylvia Robinson and her husband Joe Robinson Sr. The co-president of this new venture and its figurehead, Sylvia was a recording artist herself. Formerly known as Sylvia Vanderpool, she recorded as Little Sylvia for Savoy Records shortly after Little Esther (Phillips) left the company for Federal in 1951. Through taking guitar lessons with Mickey Baker (now the author of a renowned jazz guitar tutor book) she came to team up with him in a duo called Mickey and Sylvia. After two years and five record releases they hit big with 'Love Is

RAPPER'S DELIGHT: THE SUGARHILL GANG
KING TIM III: PERSONALITY JOCK

Strange', a record with a marked Bo Diddley feel, a catchy guitar figure and a conversation rap in the middle. Mickey and Sylvia continued as a duo until the '60s though none of their subsequent releases took off in the same way. Mickey went on to work in France as a jazz and blues guitarist. Sylvia moved into business ventures with the Blue Morocco Club on Boston Road in the Morrisania area of the Bronx and then in 1968 formed a collection of record labels – All Platinum, Turbo, Stang and Vibration – and later bought the Chess catalogue, much to the discomfort of some of its more illustrious signings like Muddy Waters.

Of the records released on All Platinum or its subsidiaries, a surprising number are of vocal eccentrics – the quavering voice of George Kerr, the strained falsetto of Donnie Elbert, the deep soul hysterics of the great (but sadly late) Linda Jones, the truly bizarre Shirley Goodman (one half of the Shirley and Lee duo) and, not least, the breathy, half-rapped seductions of Sylvia herself on 'Pillow Talk' and 'Lay It On Me'. All Platinum also released a number of monologues by artists such as Dave 'Baby' Cortez and Enoch Gregory and found room for a Last Poets-type group called The Universal Messengers, whose records came out on Turbo. Perhaps it was this liberal attitude to vocal style that gave Sylvia an open mind to rap (as MCing came to be known after 'Rapper's Delight'). Other practices at All Platinum – their low-budget commercialism ('Girls', Moments and Whatnauts's moment of ultimate sexism with its cheap but icily effective string synthesiser); the habit of using backing tracks and tacky instrumentals for B sides (turn over 'Girls' and you get 'More Girls' – the wordless version: not such a bad thing considering the lyrics); cover versions of disco hits (Gil Scott-Heron's 'In the Bottle' redone by Brother to Brother, who then went on to cover 'Every Nigger Is a Star'), these were all revived for the new rap fad. There was even a vocal group called The Ponderosa Twins Plus One, whose unusual 'Plus One' tag pre-dated Funky Four Plus One More by some years.

There are many stories about Sylvia's first confrontation with rap. One of the most romantic is that she was taken to a niece's birthday party at Harlem Disco World and subsequently signed the group who were rapping on the mike there, naming them The Sugarhill Gang in memory of her roots across the Hudson River on Sugar Hill. Double Trouble, true to their name, have a more elaborate account which probably comes closer to the actual events. Lil Rodney Cee gives his version:

Rap was travelling through the tapes so people was coming from Jersey who had family in New York. They'd hear the rap tapes and take them to Jersey. Somehow, Miss Robinson got an ear on what was going on. Her little kids loved rap music – they had all the rap tapes and they knew of us, The Funky Four, and Grandmaster Flash. They knew what was going on in New York. She said, 'Hey, if my kids like this all the kids around the world will like this!' So that's where she got the idea to make a record.

How she picked the Gang – that's another story. Hank was a bouncer at a local club we used to play at. He used to be at the door and if there was trouble he'd throw 'em out. That was Hank's job but while he was at the door he'd learn what was going on – he learned how to rap. He was working in a pizza shop in Jersey. Miss Robinson came in the pizza shop and he was in there rapping, saying somebody else's rhymes. She said, 'You wanna make a record?' and he said, 'Sure, why not?'

Mike was a friend of her older son. They went to school together. Mike was with another group that was forming out in Jersey. Master G was with a group too. At that time, being that he was a friend of her son, her son said, 'Ma, I got a friend that can rap.' He brought Mike home

DOUBLE TROUBLE

and she listened to him rap and said, 'Hey, you wanna make a record?' He said, 'Yeah.' Guy heard in the streets in Jersey that Miss Robinson was going to make a rap record and he felt that he could rap so he got in touch with her. He rapped for her and she said, 'Come on, we're gonna go in the studio.' They stayed in the studio for three days, they used Chic's record and came up with 'Rapper's Delight'.

KK Rockwell remembers his reaction to first hearing the record: 'I was walking down the block one day and it was coming out the record store speaker. I thought it was a tape. Then, I heard it was a record and I was going out of my mind. I didn't know what the world was coming to then! We was thinking of making a record at that time but we had no connections to make a record'. Financially, Sugarhill's first release was an auspicious start for the label. 'Rapper's Delight' reached number 36 in the US charts, became a huge international hit and went on to become the biggest-selling 12-inch record ever. Joey Robinson Jr (Sylvia and Joe's son, an executive in Sugarhill who was running his mother's fan club in 1977) is quoted in *Right On Focus* magazine's *Rap Music Special* of winter '83 as claiming: 'If you come up with something first, some-one's gonna go with it if they like it. We couldn't keep up with the demand for the record. It was selling an average of between 50 and 60,000 a day. To this day, we're still selling copies of 'Rapper's Delight' even if it's only 100 or 200 a month, we'll still sell copies and not one return.'

Musically, the record was less thrilling. In the early days of the 12-inch single, records used the available time to the full. Ten minutes of Lolleata Holloway, Melba Moore or Bettye LaVette was an emotional epic; 14 minutes 10 seconds of non-stop rhymes from The Sugarhill Gang was more like listening to farming news or stock market reports. Although nobody knew it at the time, their verses were recycled from groups like The Cold Crush Brothers; they were to Bronx hip hop what The Police were to The Sex Pistols, the difference being that the Bronx originals had yet to find a Malcolm McLaren figure with a stack of confrontational tactics to help them out.

Although Joey Robinson Jr is right in suggesting that success came from stealing a march on everybody else, 'Rapper's Delight' was not the first rap record. Earlier in 1979, The Fatback Band released a single called 'You're My Candy Sweet' on Spring Records. The B side was given over to a rap called 'King Tim III (Personality Jock)'. New York record stores began playing the rap in preference to the rather feeble top side, and disco station WKTU followed up with airplay. Both the single and the album were surprise hits.

Like 'Rapper's Delight' the song had novelty value for the general public, even if uptown MCs were contemptuous of it. Fatback were a Brooklyn band (part of the reason why the Bronx MCs disliked them) and their unexpected rap hit was a throwback to the brilliant minimalist funk and soul brother rap of early '70s records like 'New York Style' and 'Wicki Wacky'. By 1979 they were on the downward spiral –

success with 'street' music is bound to cause problems sooner or later – and the album containing 'King Tim III' is directionless and half-hearted. Whether they were consciously or unconsciously casting around for ideas, when Fatback heard DJ Hollywood rapping on the mike between acts they were taken with the idea. Lil Rodney Cee remembers King Tim III as Fatback's master of ceremonies – 'Ladeeez and Gennelmun . . . THE FATBACK BAAAND' – though other stories portray them searching him out after hearing a tape of his rapping over Roy Ayers's 'Running Away'. Their rap and 'Running Away' do have an uncanny similarity – identical tempo, a sing-along chorus and a bass line with a melodic hook in the first three beats of each bar. Coincidence?

King Tim's contribution was a stilted mixture of old-style MC and radio rapping, peppered with a few b boy phrases. Whatever latent talent he may have had failed to materialise. After a solo release the following year, another Fatback production called 'Charley Says! (Roller Boogie Baby)', he vanished from sight. 'Charley Says' was a better record than its predecessor but by 1980 the floodgates had opened and the competition was hot.

The energy of the Bronx scene had been spreading to other areas of New York and in 1979 rapping was widespread throughout the city. It took the success of Sylvia's first steps into the field to alert other record producers that something was happening that was worth recording. Bobby Robinson of Enjoy Records regrets his own short-sightedness:

It had been around since 1976 and I was aware of it – kids walking down the street with big boxes that you'd hear blasting all over. It was the kind of a thing where you'd hear kids do it in the street – everybody would laugh. Maybe it was because I wasn't actively recording. I kick myself because I should have been the first one out with a record. My good friend Sylvia Robinson at Sugarhill came out with the first giant rap record and she didn't know from nothing until she happened to hear it. She heard it one Saturday night and she flipped.

SYLVIA AND JOE ROBINSON AT SUGARHILL RECORDS, ENGLEWOOD, NEW JERSEY

I was working with some artists, writing and regrouping and getting ready to re-launch. Then, when I saw the success of The Sugarhill Gang and how *crazy* people went over this record, I said, well, I can't wait to get into my regular line of things. I'm gonna jump on this rap thing.

Bobby Robinson's move was significant in that he had been one of the most important record producers in rhythm and blues on the eastern seaboard of America. He was often the first to spot talent and was a catalyst in the careers of many performers who are now world famous – Gladys Knight and the Pips among many others.

At midday on a Friday in 1984, Bobby's Happy House Records is saturating Harlem's 125th Street with the explosive yearning of Otis Redding's 'That's How Strong My Love Is'. A few doors east is the Apollo Theatre, currently undergoing conversion into a venue which will broadcast videos of black acts as an antidote to the barrage of mediocre rock videos on cable station MTV. Over the street is Rainbow Records and a little further you can find Paul Winley Records. Walk back west and Bobby Robinson can be found in his apartment, currently cluttered with paperwork owing to a fire at his office. This is just one of the personal problems and setbacks which beset him at the moment but there have been quite a few during the last three decades and, as before, he has plans to bounce back:

I started in 1951. I went into the music business with the retail store in 1946 and all of a sudden, for some reason, my name started to spread nationwide as the most knowledgeable guy in black music. Any information you wanted – check with Bobby Robinson. The Apollo Theatre being only half a block from my place I met everybody in the black music business and a considerable amount of white artists who came from time to time as well. Everybody started to call me up; the A&R men from every company in the country – Ahmet Ertegun at Atlantic, Aladdin in California, the Bihari brothers, Chess out of Chicago – come to me for advice.

So finally, I said, 'If I'm such an authority I'll go into the production end of the business myself.' I didn't know anything about manufacturing or distribution but music has always been a way of life for me so I just took a chance. I gathered what little information I could get and I went into the studio and started producing doo-wop groups. We were just at the beginning of the doo-wop period. There were a couple of groups out at that time – The Orioles and The Ravens. The Ravens were a jump type rhythm and blues group and The Orioles were a sentimental kind of a thing. They were the forerunner of the doo-wops.

I got some groups together. We didn't have any place to rehearse so what I did was close the record store an hour early at 11 and lock the doors and rehearse right inside. The first group I recorded was The Mellow Moods – a standard tune, 'Where Are You Now That I Need You'. I started to get very good success immediately. Once you start going everybody starts to run to you so then followed The Vocaleers, The Scarlets, The Teenchords. Altogether I introduced about 13 or 14 groups in that category.

Later on, Bobby produced hits by The Channels ('The Closer You Are') and The Charts ('Deserie'). In the bible of the doo-wop era, *They All Sang On the Corner*, Philip Groia describes how The Charts got themselves booed off stage at The Apollo Theatre amateur night 'for singing what the audience believed was a "weird" song.

"Deserie" was a drag as it "wah-wahed" along with no channel [bridge] . . . They sang it right through the booing, onto the Everlast label and into three and a half million copies of the novel recording. No more hanging around corners anymore.' Unfortunately, as Groia points out, The Charts were too young to keep control of their success. They sold the rights of 'Deserie' to a photographer and after four more records for Bobby Robinson they vanished. The parallels with the rap scene are clear. Having lived and worked in the middle of both phenomena, Bobby draws the comparison:

Doo-wop originally started out as the black teenage expression of the '50s and rap emerged as the black teenage ghetto expression of the '70s. Same identical thing that started it – the doo-wop groups down the street, in hallways, in alleys and on the corner. They'd gather anywhere and, you know, doo wop doo wah da da da da. You'd hear it everywhere. So the same thing started with rap groups around '76 or so. All of a sudden, everywhere you turned you'd hear kids rapping. In the summertime, they'd have these little parties in the park. They used to go out and play at night and kids would be out there dancing. All of a sudden, all you could hear was, hip hop hit the top don't stop. It's kids – to a great extent mixed-up and confused – reaching out to express themselves. They were forcefully

BOBBY ROBINSON'S RECORD STORE, 125TH STREET

THE CLOSER YOU ARE: THE CHANNELS
Photo: courtesy of Charlie Gillett

BOBBY ROBINSON AT HOME

trying to express themselves and they made up in fantasy what they missed in reality. The older guys who created doo-wop – it was a little different. They weren't so aggressive and volatile.

From doo-wop Robinson moved into rhythm and blues with Wilbert Harrison's 'Kansas City' ('after that it was a whole new ball game'), Buster Brown, Elmore James and Lightning Hopkins. Through the '50s he had formed a number of labels starting with Red Robin, then Whirlin' Disc followed by Fury ('I was pretty furious at some of the things that had happened with the Whirlin' Disc setup so I formed Fury as a label'), Fire and then, in 1963, Enjoy. The first record on Enjoy was the driving tenor-saxophone instrumental 'Soul Twist' by King Curtis, one of the major black instru-

mentalists to span the eras of '50s and '60s jazz and R&B through to '70s soul. Curtis, who died a violent death in 1971, was one of the artists who benefited from Bobby Robinson's ear for the commercial. After a brief period of success on Enjoy, King Curtis decided that greater rewards lay elsewhere and Bobby Robinson granted him a release from his contract to move to Capitol Records. This was a pattern that was to reassert itself in the '70s with most of the rap groups which recorded for Enjoy.

During the 1960s Bobby reactivated the Everlast label (previously run by his brother Danny) and had a million seller with Les Cooper's dance-craze disc 'Wiggle Wobble'. Successes became thinner on the ground and the operation ran into what he describes as a 'quagmire'. With the retail store still doing business he became a $100-a-day consultant for Pickwick International, a huge budget record company in Long Island, packaging black music records in a series called Soul Parade. He also made many lease deals for his back catalogue, which he now regrets. Like many older producers and artists, disco was a music which had little appeal for him:

I'll tell you very frankly, I didn't have too high a regard for disco because what it was to me was like taking good-age Scotch and pouring it two-thirds with water. When I've got to sit down and produce music and count how many beats goes to a minute to hell with it. Black music is like a sixth-sense thing. You've got to feel it. I don't care how many beats it is. When they would take

one line and say it over 130 times and that was a song – that really bugged me. It was a craze that caught on. The whole world was dance crazy. A lot of it was good but to me it just didn't have the substance that I thought music should have.

As disco began to wane as a fad Robinson felt that the time was right for him to release records again, and the charting of 'Rapper's Delight' pushed him into searching out some MC groups for himself. His scouts reported back to him from the deepest Bronx:

There's a group called The Funky Four that have got a girl rapping with them called Sha Rock. That's a novelty 'cos she's the only girl out there. So I got that group first. We rehearsed in a garage – you press a button and the doors slide up – the guy backed his car into the street. We set the band up, the drums and guitar and everything; it was cold. It was mid-October and it was kind of chilly, so we let the gates down and we rehearsed. The Funky Four record took right off – called 'Rappin and Rockin the House'.

Released in 1979, the rhythm track for 'Rappin and Rockin' the House' was a version of Cheryl Lynn's debut, 'Got To Be Real', a single which had topped the R&B charts in January of that year. The drummer and bandleader on the session was Pumpkin, a young multi-instrumentalist who had started out playing jazz in high school and worked with a number of jazz fusion groups, including Triad, playing drums, bass and synthesiser. Funky Four's DJ Breakout had remembered Pumpkin always playing in a garage and recommended him to Bobby Robinson for their first (and only) Enjoy session. Clocking in at a length of 16 minutes, the record is a marathon to top 'Rapper's Delight'. Apart from a spectacular drum break by Pumpkin, the entire length is given over to rapping.

In the rush to get rap onto disc the most logical way to transfer live throwdowns onto tape was to take the favourite instrumental B sides that were being used by MC crews at the time, re-record them in their simplest form (guitar, bass and drums playing the chords and rhythmic structure), then overlay the rapping. The raps started about eight bars in and could usually be heard fading into the distance on the run-out groove. 'Rappin and Rockin the House' suffers from its lack of contrast but the feel is more innocent and the vocal interplay more dynamic than the Sugarhill debut, making it the more likeable release. Funky Four Plus One More were Lil Rodney Cee, KK Rockwell, Sha Rock, Keith Keith and Jazzy Jeff with DJ Breakout. KK Rockwell sketches in their history: ' I got started with Breakout. About seven or eight years ago there was just me and DJ Breakout. He got a partner, then along came Keith Keith, then Sha Rock, then we put Rahiem with us. He left us for Grandmaster Flash and that's when Rodney and Jeff joined with us and we turned to the Funky Four Plus One More'.

Their first experience as recording artists fell short of their expectations, although there seem to be no hard feelings directed at Enjoy. Rodney explains their disappointment:

We were young at the time. When we signed the contract we were 16 and 17. Nobody was older than 17 in the group. We signed with Enjoy and it didn't turn out the way we expected it. All I knew, this guy came to me, he wanted to make a record and he told me I'm gonna be rich. That's what I expected. I expected to be rich for making a record and it didn't materialise. We made a nice little bit of money – it wasn't all that bad. We did a couple of shows. We went down south where it didn't turn out right because rap was new across the country. Right here in New York it was well accepted so we could play here and make crazy money.

It is hardly surprising that Funky Four's first release was so long (the longest single ever made?). For their live shows they were publicising themselves by handing out flyers and then performing from midnight to three or four in the morning, rapping straight through. Their dance routines were inspired by The Temptations. Ted Fox, in his book *Showtime At the Apollo*, talks about The Temptations' influence and the Apollo's effect on the Motown acts' stagecraft:

What really ignited the Motown revues at the Apollo was the slick sophisticated choreography of the great male groups like The Four Tops and especially The

SLICK, SOPHISTICATED CHOREOGRAPHY: THE TEMPTATIONS *Photo: courtesy of Charlie Gillett*

Temptations. 'The Temps were known for that,' said Gladys Knight, 'and the Apollo Theatre perpetuated that style because it became popular with the audiences there, and they just ate it up.' Gladys Knight and the Pips had been on the scene professionally for ten years be-

fore the Motown revues began, but didn't join the Motown caravan until the mid-sixties. The Pips' dancing ability, fine-tuned by Honi Coles' partner, Cholly Atkins, was a tremendous influence on The Temptations.

The big attraction of The Temptations for The Funky Four was their professionalism. Though rap was relatively amateur it was fiercely competitive, and the group were aware that an entertaining stage show would give them an edge over the MCs who simply stood and ran their mouths. The dance steps were combined with raps to make little routines, some of them based on TV theme tunes like 'Gilligans Island'.

Bobby Robinson's scouts initially recommended two groups – The Funky Four Plus One More and Grandmaster Flash and the Furious Five. Flash remembers with some amusement the time Bobby came to see them play:

> When that record ['Rapper's Delight'] came out, little carry-your-records-in-a-trunk producers were coming out of the woodwork looking for any group that could do this. So I said to myself, I know my fans' age range is between 15 and 21. There was this little *old* man in the back – he was too old to be partying. Either he was in there looking for his daughter or son or he was the fucking cops. My manager went up to him after – could he help him? So he says, 'Why sure, I want to speak to these guys. I'm interested in cutting a record with them.' His name was Bobby Robinson.

The record was 'Superrappin''. Around the time of its release another 12-inch single appeared by a group calling themselves The Younger Generation. On Brass Records, it was called 'We Rock More Mellow' and was produced by Terry Lewis. This group was also the Furious Five – Melle Mel, Cowboy, Rahiem, Mr Ness and Kid Creole – under an assumed name. Considering the brief time lag between the two records, the differences are striking. The backing track for the Younger Generation tune is a leaden disco thumper with a shaky four-on-the-floor bass drum, and the rapping is a strictly follow-my-leader effort with the MCs sounding like the session was beginning to depress them. In contrast, 'Superrappin'' has the kind of pumping rhythm that characterised rap in its early days on disc – a brisk 114 bpm with the bass drum playing syncopations that hadn't been heard in dance music for some years.

The Furious Five's rapping style was a revelation. Lines were divided up between individuals and cut in with unison ensembles and solos which highlighted the different vocal qualities and styles. They also duplicated Flash's spin-backs and quick cuts, repeating syllables as if the stylus was dropping back into the same groove – 'That Flash was on the beat box going . . . an . . . an . . . an . . . an . . . sha-na-na'.

The group had been asked to make a record some years previously but Flash was reluctant, thinking that a used beat and some talking was no competition for the plush orchestral sound that was predominant during that period. He has reservations about 'Superrappin'':

> I enjoyed 'Superrappin'' to a point and then again I didn't. It could have been done better 'cos if you listen the tempo speeds up after a while. The band goes out of wack a little bit. After a while we

were waiting to hear 'Superrappin'' on the radio because this other rap record, The Sugarhill Gang, they were on the air. What power do Sugarhill have to get something on the radio like *that* and we can't get *ours* on it? Ours sounds better than theirs. Bobby didn't really have the push to get us out there. We got kinda angry with him and we went to the Hill.

Bobby Robinson had suffered, in fact, from his long lay-off from the business:

I'm off and running with Enjoy and with two smash hit records. I really wasn't organised on a national basis because I'd been out of it for a while. I could have had much bigger records had I really been geared. I operated most of the eastern seaboard from here to Florida. I spread a little bit west but I wasn't really geared with the national distribution linkage. I found myself caught up in it. I thought it was a fad that will last a little while and blow over and I'll get into my other thing. I had no idea it would be as long drawn-out as it has been.

The radio stations were all very touchy but I'll tell you the truth – I didn't miss it because with the rap records, luckily for a lot of small companies who had trouble with airplay and credibility, the rap thing was like wildfire without the radio. You see, you cover all the discos and disco pools and mobile jocks – everybody that's got a mike in their hand, give 'em records. And stores – in-store play – put 'em on the speakers outside in the street and the kids would line up. So I broke the records wide open without the air.

Although Bobby was fast off the mark, the time it took him to realise what was going on cost him another first. After Flash and the Five he paired The Treacherous Three with Spoonie Gee. One side was the tongue-twisting 'The New Rap Language', a rap with a nod to Mary Poppins which set a new style of quickfire rhyming against a 112 bpm beat with a slowish feel. On drums was Pumpkin, and featured on congas was Pooche Costello, Spoonie Gee's brother (currently answering the phone at Enjoy Records). The other side was 'Love Rap', a solo rap by Spoonie Gee, with just voice, drums and congas. One of the very few

LOVE RAP: SPOONIE GEE AT DANCETERIA

commercially released raps with only beats for backing, it has been a consistently big seller for Bobby right up until the present. He confesses how he missed out once again:

Spoonie was raised right here in this house. Pooche Costello, the conga player, that's Spoonie Gee's brother. Their mother was my wife's baby sister and they lived down the hall – same floor, last apartment. She died suddenly and Spoonie was 12, Pooche was about 14, and my wife took them in and gave them that back room there.

He did his first rapping right in this room – wearing out my records! He'd sit over in that corner day after day. He'd play my records. My wife used to run him out of here sometimes. She'd say, 'Get out of here with that noise. All day long that yap-yap-yap.' He put together that very first thing that he did in this room to my music but I was so involved at the time. I had three or four things going on. This guy, Peter Brown, he was in my record store one night and he said, 'I'd like to cut a rap record', and somebody says, 'Spoonie can rap'.

As a result of this scene from an M.G.M. musical, Spoonie Gee cut 'Spoonin' Rap' on Sounds of New York USA, one of Peter Brown's bewilderingly full hand of labels. It also appeared on an album on Queen Constance Records called *The Big Break Rapper Party* and was remixed and re-released in 1984 on Heavenly Star. For Brown (not the Peter Brown who recorded 'Do Ya Wanna Get Funky With Me'), record pro-

duction was a hustle among hustles. His other labels included Golden Flamingo and Land of Hits, the records frequently classics of low-budget incompetence. If the label said 33 it was 45; singers sang and rappers rapped out of time; drummers lost the beat, and the sound was as garage as they come. A number of these releases had appeal as golden turkeys, but from amidst the general mass of garbage Spoonie Gee shone through as a real talent.

Spoonie is currently working as a supervisor in a rehabilitation centre for the mentally disabled where he is known by his real name of Gabe Jackson (his nickname came from his fondness for eating with a spoon when he was a small boy). 'Spoonin' Rap' was the first release on a journey through three different labels before his current signing at Aaron Fuchs's Tuff City Records. He already sounds self-assured, fluently rolling out the seduction routine that has become his trademark over a slinky backing track of bass and drums, some flexatone and whistles. With his tall tales, sexual boasting and badman stories, Spoonie is closest to the mythical Jody, the woman stealer and death dealer. However regrettable outsiders might find the sexism of his songs, they are part of a line in black oral literature and song which extends at its furthest limit to Spoonie's favourite form of music, the romantic soul ballad: 'I'm into all types of music but I like the type of music I can lay back to and listen. I like old records, old and new, but I like slow ballads. I'll take slow music over fast music any day. I like Marvin Gaye, Nat King Cole, Brook Benton. I like, God bless the dead, Jackie

Wilson. I even liked Elvis. I can't forget Barry White'.

If Spoonie identifies with the balladeers, Kurtis Blow sees himself as being somewhere between Chic and James Brown. The sound of 1979 was rappers splashing into wax, and Kurtis leaped with the leaders. His 'Christmas Rapping' appeared on Mercury at the end of the year. The bass line was a distant cousin to 'Good Times'; the guitarists obviously knew a thing or two about Nile Rodgers and Jimmy Nolan (the late great guitar chair with the JBs), there was even an echo of Junior Wells's 'Messing With the Kid', not to mention a key change and a very funky piano player, Denzil Miller. Rap on record had come a long way in a few months.

Kurtis was another soloist with Harlem origins, a mobile jock playing James Brown records in Queens who was struck by DJ Hollywood's popularity at the 371 Club in the Bronx. For a brief period he worked with Grandmaster Flash, and in summer '79 was spotted at The Hotel Diplomat by his producers, JB Moore and Robert Ford Jr, and offered a deal.

Rap was a performance medium. It was a throwback to the days when musicians made singles which approximated to their live show, albums were hastily-thrown-together hotch potches of hits with filler, and overdubbing was virtually unheard of. Signing to Mercury, with its Polygram distribution, and working with a team of lyricists which included Moore and Ford as well as his manager, Russell Simmons, Kurtis was the first to combine hip hop with a '70s concept of production and marketing. In 1980 he released an album which obviously attempted to cross him over to a broader audience. The songs took basic b boy rhymes and moulded them into themes with a humorous or moral twist. There was even a rock song – Bachman Turner Overdrive's 'Takin' Care of Business' – and a ridiculous ballad with Kurtis revealing a surprisingly frail voice.

The big track was 'The Breaks', a 1980 hit which gave rap some of the tautness of a comedy routine (partly through being inspired by Eddie Lawrence, a white comic). Thanks to Roddy Hui's engineering, the track had a terrific clarity. The bass and drums were used as a foundation, reggae style, for a clever arrangement of the other instruments, in particular the fierce percussion breaks traded off between Jamie Delgado's timbales and Jimmy Bralower's tom toms. Kurtis Blow may not have been 100 per cent proof Bronx hip hop, but his early records helped set the style in post-disco dance music.

One of the constants of rap is its machismo. On the front cover of his first album Kurtis is bare-chested, hung with gold chains showing off his pectorals. The look is 'tough' and the eyes are sincere but steady. Considering the rich heritage of female vocalists in black music it is surprising that women rappers have not had greater success. In the early days of hip hop Grandmaster Flash remembers there being more female crews than male. Of the few fixed groups in those days one was entirely female – The Mercedes Ladies (Zena Z, Debbie D, Eva Deff and Sherry Sheryl, with RC and Baby D as DJs). Rodney and

Kevin of Double Trouble recall their rise and fall: 'They were from the Bronx. But they came in and went out fast,' says Rodney. Kevin elaborates: 'Slowly but surely their name was getting out there. People was getting to know them but they gave up. They even played with us one time and it was packed. Right there, that's a lot of publicity for them. They should have stayed with it. The girl DJ was good – she definitely should have stayed with it. Sha Rock stuck with it and she mastered it.'

Since rapping has strong roots in the predominantly male activities of toasts and dozens, it is not surprising that men see it as the musical equivalent of a sport like baseball. They are prepared to accept that women can do it but see the competitive element as the final deterrent. Flash has a paternalistic attitude to it:

> There was the Mercedes Ladies, Sha Rock, Lisa Lee – there was quite a few, but a lot of them gave up. See, what it is in this highly competitive sort of entertainment there's very few females I see made it. I even tried to show some of them the proper way of going about it. I've seen one DJ – she was pretty good. She thought she was as good as me. That's good to have that type of spirit. She was good but she just stopped. Now she's on West End Records – Baby D, D'bora. She was pretty good back in that day. She was the DJ for the Mercedes Ladies, a whole female crew, and that's what they need right now. I'm talking about a real good DJ and some good MCs that really know how to shake it and

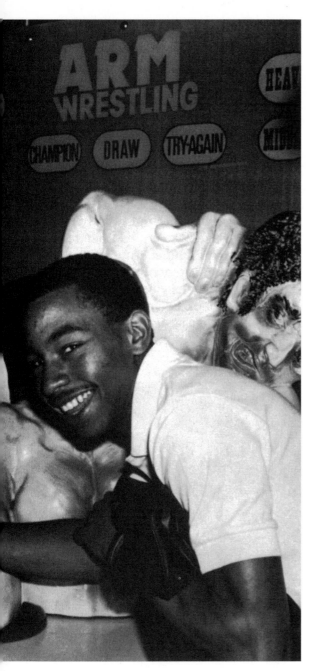

entertain the crowd. They'd make money. They'd make a killing right now 'cos what's happening right now is everything is becoming repetitious.

Women associated with the scene, on the other hand, feel that men tend to disapprove of their standing in front of a crowd bragging and boasting. But in some cases they go along with the men: shouting about yourself might be all right when you're young but as you get older it's 'unladylike'. In the first few years of recording a high proportion of raps featured girls – Funky Four Plus One More, Lady D on Reflection Records, The CC Crew on Golden Flamingo, Naomi Peterson on Heavenly Star, Cosmic Force and Paulette and Tanya Winley on Winley Records, Philadelphia DJ Lady B on Tec Records and Sequence on Sugarhill.

At Danceteria on West 21st the diminutive duo Double Trouble and dancers Electric Force are hosting a 'graffiti wedding celebration' in honour of Rodney's marriage to Angie B of Sequence. At the end of the show Angie B and Cheryl the Pearl come out to perform a song, handing out copies of their album and explaining that their third member, Blondie, is in Los Angeles right now. Although their voices don't yet have the emotional depth of a gospel group like the Barrett Sisters, they certainly look the part. Sequence were originally a singing group from Columbia, South Carolina, whose break came when they went to a Sugarhill Gang concert in the

ARM WRESTLING AT THE FUNHOUSE

summer of 1979. One of the Gang's road managers took a liking to Angie B but found himself having to listen to the whole group giving an impromptu performance of a song they had written called 'Funk You Up'. Probably feeling out of his depth, he took them backstage to meet Sylvia Robinson, who auditioned them then and there and within three weeks had sent them plane tickets and recorded their tune.

'Funk You Up' is one of the classic boasting raps, with Blondie (not the Debbie Harry version) telling the boys in the house not to ring her bell if they can't fulfil her needs. Culture heroes like Fred Astaire and Ginger Rogers, Fred Flintstone and Yogi Bear are invoked, and the Sugarhill houseband sound extremely powerful, with Doug Wimbish's visceral bass tangling with the voices.

On all of the early rap records featuring women, the women rap as well as the men – in some cases far better. 'Vicious Rap' by Sweet Tee, in particular, is a refreshing blast of old-style R&B. The drummer plays with the snares off, there's an organ stabbing away underneath the guitar (probably played by Dave 'Baby' Cortez) and Sweet Tee raps out a tough story of false arrest. The sound may be boxy and lacking in production, and the tempo speeds up, but the excitement is there.

Sweet Tee, who also raps with her sister on 'Rhymin and Rappin' had her records produced by her mother, Ann Winley, and released by her father, Paul Winley. This family enterprise can be found on 125th Street. If you look up you see a smart logo and a painted sign saying PAUL WINLEY RECORDS INC. Look down and you see a

SEQUENCE AT DANCETERIA

different picture. Winley Records has obviously seen better days. The storefront has an unkempt display of record sleeves – Afrika Bambaataa, Malcolm X, Martin Luther King, Gloria Lynne – and inside are the signs of having worked on the far edges of an already marginalised field of music. Despite his notorious reputation among certain sectors of the New York record business, Paul Winley is a friendly and obliging man with a resigned, philosophical attitude to the consequences of cutting corners in matters of copyright. He describes his starting point in music:

I started in the business from writing songs. My brother had a group called the Clovers and I started writing songs for them in Washington. They used to come to New York to record for Atlantic – and I used to come up with them. I met Ahmet Ertegun and all of us became very good friends. Everybody at Atlantic at that time was like family so after moving here from Washington in '52–'53 I just stayed. I used to spend a lot of time at Atlantic. They had artists like Ray Charles, Ruth Brown, Joe Turner – I remember writing songs for Ruth Brown and Joe Turner.

From Atlantic I hit the street and started writing around the Brill Building which was 1619. In the old days that's where all the songwriters and all the

PAUL WINLEY

PAUL WINLEY RECORDS, 125TH STREET

black entertainers would meet – on Broadway, 49th and Broadway, which is now Colony Records. We would congregate round there, write songs and shoot the breeze. I did that for a number of years, then in 1956 I started my own record company. A lot of publishers to survive at that time went into starting their own record companies. In order for a songwriter to give a publisher a song he had to damn near have a record. There was a group of songwriters. There was about six or seven of us – there was a feller named Otis Blackwell who wrote for Elvis. There was a feller named Winfield Scat who wrote 'Tweedle Dee'. There was a feller we considered our teacher – his name is Jesse Stone but they called him Charles Calhoun. He wrote 'Shake Rattle and Roll', 'Money Honey', a lot of songs. He was the real backbone of the songwriters.

Winley had a songwriting partnership with Davey Clowney, later known as Dave 'Baby' Cortez, and the two of them started recording doo-wop groups:

First thing I recorded was by 'Baby' Cortez, then a feller named Little Anthony. He had a group called the Duponts – we recorded them. Nothing happened too much and then we recorded The Paragons. A friend of mine wanted me to hear these kids out in Brooklyn and they were real hoodlums, real zip-gun street-warring hoodlums, you know, but at the time I was young and crazy myself so it didn't make any

difference. We got together and listened to them and the guy that sang lead had a song called 'Florence' and they could never sing the damn thing twice in the same way. We finally got 'em into the studio and we recorded 'Florence', and there was another group from the east side here called The Jesters who recorded, so I had two good groups. Then another group came along, with a good song, called The Collegians – they made a record called 'Zoom Zoom Zoom' for me. We had a lot of good things here and there in the '50s, and then in the '60s we recorded The Jesters who rearranged their group and re-recorded a thing called 'The Wind'.

With Moms Mabley for his godmother and other comics like Nipsey Russell, Pigmeat Markham and Flip Wilson as friends, Paul was very aware that rap was just another chapter in a rich tradition of black vocal artistry:

Rapping goes back. Rapping is an old thing. Like a lot of black singers couldn't sing but they could talk. My brother, the one who used to be with The Clovers, is singing now with a group called The Inkspots – the original management group of The Inkspots. If you go back to that era, the part my brother does is the bass 'cos he was bass with The Clovers, so now he talks. James Brown did rapping, Isaac Hayes did rapping, Millie Jackson did rapping – rapping is nothing new.

Apart from recording his own family in the late '70s, Winley also put down tracks by two of Afrika Bambaataa's MC crews, Cosmic Force and Soul Sonic Force. 'Zulu Nation Throwdown' by Cosmic Force was released in 1980. Neither Winley nor Bambaataa are too happy about the record, and Bambaataa doesn't bother to hide his contempt for the company:

A wack company. It was jive. He put out a record called Afrika Bambaataa's 'Death Mix'. That is a tape like – suppose she came to my party and made a tape and she made a copy for you and you made a copy for me and I took the tape and gave it to him and he put it on record. It sounds like doo doo! He had the nerve to put on the back, 'I'm sorry for the first two records I did with you. You my friend' and all that. It was really a bootleg type of mess. We didn't get any money for the first record. The first two he made was ugly anyway. I went to him saying I could make his company move. I had ideas but he didn't pay us no mind.

'Zulu Nation Throwdown, Part One' helped us to get downtown. A lot of the new-wave people liked it. It surprised me 'cos I couldn't stand it until I heard it on the Ritz system. I started coming to clubs and they were playing it a lot and I started liking it. Then we made Part Two with Soul Sonic Force which never went no-where. This company was just terrible.

Despite Bambaataa's dislike of Winley Records, it was the only company prepared to release his material in the early days. He had been working on a version of Sly Stone's 'Sing a Simple Song' in the Sugarhill Studios with George Kerr (an intriguing project which came to nothing), but what he was hearing about Sylvia Robinson was anything but encouraging. Sending a tape to Enjoy proved fruitless, so Winley was the next stop.

The Cosmic Force 12-inch is high on charm, with a Chitty Chitty Bang Bang throwaway and some strong lines in a James Brown mould from Lisa Lee:

Rock it to the sounds that make you dance
Make the ants crawl in your pants
Put you in a music trance.

In his sleeve notes for *The Best of Winley Records* on Relic Records, Donn Fileti's analysis of Winley's doo-wop approach in relation to bigger companies could just as easily apply to the '70s:

There's a kind of down-to-earth, almost amateurish quality to the records that Winley produced in the late '50s which made them almost impossible to duplicate; his sound could only have come from an imaginative independent operator – the major labels thought the group sound was easy to copy but their abject failure with New York-type vocal groups was partly in trying to employ expensive production values for street-corner harmonizers, which Winley disdained (and could not afford). The Paul Winley sound is unique, and could only have come out of New York City.

Winley describes his entry into the rap market:

In the '70s when the rapping started I put out some records called *Super Disco Brakes* and the kids would use certain breaks in these records to rap. I recorded my two daughters. One of my daughters was a rap fanatic. Every time I looked at her she had her head in her notebook. I said, 'Well, how much homework you got? You really must love school!' But she was actually writing rhymes. That's Tanya. Paulette wasn't into that – she was more into singing.

A couple of dealers who used to buy these records from me said, 'Hey Paul, why don't you make one rap record because these kids – *anything* – if you put out something with the raps it'll go.' I said, 'But every kid on the block is rapping.' They said, 'But they just want to hear it on record.' That's the reason I hesitated. I would have recorded rap before Sugarhill was even thought of – long before Bobby Robinson cut rap – because these guys didn't know what was going on. I was in the street selling my break records so I was very familiar. I knew they were buying the records to do the raps off.

Given the extraordinary subsequent influence of hip hop all over the world – scratch mix seminars in Japan, rap radio in Holland, breakdance fever in Germany, smurf madness in France, rap clubs and crews in Britain – the reticence of rappers and label owners to record is puzzling. In many cases there was a resignation to being shut off from the mainstream – physically, politically, culturally – at a time when much black music had crossed over to a non-black audience. In the middle '70s an enormous amount of black music was achieving sales in the international mass market. Although all of it derived from strands of the black music tradition, the degree of success tended to be proportional to the absence of rawness, and the phrase 'too black for the charts' became common music-business jargon.

With Sugarhill proving that there was a new market for streetcorner sounds, the old-time entrepreneurs dusted off the ancient contracts and moved in. Jack Taylor, from Rojac Records, who in the '60s had recorded Big Maybelle records like 'Don't Pass Me By', recorded pioneer MC Starski, and Danny Robinson, Bobby Robinson's brother, briefly revived his Holiday label (home of The Bop Chords in 1956) for The Nice and Nasty Three's 'The Ultimate Rap' in 1980. The early records are confusing, partly because they transferred a sound-system-based music onto disc and partly because some of the artists were recorded not so much for their talent but because they happened to hang out down the block from the record company. Although most hip-hop innovators had found their way onto disc by 1980, it was initially difficult for a casual listener to tell who were the opportunists and who were the originals. It may not all have been good but it was definitely fresh.

8. Version to version

One of the first signs that the early flurry of rap recordings had registered an impact outside of its own back yard was the release of a cover version of 'Rapper's Delight' on Joe Gibbs's reggae label in 1979. 'Rapper's Delight' and 'Rocker's Choice' by Xanadu and Sweet Lady is rapped, quasi-Bronx style, on one side, and toasted, Jamaican style, on the other. Given the Caribbean background of three of the prime movers in hip hop (Kool DJ Herc, Afrika Bambaataa and Grandmaster Flash), the similar foundation of rap and reggae in sound systems and radio DJs, and the number of Bronx, Harlem and Brooklyn residents with roots in the West Indies, it is surprising that there were not more crossovers of this type. According to Jervis Anderson's book, *Harlem: The Great Black Way*: 'In the nineteen-thirties, more than twenty per cent of Harlem's black population were people from the West Indies.' Tempting as it might be to imagine that hip hop emerged simply through the influence of Jamaican toasters like U Roy and Big Youth, it was, in fact, more subtle than that. Most rappers will tell you that they either disliked reggae or were only vaguely aware of it in the early and middle '70s. Although Jamaican-run record companies like Clocktower (now defunct after the killing of label boss Brad Osbourne), Bullwackies and Clappers exist in New York, there have been remarkably few musical collaborations between reggae and funk.

In the same way in which salsa has been plundered but rarely met on its own terms, reggae has been an influence on isolated records ('Rock the House' by Pressure Drop on Tommy Boy or Sugarhill's remake of 'Love Is Strange' by The Word) or on studio techniques. Dub mixes began to appear in 1982, particularly from The Peech Boys, François Kervorkian's mixes of Forrrce and D Train, and Nick Martinelli and David Todd's mixes of Raw Silk and Brenda Taylor.

With sound systems at their heart, reggae and rap share a partial reliance on previously recorded rhythms. In all the stories of pre-disc hip hop the only musicians are the ones on the DJ's records. The rock or soul impulse to form a band, rehearse and play gigs was supplanted by the magic attraction of the twin turntables. Ask the majority of DJs and MCs if they play an instrument and they'll probably offer 'beat box' as a reply. This is changing gradually as groups develop their ideas in recording studios, but in its basic form hip hop has stayed true to its house-party origins.

The time it took for record companies to move in on hip hop in New York allowed a huge build-up of innovative techniques and quirky styles which then had to be translated into a playable instrumental form and adapted for mass public consumption.

Though many of the rap/scratch records that have been released since 1979 sound unique, they are mostly polished versions of the kind of thing every kid on the block was doing. This is particularly true of Malcolm McLaren 'Buffalo Gals' single and its follow ups, the *Duck Rock* album and other related projects like Art of Noise. All of them were crucial in bringing acceptance of hip-hop attitudes to a very wide audience (and, to be fair, had an influence back into hip hop). *Duck Rock* was a hi-tech version of the kind of inspired musical collisions that were commonplace at the time when McLaren's attention was focused on scandalising the world with The Sex Pistols.

In the who-dares-wins delirium of the house parties, Bambaataa mixed up calypso, European and Japanese electronic music, Beethoven's Fifth Symphony and rock groups like Mountain; Kool DJ Herc spun The Doobie Brothers back-to-back with the Isley Brothers; Grandmaster Flash overlayed speech records and sound effects with The Last Poets; Symphonic B Boys Mixx cut up classical music on five turntables, and a multitude of unknowns unleashed turntable wizardry with their feet, heads, noses, teeth and tongues. In a crazy new sport of disc jockey acrobatics, musical experiment and virtuosity were being combined with showmanship. Earlier in black music history the same potent spirit had compelled Lionel Hampton to leap onto his drums, Big Jay McNeely to play screaming saxophone lying on the stage and the guitar aces – T Bone Walker, Earl Hooker, Johnny Guitar Watson and Jimi Hendrix – to pick the strings with their teeth or behind their heads.

A few small groups of studio musicians were given the job of converting all this sound-system mayhem and verbal wildstyle into marketable recordings. The All Platinum set-up in Englewood had maintained two studios as well as a house band called Wood, Brass and Steel, all of which transferred to Sugarhill with the incorporation of the new company. Keith LeBlanc, a white drummer, bassist Doug Wimbish and guitarist Bernard Alexander formed the early nucleus of the Sugarhill band, along with a horn section called Chops. Later additions included guitarist Skip MacDonald, percussionist Ed Fletcher (Duke Bootee of 'The Message' and 'Survival' fame) and keyboardists Gary Henry, Duane Mitchell, Reggie Griffen and Clifton 'Jiggs' Chase. Jiggs, whose dues include the organ chair in flautist Joe Thomas's '60s soul jazz group (comping behind the soloists on Hammond organ), has also been the arranger on most of Sugarhill's rap output as well as mixing tracks with engineer Steve Jerome. The biggest credit is generally given to Sylvia Robinson as producer and co-writer, though some Sugarhill artists (mostly those who have fled the company) question the extent of her actual contribution. What all give her credit for is her ability to spot records with strong, usable rhythms for potential raps.

When Flash and The Furious Five moved from Enjoy to Sugarhill, signing their contract on the bonnet of a car, Sylvia offered them a backing track for their first release, a single called 'Freedom'. Flash explains the circumstances:

What was hot from the b boy scene was this record called 'Get Up and Dance' by this group called Freedom, on TK Records. This was what all the DJs were cutting – disco DJs and b boys DJs. What she did is she took it and recut it, reconstructed it herself, and she had it on 24-track tape in the studio, so when I met Sylvia Robinson, me and Raheim, she was saying she could get us on that record if we signed.

Funky Four Plus One More also moved from Enjoy to Sugarhill, losing the last word from their name somewhere in the Hudson River but still clutching their idea for a rhythm track. Their debut for the new label was 'That's the Joint', a slower re-arranged version of 'Rappin' and Rockin' the House', with LeBlanc's bass drum and Wimbish's bass kicking at the front of the mix. Although 'Freedom' was credited to its original writers, 'That's the Joint' was given to Funky Four, Sylvia and Jiggs. The general rule among companies was to ignore copyright on the original rhythm until there was trouble. 'Rapper's Delight', for example, was initially credited to The Sugarhill Gang and Sylvia, but later pressings gave total authorship to Chic's Bernard Edwards and Nile Rodgers, the writers of 'Good Times'.

Edwards and Rodgers have seen 'Good Times' reappear on numerous occasions in various guises. An Atlanta disc jockey named Vaughan Mason released a floor-shaking riff called 'Bounce, Rock, Skate, Roll' on Brunswick in 1979 which was clearly based on 'Good Times'. Like an omen of things to come, it was the funk equivalent of heavy metal – guitar, vocals and percussion all extraneous dressing on the demolition-derby bass at its immovable centre. Mason, who claimed authorship of this multi-imaged riff, then saw his track

reappear on the launch release for a new label called Sound of New York (not to be confused with Peter Brown's Sound of New York, USA). It was used as a backing track for a rap called 'Rap, Bounce, Rockskate' by two young MCs called Jerry Miller and Eric Isles, working under the name Trickeration. Authorship this time went to the company's president and vice-president, Gene Griffen and Bill Scarborough respectively.

The big hit of 1980 was Queen's 'Another One Bites the Dust', a song which pushed the Chic riff a little bit further from its origins and gave mixers the opportunity to slip from one version to another. This culminated in Grandmaster Flash's challenge to the world, 'The Adventures of Grandmaster Flash On the Wheels Of Steel' (Sugarhill, 1981), a devastating collage of Queen, Chic, The Sugarhill Gang's '8th Wonder', The Furious Five's 'Birthday Party', Sequence and Spoonie Gee's 'Monster Jam' and Blondie's 'Rapture'. It also overlayed a Disney-sounding story, the source of which Flash is keeping a firm secret.

All of the tracks used by Flash for his in-studio cut-up tie together – 'Monster Jam', 'Birthday Party' and '8th Wonder' all share the distinctive Sugarhill band sound. 'Birthday Party' is a do-over of 'Freedom' with a bridge sounding suspiciously like McFadden and Whitehead's 'Ain't No Stopping Us Now', and 'Monster Jam' is yet another 'Good Times' derivation which links the Queen and Chic tracks. The Blondie song, their homage to hip hop, is used for its namecheck of Flash – the

Grandmaster drops the needle back on the beginning of 'Flash is fast' three times just to prove how fast he is.

The passage of years since the bombshell release of 'Adventures' makes it easier to hear the differences between Flash's techniques and those of the newer-mix DJs. His scratching, in particular, has a harsh and grainy quality and a terrific rhythmic drive. Comparing him with scratch DJs like Grandmixer D.ST or Whiz Kid is like comparing John Lee Hooker's guitar playing with B.B. King's. The instrument and the musical genre are the same but the individual approaches are a mile apart.

'Adventures On the Wheels of Steel' was the first record really to show that rap was something other than an offshoot of disco. Where other releases *translated* hip hop, 'Adventures' was as close as any record would ever come to *being* hip hop.

Alongside 'Good Times', one of the other big version rhythms was Taana Gardner's 'Heartbeat'. Rap had applied the brakes to disco's pace and taken off its frenetic edge. 'Heartbeat' more or less ground it to a halt. Introduced by a disturbingly unsteady heartbeat and claps like gunfire, 'Heartbeat' seems to hang on to its funereal rhythm like a cardiac-arrest victim clinging to life. On any other record it might have been a disastrous move but the tension and slowness in the rhythm worked with Taana Gardner's strange quivering voice to create a pervasive trance atmosphere that is intensely compelling. The record sold in enormous quantities for West End Records and established three volatile careers – those of Taana Gardner, Kenton Nix (pro-

ducer and writer, and currently a boxing trainer) and Larry Levan (Paradise Garage DJ and producer for The Peech Boys). Dennis Weeden, who played guitar on the session, remembers its impact:

> 'Heartbeat' was one of my greatest experiences and I must say it sure was an inspiration because when I did that record I had no idea it was going to jump off like it did. When we were in the studio recording it I said to myself, 'Now come on – this is never gonna make it.' It was just that type of tune where it seemed like it was not gonna happen, and then the next thing I know they were playing it five, six or seven times a day, just rotating, rotating different mixes. Didn't it revolutionise the whole thing? It turned everything around.

Dennis also played on Sweet G's 'A Heartbeat Rap', which used the same heartbeat (still pumping) and clap tracks as the original. Other rap versions of the rhythm included 'Life On the Planet Earth' by Pee Wee Mel and Barry B on 12 Star Records and 'Feel the Heartbeat', an excellent Enjoy release by The Treacherous Three (Kool Moe Dee, Special K and L.A. Sunshine) who made their debut with Spoonie Gee.

For radio play, Taana Gardner's 'Heartbeat' is sometimes played back-to-back with another Kenton Nix composition and production, Gwen McCrae's 'Funky Sensation' released on Atlantic in 1981. Again the rhythm and distinctive bass riff were ideal for MCs, and a version followed on Tom

Silverman's Tommy Boy Records, a fledgling label then sited on East 85th Street. 'Jazzy Sensation' was an important record in that it brought together Afrika Bambaataa and his MCs The Jazzy Five with two white disc jockeys who were to have a profound influence on dance music of all kinds in years to come – Arthur Baker, who produced the record, and Shep Pettibone, the mixer and arranger. Apart from the Winley release, various Bambaataa MCs had previously recorded as Cotton Candy on Tommy Boy, but this was the first record that did justice to their abilities – not to mention Bam's imaginative ideas.

'Jazzy Sensation' has three mixes, one with the Jazzy Five's rap, one by Kryptic Krew featuring Tina B, and one an instrumental, and all move away from the dominant Sugarhill/Enjoy sound, using unusual sounds like friction drums, car horns and electronic clave. Tina B's rap, and particularly the instrumental, with synthesiser revoicing over the original percussion track, suggested that the guitar, bass and drums trio might be on the way out. Of the two individuals responsible for the music track, Pettibone was a pioneer of the radio mastermixes heard on Kiss FM. Mastermixing was a parallel development to the b boys' cutting and scratching, a way of intercutting and juxtaposing records in a way that completely transformed them and collaged them into long sequences. After 'Jazzy Sensation' Pettibone moved towards the dub style as well as reviving classic disco sounds by singers like Loleatta Holloway for a permanently appreciative audience of club dancers. Arthur Baker, on the other

SHAKEDOWN SOUND: ARTHUR BAKER

hand, became a crucial figure on the rap scene.

Baker began in music as a club disc jockey in Boston, playing Philadelphia soul. After a while he moved into record production:

The first thing that I really did, I had every relative who would speak to me give me $1,000. I was in Boston – everything was a lot cheaper. I did like 10 cuts. I went in totally over my head. I didn't know what I was doing – I had strings and

summer. I started meeting new musicians and getting turned on to different things – the rap music. This was like summer '79. This guy Joe Bataan, who's like a salsa musician – we were going to do an album for London Records, co-producing, so the first thing we went in to do was a rap record, 'Rap-O-Clap-O'. He took me up to all these rap clubs and he said, these were the words, 'Someone's gonna make a million dollars on this rap music.' I just said, 'No way!' I liked it, but . . .

So we did 'Rap-O-Clap-O' but what happened was London Records went under and he took the tapes and I didn't know what happened to them. I moved back to Boston and then six months later the record came out. I got no credit on it. Marty Sheller ws the arranger but that record – there really wasn't much to it. All it was was a rip off of 'Got To Be Real' – Cheryl Lynn's record.

Joe Bataan is a musician like Jimmy Castor who embraces many different aspects of New York music. An ex-leader of Spanish Harlem gangs The Young Copasetics and The Dragons, he was one of the driving forces behind Latin soul in the '60s. His *Riot* album from 1969 is an exultant mix of bugalu, doo-wops like 'Daddy's Coming Home' and high-spirited R&B. Featuring his group The Latin Swingers ('from 98th to 110th Streets') and pupils from Taft High School, its mood spells out the positive side of the urban gangs. The sleevenotes say it all: 'P.S. The Riot is a song of joy and good feelings ex-

horns and spent all this money. I didn't have enough to finish it so I hooked up with Tom Moulton and he offered me like $2,500 for seven songs, 10 songs, whatever the hell it was. I jumped at it 'cos that was a way to pay my debts. I didn't make any money but I at least paid my debts.

I did a few records for Emergency. 'Happy Days' by Northend and Michelle Wallace. I had all these records and I was doing a few more little things. When I did 'Happy Days' I moved down here for the pressed thru music and not of violence.' The arranger on 'Rap-O-Clap-O', Marty Sheller, worked on another Latin rap, Tito Allen's 1980 'Salsa Rap' on Alegre which, along with the rapping on Bataan's *Mestizo* album, is about the extent of rap's penetration into the older-generation Latin music.

Arthur Baker tells how his introduction to rap led him to get more fully involved:

I was aware of this stuff from when it first happened. Then I did another record called 'Can You Guess What Groove This Is' by a group called Glory. It was on Posse Records and it was one of the first medleys. It had 'Good Times' and all this stuff and it was done around the time of 'Rapper's Delight'. So I was into that but I didn't really get involved until I moved to New York. Then, two months later, I hooked up with Tom Silverman and we were gonna go in and do two rap records. I had no money so he was going to finance it. We were going to do 'Genius of Love' and 'Funky Sensation' – a rap on that. The night we went in we heard that four other people were doing 'Genius of Love', so we just did 'Funky Sensation'. So from there I hooked up with Bambaataa. We did 'Planet Rock'. I did 'Walking On Sunshine' and we started Streetwise Records.

Baker sees the versioning of other people's tunes as being a kind of jazz: 'The way I look at it, it's sort of like a jazz music. It's like rearranging. Like when John Coltrane does 'My Favourite Things' it doesn't sound like it's gonna sound if some lounge singer does it. They rearrange it and it comes out differently'. As Arthur suggests, there was a bandwagon-jumping attitude to using popular rhythm tracks. It was similar, in some ways, to the cover-version syndrome of the '50s and early '60s (not to mention the early '80s), though in contrast to the Pat Boone/Paul Young type of approach, rap versions usually threw a completely new light on the originals.

Interesting complications arose as white musicians moved out of rock and into funk. Blondie and Queen were both recycled by Grandmaster Flash in 'Adventures On the Wheels of Steel'. Flash and The Furious Five also used Tom Tom Club's 'Genius of Love' for 'It's Nasty', and Tom Tom Club, a Talking Heads spin-off, had their own rap hit, 'Wordy Rappinghood', in 1981. It was 'Genius of Love' which had everybody rushing into the studio to redo its bumpy, nursery-school funk. One of the most intriguing 'genius' records was Dr Jeckyl and Mr Hyde's 'Genius Rap' on Profile Records. Profile is a New York company which started out in May 1981 with an English record by Grace Kennedy. Their second release was a rap called 'Young Ladies' by Lonnie Love, who later drank the potion and turned into the Mr Hyde half of the 'Genius Rap' duo.

In the Profile offices somewhere near the top of a high-rise on West 57th, 26-year-old co-president Cory Robbins is explaining how 'Genius Rap' came to be made. It's an object lesson in independent record production. If Arthur Baker looks like he should be playing drums in a heavy-metal group, then Cory makes a credible Beach

DR JECKYL AND MR HYDE

Boy (in their younger days). With a background in DJing upstate New York, there are no doubts about his ability to spot good dance music. His confidence in Dr Jeckyl and Mr Hyde was justified by their third release ('the first two records, which we thought were great, were total stiffs') which was made in 11 days from conception to the stores. Produced extremely cheaply, it went on to sell 150,000 12-inch copies. Although the Jeckyll and Hyde duo may have been overstating their case in 'Genius Rap' when they bragged about penthouses overlooking Central Park and pictures on the cover

of *Jet* and *TV Guide*, it was a success of sufficient dimensions to establish them in the easy-come, easy-go rap hall of fame.

Versions are obviously a convenient way of making records as most of the ideas have already been worked out in the original. Some of the most interesting covers are those that offer an alternative viewpoint (answer record style) to the lyrics of the existing song. Sylvia Robinson made a brief return to recording with 'Good To Be the Queen', her answer to Mel Brooks's rap 'Good To Be the King', and in Brooklyn, Reelin and Rockin' Records produced a

IF WOOD COULD RAP: WAYNE AND CHARLIE

time and had eventually managed to convince the partners that he had talent and, in the words of Giammanco, 'the knowledge and feel of the street'.

Bon Rock's trio comprises one male and two females – Bon Rock, Tania Battiste and Diane Hawkins. 'Searchin' Rap' was a twist on the theme of Unlimited Touch's 'Searching To Find the One' on Prelude. Where Unlimited Touch, in a beautiful but lyrically dubious song, were out looking for a strong man, Tania and Diane were looking out for themselves, 'born between two 45s' and learning to cut up with the best at the Audubon Ballroom. Their 'Junior Wants to Play' (released through Tommy Boy) revamped Junior Giscombe's 'Mama Used to Say', but this time Junior was dragged away from sensible maternal advice and turned into a hip young hedonist whose attempts at sweet-talking women got him a solid 'Oh no, not tonight darlin'' rejection.

Rap was also busy plundering its own stockroom. The confusing interchangeability of MC clichés like 'shock the house' and the similar feel of much of the music made it hard enough for the casual listener to distinguish individual records, let alone choose good from bad. As with any genre, the verbal and musical crosstalk could be seen from a number of viewpoints – either it had an 'archaeological' richness which was fun to unravel or it was lost in repetition. Probably both interpretations are true. A record like Wayne and Charlie's 'Check It Out' (Sugarhill, 1981) has all the clichés, but it's interesting for being a ventriloquist and his wooden dummy offering a new (uncredited, naturally) angle on Kurtis Blow's

group called Bon Rock who seemed to specialise in turning some of the conventional messages of dance music on their head.

Situated on Fort Hamilton Parkway, Reelin and Rockin' is run by Ed Pavia and Anthony Giammanco, a team who have worked together in the music business for 20 years running a Brooklyn record shop called Now Music. Pavia also gave guitar lessons and through giving concerts of his pupils realised that he and his partner might as well be making records instead of just selling them. Their first release was 'Searchin' Rap' by Bon Rock and the Rythem Rebellion. Bon Rock had appeared in the record shop from time to street-smart protest 'The Breaks'. If wood could rap . . .

Other records attempted to move beyond the simple funk basis of rap and create a music that evoked turntable cutting. One of the wittiest was the Disco Four's 'Country Rock Rap'. Better known for their later electro-rap releases on Profile, the group included Bobby Robinson's son, so fittingly the record came out on Enjoy. 'Country Rock Rap' is another Pumpkin music track – a jaunty banjo hoedown with a hilarious story of yahoo-yelling cowhands leaving the farm to rock the disco till the break of dawn. King Tim III had evoked squaredance with his 'grab your partner, swing her round' lines in the very first rap record, but nobody had gone quite as hee-haw mad as The Disco Four. Naturally, it took a white person to take the idea to the top of the charts. Malcolm McLaren's 'Buffalo Gals' was undeniably more commercial than 'Country Rock Rap' but it is still depressing that the experimentation in hip hop needed opportunists, white or black, to take it into the mainstream pop charts.

The Disco Four's redneck rap, along with similar fusions like The Cold Crush Brothers' 'Punk Rock Rap', had its origins in Bronx sound systems. The breadth of music being used to create break-beat music – the fertilising ground for such records – is partially shown by Paul Winley's *Super Disco Brakes* anthologies, produced by DJ Jolly Rogers for Jolly Rogers Records (a message in there somewhere, maybe?).

Winley knew from his background in the very early discos that popular dancefloor records could be hard to find for the average punter, especially if DJs were blacking out the centre labels or soaking them off. He was also familiar with navigating 'obstacles' like copyright or union restrictions:

I promoted a lot of shows – me and disc jockeys like Jocko. We ran shows at the Audubon. We were running discos before discos were ever popular. I'm talking about 1962. We used to call them record hops and they were eliminated to skating rinks and different places, but in a class A union ballroom you couldn't put records. I used to own a dancehall and the union wouldn't allow you to play records. Me and Jocko, we used a place called the Audubon Ballroom, 166 and Broadway, that's where Malcolm X got killed. In fact I was giving shows when Malcolm got killed that Sunday.

We had trouble with the union so I had a group of fellers and we used to just grab the delegate and give him $50 and say, 'Do you wanna take this or do you wanna hang out the window?' He got to know us so he'd come up every Sunday for his 50. This went on for years and eventually disco became a very big thing.

Super Disco Brakes, a four-volume set of poorly transferred disco classics mixed with Winley product, contains tracks like 'Funky Nassau' by West Indian group The Beginning of the End (mysteriously attributed to Dyke and the Blazers on the centre label), 'Funky Drummer' by James Brown and other b boy source material by The Meters, whose New Orleans fatback funk was one of the main roots of hip-hop beats, Creative Source (disguised as Creative Service), the JBs and The Blackbyrds.

Some of the major breaks records are included – Magic Disco Machine's 'Scratchin'', Dennis Coffey's 'Scorpio', Captain Sky's 'Super Sperm' and Bob James's 'Mardi Gras'. There are two African tracks, 'Soul Makossa' (Winley was the first to jump on the New York disco craze for Manu Dibango's Cameroon Afro Quelque Chose) and 'Easy Dancin'' by Wagadu-Gu (reputed to be by Nigerian highlife star Prince Nico). Grouped together on Volume Three are Gil Scott-Heron's disco hit 'In The Bottle', a track from Lightnin' Rod's *Hustler's Convention* album on Douglas (basically a Last Poets record but credited to Alan Douglas on *Disco Brakes*) and the legendary 'Apache'.

Many of these tracks inspired later rap recordings. Bob James's cover of Paul Simon's 'Take Me to the Mardi Gras' begins with a tremendously atmospheric percussion break before lapsing into MOR sweetness. The break was the part that the b boys played, and in 1982 The Crash Crew released a single on Sugarhill called 'Breaking Bells (Take Me To the Mardi Gras)' which, despite giving writing credits to Paul Simon, bore almost no resemblance to either his song or Bob James's cover.

Captain Sky (christened Daryl L. Cameron) recorded the kind of George Clinton-inspired comic-strip funk the b boys and b girls liked. 'Super Sperm' (actually called 'Super Sporm' on the sleeve of *The Adventures of Captain Sky*, presumably for the sake of propriety) gets a namecheck in 'Rapper's Delight' and is claimed as one of the influences on Afrika Bambaataa's 'Planet Rock' along with Kraftwerk and a track called 'The Mexican'. More of 'The Mexican' later, except to say that Funky Four tried to make a decent record from it, called 'Feel It', and failed.

The record on which everybody concurs – the quintessential hip-hop track – is 'Apache' by The Incredible Bongo Band. The song was written by an English ex-grammar school boy, a singer named Jerry Lordan, and was recorded in 1960 by both guitarist Bert Weedon (strictly no relation to Dennis who played on 'Heartbeat') and instrumental group The Shadows. The Shadows' version, starring Cliff Richard on bongos, was a million seller later covered by The Ventures, an American guitar group who specialised in covering records as they started to move up the lower reaches of the charts. If a song got to the top then The Ventures could release their instrumental immediately and cash in. In 1974 The Incredible Bongo Band, a Jamaican group who had international disco hits like 'Let There Be Drums' and 'Bongo Rock '73', recorded their version. It emphasised the 'big beat' feel of the original – a bit less Hollywood Red Indian hub-a-hiya – and extended the percussion breaks into mini bongo symphonies. Cover-cover-cover versions of 'Apache', evidently oblivious to the song's past in white instrumental music, began to appear on Sugarhill in the '80s – first the Sugarhill Gang's 'Apache' and then West Street Mob (Joey Robinson Jr's group) with 'Break Dancin' – Electric Boogie'.

An underground movement indirectly inspired by a Cliff Richard percussion break might give the impression of a lemming-like abandonment of black traditions, but in a perverse way these cut-ups of unlikely records, whether by The Monkees or Yellow Magic Orchestra, were a recreation of the forthright emotion that at times looked like becoming a rarity in the mainstream of black music. They were a way of tearing the associations and the pre-packaging from finished musical product and reconstructing it, ignoring its carefully considered intentions and restitching it into new music. As the process of recording music became increasingly fragmented in the '70s – a drum track laid down in Muscle Shoals, a back-up vocal in California, a lead voice in New York – so the implication began to exist that consumers might eventually be able to rejig a track according to their own preferences.

The b boy DJs and MCs were half-way between consumers and performers (until they became stars) and their response to packaged music was to violate it with cutting and rapping. If there was a model for the final results then it was the proto-raps being played as break beats.

One of Afrika Bambaataa's favourite records is 'Tramp' by Otis Redding and Carla Thomas. It's a tune with an intense Southern feel – the lyrics (written by bluesmen Lowell Fulsom and Jimmy McCracklin) have a familiar theme. Carla pours scorn on Otis for his rural Southern ways, his overalls, his boots and his long hair. Otis roars back his defence over Al

Jackson's funky drum breaks, offering Carla a choice of rat, squirrel or frog in return for her demands of mink and sable. Basically a talking record, it is a satire that harks back to the husband and wife comedy teams – Butterbeans and Susie or Stringbeans and Sweetie May – or the venomous dialogue of songs such as Big Maybelle's 'Gabbin' Blues' from 1952. The imposing Maybelle is being tormented by a gossip – 'here comes ol' evil chick, always telling everybody she come from Chicago. Got Mississippi written all over her'. Her defence, like Otis's, was her pride and the threatening power of her awesome voice.

No matter how far Bambaataa and others like him may go in their outlandish selections of source material or their desire for internationalism, the music always returns to two basic elements – a funky drumbeat and some spoken or chanted words. Both spring from an abundant Afro-American tradition.

9. Tough

The release of two Last Poets records in March of 1984 was a reminder, should one be necessary, that rap had very recent predecessors. Both releases were 12-inch singles – 'Super Horror Show' by the Last Poet and 'Long Enough' by The Last Poets. A different last poet was behind each record – 'Long Enough' by Jalaluddin Mansur Nuriddin on a Brooklyn label called Kee Wee, and 'Super Horror Show' by Abiodun Oyewole on Nia, a label normally associated with Captain Rock and the Fantastic Aleems production team. With a percussion intro reminiscent of early Last Poets records, a strong synthesiser/beat-box music track and an 'I've had it' lyric, 'Long Enough' is the stronger of the two. Ironically, 'Super Horror Show' is a pale imitation of 'The Message', the Grandmaster Flash and the Furious Five hit of 1982 which set the ball rolling for the message rap fad through its enormous international success.

By the time The Last Poets were interviewed by Jonathon Cott for *Rolling Stone* magazine in 1970, Abiodun Oyewole had left the group. He can be heard on their first album for Douglas, a New York company run by Alan Douglas who also recorded music by John McLaughlin and Jimi Hendrix. The Harlem-based Poets were at

THRILLER BREAKER AT THE ROXY

that time Alafia Pudim, Omar Ben Hassan and Nilaja, the percussionist (all of them later changed their names). They described themselves as being part of a new age for poets – prophetic of the way in which wall poems and street verse would be set to dance-music tracks and climb not only the R&B charts but also pop hit parades all over the world.

There was little chance of the same success coming to The Last Poets when they released titles like 'Niggers Are Scared of Revolution' or 'White Man's Got a God Complex'. They took streetcorner rap with its potential for verbal violence and used it as an assault on what they saw as black apathy, self-exploitation and stereotyped roles. Direct or indirect, it was an attack on white society also, and Nilaja is quoted as saying, 'If I were white I wouldn't come hear us. Just like I wouldn't go hear George Wallace.'

Their ancestry lay in the tough-voiced black writers who had earlier set poetry in a musical context or used lyrics and music to create a specifically political message – Imamu Amiri Baraka's 'Black Dada Nihilismus' with The New York Art Quartet, recorded in 1965, as well as his work with Sun Ra; Archie Shepp's poems for Malcolm X, 'Malcolm, Malcolm, Semper Malcolm' from his Impulse album *Fire Music* and 'Poem For Malcolm' recorded in Paris in the late '60s; the Abbey Lincoln/Max Roach collaborations including *We Insist – The Freedom Now Suite* recorded for Candid, and, going back to before the '60s Civil Rights battles, a moving set of recordings of Langston Hughes reading his poetry with two jazz groups – one including Red Allen and Vic Dickenson, the other with Charles Mingus and Shafi Hadi.

The Last Poets were virtually the sole occupants of a lonely territory between the jazz poets and the commercial singers who had spoken out during the decade of Civil Rights and Black Nationalism – Nina Simone, James Brown, Curtis Mayfield. Their poems reflected their position – 'Uncle Sam's Lament' from the *At Last* album mixes free jazz with references to James Brown's 'Ain't It Funky' and Jimmy Castor's 'Hey Leroy, Your Mama's Callin'', and one of their hardest tracks, 'This Is Madness', is full of references to 'Trane, Bird and King Pleasure's 'I'm In the Mood for Love'.

In *Die Nigger Die*, H Rap Brown, ex-minister of justice in the Black Panthers and chairman of the SNCC (Student National Co-ordinating Committee), wrote: 'The street is where young bloods get their education. I learned how to talk in the street, not from reading about Dick and Jane going to the zoo and all that simple shit. The teacher would test our vocabulary each week, but we knew the vocabulary we needed. They'd give us arithmetic to exercise our minds. Hell, we exercised our minds by playing the dozens'.

Jonathon Cott's *Rolling Stone* feature, 'The Last Poets and Apocalypse', makes a similar point:

But what The Last Poets do onstage is nothing more than heighten the form of a new Black urban street poetry. At a New

York high school assembly commemorating Malcolm X's death two months ago, the 'predominantly Black' students hooted the principal down, and kids got up on stage and read their poems – charged statements like those of The Poets, rhythmically asserting black consciousness while revealing the breakdown and proving unworkable the New York City school system.

The Last Poets made their streetlife connection clear with an album called *Hustlers Convention* (attributed to Lightnin' Rod)· released on Douglas in 1973.

Hustlers Convention is a modern-day toast, the story of a gambler, Sport, and his crime partner, Spoon, who win at craps, pool and poker at a hustlers' convention in Hamhock's Hall. The story ends with Sport freed from a 12-year stretch on Sing Sing's death row after a shoot-out with the cops. By the time he's released he has had time to think about the foolishness of being a small-time hustler.

Music on the album is provided by an impressive list of names including Kool and the Gang and Eric Gale; with its sound effects and atmosphere it brings to mind other black audio-dramas like *Roi Boye and the Gotham Minstrels* by saxophonist Julius Hemphill (one of the musicians on *Hustlers Convention*), David Porter's *Victim of the Joke* soul opera and Melvin Van Peebles's soundtrack albums *Sweet Sweetback's Baadasssss Song* and *Don't Play Us Cheap*.

In the middle '70s, *Hustlers Convention* was being used as a break record by hip-hop DJs. They were also using Gil Scott-Heron tracks. Both Gil Scott-Heron and The Last Poets are seen by most Bronx rappers as the godfathers of the message rap. As a writer, Scott-Heron published novels and a rap poem – 'Small Talk at 125th and Lennox' – before putting the words into a musical context. Early rap poems such as 'Sex Education: Ghetto Style' and 'Whitey On the Moon' were in The Last Poets mould (though strong in their own right) with conga backup. Other raps like 'The Revolution Will Not Be Televised' used more instruments (drums, bass, flute) but they were still hard-hitting political broadsides which contrasted sharply with his mellow and melancholic songs. The content was the same in both, but the effectiveness of the rap format was driven home by the release of the *Reflections* album in 1982, with its rap attack on Ronald Reagan in 'B Movie'.

At Tuff City Records in the strictly B movie landscape of Long Island City, Aaron Fuchs – long-time R&B collector and writer of the Motown chapters in Allan Betrock's *Girl Groups* book – is being forthright about an aspect of rap he disdains:

AARON FUCHS: TUFF CITY HEADQUARTERS

The only trend I do not like in rap right now is the message rap. I consider the message rap the equivalent of what strings were to rock 'n' roll in the late '50s – a capitulation to the adult norm who can't accept the music on its own terms. The people who considered 'Sixty Minute Man' by Billy Ward and the Dominoes, 'Annie Had a Baby' – as the pinnacles of '50s R&B now are super uptight over the – in quotes – hotel/motel lyrics of rap. Rap is definitely as true to the essence of rock 'n roll as anything that's out there today.

Although Kurtis Blow recorded a couple of message raps in 1980 ('The Breaks' and 'Hard Times'), it was Grandmaster Flash and the Furious Five at Sugarhill who turned it into a trend. 'The Message' appeared in the late summer of 1982. It was partly a response to Afrika Bambaataa's 'Planet Rock', a record that came from behind the frontrunners and left them all standing. Instead of moving with the Kraftwerk-influenced sound, 'The Message' used a backing track more in line with groups like D Train and The Jammers – a hard, slowish beat that was electronic enough to drag Sugarhill into the new age of dance music. Mostly the creation of Ed Fletcher (known as Duke Bootee) and Melvin Glover (Melle Mel), it recycled a number of lines from 'Superrappin'' but was otherwise a strikingly original song which combined shock images of violent and decaying New York with enough melodic and percussive hooks to make it a highly commercial proposition.

It has always been debatable just how much listeners take in the lyrics of songs. Sung vocals have a tendency to blend into the instrumental music, so that often the only words that are remembered are those in the title. For obvious reasons this problem is even bigger in dance music. Rap vocals, on the other hand, have a separation from the music – it is possible to communicate in more detail and with a greater directness. 'The Message' managed to harness this potential to a pop sensibility as well as a hardcore dance track. It cut straight across the stagnation in rap lyricism.

Rap before 'The Message' wasn't all hotel/motel/Mercedes/young ladies. Aside from Kurtis Blow, there were records here and there which went beyond bragging and boasting. Community People's 'Education Wrap' on Delmar Donnell's Delmar International Records updated James Brown's 'kids, stay in school' lecture, and Sweet Tee's 'Vicious Rap' showed that there was one kid who was 'gonna scream and shout and let the government know what we all about'. The toughest talk, though, came from Brother D with his 'How We Gonna Make the Black Nation Rise', a release on Clappers. The Clappers label was started by Lister Hewan Lowe, a Jamaican who had moved to New York after working with Augustus Pablo on the Yard Music label. Brother D, a young maths teacher named Daryl Aamaa Nubyahn, recorded a hip-hop tune to reflect the philosophy of a political and cultural organisation called National Black Science, realising that despite rap's being the happening music in his neighbourhood of the Bronx, it wasn't saying

MELLE MEL AT THE ROXY

much beyond personality commercials. Taking one of the two most popular rhythms of the time, Cheryl Lynn's 'Got To Be Real', Brother D produced something that was a considerable departure from the usual formula:

> The Ku Klux Klan is on the loose,
> Training their kids in machine gun use.
> The story might give you stomach cramps
> Like America's got concentration camps.
> While you're partyin' on on on on and on,
> The others may be hot by the break of
>   dawn.
> The party may end one day soon,
> When they're rounding niggers up in the
>   afternoon.

Another Clappers release was 'Ms D.J. Rap It Up!' by She. She has a lot of faces. On the subway she is liable to be recognised because of her role as Thomasina in NBC's daytime TV soap opera *Another World*, but she also goes under the name Ms D.J. as well as her legal name, Sheila Spencer. A church choir singer in Brooklyn from the age of five until her late teens, Sheila is a trained actress who has also provided background paaardddy vocals for Kurtis Blow's first album and worked as a Muhammad Ali boxing cheerleader (an admirable training for an MC). Her record was a conscious attempt by her producer, Dennis Weeden, to get a solo female rapper onto the market.

Though rapping is a macho stronghold there have been a few women with lyrics that struck back. Sula's 'Jungle Rap' asked Tarzan why he had to play with such a hard

hand, and Lady B told her story of how she and Superman had a fight and she hit him in the head with some kryptonite. Lady B's record was first released on a Philadelphia label called Tec, mixed by Nick Martinelli (now well known for his mixing collaborations with David Todd on West End) and then picked up by Sugarhill and re-released in a slightly speeded-up version. Called 'To The Beat Y'all' it also told a tale of Jack and Jill going up the hill to play but ending up with a baby because 'stupid' Jill forgot the pill. Sequence came straight back with their 'Simon Says' – a warning about boys who want to 'pump' every day but refuse to take responsibility for the babies they help to create. It also took a few lines from 'The Clapping Song', the Shirley Ellis song that went gold in the mid '60s.

Shirley Ellis; along with her writer Lincoln Chase, was another forerunner of rap. The wordplay songs, 'The Name Game' and 'Ever See a Diver Kiss His Wife While the Bubbles Bounce About Above the Water', were nearly 20 years ahead of Z-language raps like Frankie Smith's 'Double Dutch Bus', UTFO's 'Beats and Rhymes' or graffiti artist Rammelzee's tricknology rap 'Beat Bop'. The Kangol Kid, one half of UTFO, is a breaker and popper who specialises in what he calls 'disability moves'. UTFO dance with Brooklyn rap group Whodini but they also rap themselves. Kangol explains the word game behind their first record: 'Another new thing is Z-rap. It'd be like a code language. I would talk to him and his name's Doctor Ice. I would say, "Dizoctor Izice. Yizo hizo bizoy wizon't youza kizoy mesover herezere?" – that's just saying, "Yo, home boy, why don't you come over here?" and what I did is make a rap out of that language. In New York they'd understand but Europe they just have to get up on it now'.

'Beat Bop' by Rammelzee Vs. K-Rob was initially released as a limited pressing by artist Jean Michel Basquiat on Tartown and then picked up by Profile Records for wider distribution. Rammelzee's name is a conjunction of Ramm-elevation-Z (Z being a symbol of energy which flows in two directions); his graffiti paintings and drawings are unusual even for the hip-hop art scene. 'Beat Bop' is rapped in what he calls slanguage – a stream of consciousness rap between a gangster and a child who debate the pros and cons of school. The music is a slow trance beat drenched in washes of echo which drop and clear like mist – the nearest parallel is the hypnotic Yoruban Fuji, Apala and Waka drumbeat musics from Nigeria. The language glides bafflingly in

FLASH, RAHEIM, KID CREOLE AND THE NEW RECRUITS

and out of hip-hop cliché, social realism and pure nonsense – Rammelzee, the Screamin' Jay Hawkins of rap:

Bunny rock a ya don't stop,
That long fingernail at the end of my tail
Oh my pinky cocaine make it slip-a-my lip,
Just make you freak when the paniwani was flip
Like the little pat to the dab'll make you my hip.
Shake shake rock body rock a hip an-a-hop,
Like a – RTMs my –
Nose don't care about the rhythm that breaks.
(approximate transcription)

Profile also released 'Street Justice' by The Rake (known to his family as Keith Rose). It was a story rap which ignored the clichés and the nonsense and went for the social realism. Amazingly enough, this grim scenario of a vigilante bent on revenge after his wife is raped and the attackers are let off was written by two professional songwriters, Blatt and Gottleib, who wrote 'She Was My Girl' for The Four Tops. 'Street Justice' was fairly typical of the subject matter current in rap after 'The Message'. The follow-up to 'The Message' was another Ed Fletcher/Melle Mel collaboration called 'Message 2 (Survival)'. With hindsight it was the first sign of the imminent split within Grandmaster Flash and the Furious Five, though Sylvia Robinson's insistence on·

Melvin's rapping solo on 'The Message' was the beginning of divide and rule. 'Message 2' was in the style of the sequels and prequels that had become an obsession in cinema. More *Halloween II* than *Rocky III*, it was bad news in more ways than one. Chic's 'Good Times' had finally been replaced (commercially) by the hard times.

It has been suggested that record companies go through phases of releasing songs with political or protest lyrics and that 1982 onward is one such phase. Distinguishing worthwhile bandwagon jumping from sheer cynical opportunism can be tricky – besides which, the eventual effect of a record can be very different from the original intentions, good or bad. Among the more incisive high-pressure raps which were thrown up by message-ism were 'The Bottom Line' by South Bronx on Rissa Chrissa, 'Problems of the World' by The Fearless Four (very striking lyrics by DLB), 'You Gotta Believe' by 'Love Bug' Starski (more survivalism than protest) on The Fever label, 'Bad Times (I Can't Stand It)' by Captain Rapp on Becket Records, 'It's Life (You Gotta Think Twice)' by Rock Master Scott and the Dynamic 3, and Run-D.M.C.'s 'Hard Times', both on Profile.

The contradictions of a money-minded craze for gory social realism and criticism of the Reagan administration, with its callous cutbacks in social programmes, are hard to resolve. The juxtaposition of protests about rape victims with rampant machismo or hard-times lyrics sung by kids in expensive leather outfits and gold chains can be hard to stomach. With Jesse Jackson's decision to campaign for the 1984 Democratic nomination in the race for presidency came a new mood in American black politics. The long-overdue granting of a commemoration day for Martin Luther King led to the release of Stevie Wonder's tribute, 'Happy Birthday', with a B side of the Civil Rights campaigner's speeches, including 'I Have a Dream'. Also from the soulside came a tribute from Bobby Womack, and in the rap field, reflecting the hip-hop technique of overlaying beats with speeches by black leaders, came 'Martin Luther', a Kraftwerk-meets-desert-funk-and-black-politics 12 inch by the Las Vegas-based Hurt 'Em Bad and the S.C. Band.

The Jesse Jackson campaign was supported by Face 2000 with 'Run Jesse Run' and Melle Mel with 'Jesse', the latter a collaboration between Melvin Glover, Reggie Griffin, Sylvia Robinson and one of The Isley Brothers, reflecting the Isleys' business tie-ups with Sugarhill. Most surprising of all was the late 1983 posthumous release by Malcolm X on Tommy Boy Records. The record was a hard beat-box track put together by ex-staff drummer at Sugarhill, Keith LeBlanc, with equally ferocious speeches by Malcolm X. Inevitably, it trailed controversy in its wake, with a court battle between Sugarhill and Tommy Boy over legal rights to the speeches and dissenting voices from within the black community about the disrespect they felt the record showed to one of their leaders. Paul Winley, who had released speeches by both Martin Luther King and Malcolm X, had this to say: 'It's just like taking one of your idols, one of your heroes and boogie-ing behind 'em. It's just like taking the Pope's speech and putting some disco music behind it – here's John Paul, baby!' Others felt that Black Nationalism from a white drummer and a white record company was an insult.

Nevertheless, it was sanctioned by Dr Betty Shabazz, the widow of Malcolm X, and caught the mood of its time perfectly. 'No Sell Out', along with Afrika Bambaataa's rebel optimism of 'Renegades of Funk' and the militant break music from the hip-hop minimalists, were the strongest contenders in the new spirit of 1984 punk.

10. Whiplash snuffs the candle flame

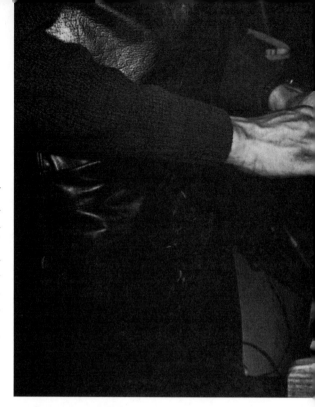

ROCKIN' TO THE SOUNDS OF THE BEATBOX

Fresh as the first rap records were, they were tame compared to the uncensored beats and rhymes of the parks and high schools. What was a DJ to do on a record? 'Superrappin'' threw a clue into the wind but nobody caught it – The Furious Five chant 'Flash is on the beat box' but the drum machine stays mute. Funk was still powered by a set of traps. Flash was a pioneer in combining turntable trickery with beat-box improvisations, using an ancient keyboard percussion box made by Vox, an English company whose name can be spotted on the amplifiers in old footage of The Beatles. It was a bootleg record that pulled electronic drums out of the Bronx. 'Flash To the Beat' by Flash and the Five on Bozo Meko Records was recorded off the sound system at Bronx River Community Centre by Afrika Bambaataa. It puts most so-called noise records to shame.

The response at Sugarhill was to rush the group into the studio to record an official version. 'Flash To the Beat' (Sugarhill) is less celebrated than Flash and the Furious Five hits but is nonetheless superb. For nearly six minutes the Furious Five trade off catch phrases, parodies of Brit-speak (a great source of amusement to rappers), solo singing and unison chants against a seething beats-only backdrop of drums, Latin percussion and Flash's chattering, popping percussion box fed through an echo delay. At five minutes 50 seconds the group start to sing 'the bass is with the beat box playing' and in crashes Doug Wimbish with a vicious riff that stays with the record for the remaining five minutes.

Despite many claims to the contrary, much of the early serious use of drum machines was in black music. Electronic rhythms were mostly an accessory for organists (the kind of thing heard on Timmy Thomas's 'Why Can't We Live Together') but in the early '70s two musicians in particular, Sly Stone and Stevie Wonder, used drum machines as a part of finding greater independence – learning to exploit new technology and the developing multi-track

almost insulting volume, sometimes almost drowning out the mumbled vocals. It imbues the songs with a mechanical feeling which only adds to the sense of alienation throughout the whole album. The drum box mixes perfectly with Larry Graham's slapping and popping bass (also way ahead of its time), but the personal mix in the group was less than happy and Graham left shortly after contributing uncredited work to the follow-up album, *Fresh*, and formed his own group.

Graham Central Station pursued many of the ideals of The Family Stone – musicians of mixed race and gender playing rock-tinged heavyweight funk – and on a track called 'The Jam' from 1975 one of the lead vocalists, Patryce 'Chocolate' Banks, takes what may have been the first drum-machine solo in record history:

Uh F. U. N. K. box
It's an F. U. N. K. box-box-ah
Play it on a funk box y'all
My name is C. H. O. C. L. E. T.
Chocolate.

studio facilities to further it. Sylvia Robinson and The Moments were also up there among the earliest musicians to record with drum machines so it's hard to know why it took them so long to get around to recording 'Flash To the Beat'.

Sly Stone used the drum box extensively to build up tracks, playing most of the instruments, including acoustic drums, himself, and then deciding whether to leave the machine in or out of the final mixdown. *There's A Riot Going On* (Epic, 1971), Sly's druggy masterpiece, is characterised by the drum-machine sound. On songs like 'Time', 'Spaced Cowboy', 'Family Affair' and 'Africa Talks To You "The Asphalt Jungle"' it ticks, hisses and tocks away at an

'The Jam' was a favourite b boy break record, as were many Sly and the Family Stone cuts. Sly's coke- and smack-brained ideas made a big impression in the asphalt jungles of New York (although musically speaking only – hard drugs were mostly disapproved of). On top of that the drum machine was the perfect instrument to blend into the concept of an MC show. Plug it in by the record decks and the DJ could move from one set of controls to the other without losing the flow. Flash was honing

GRANDMASTERS – MARQUEE IN TIMES SQUARE

the combined arts of cutting, scratching and manually operated beat box. Being a DJ was starting to look like an Olympics event. Flash tells the story of his name:

> Somebody was telling me that there a Grandmaster Flowers out there before me but I was named that from my fans. It was '74, on my birthday. There was this guy named Joe Kid. He was one of the troublemakers in my party but he was a good friend of mine. He said, 'Flash, for

KRAFTWERK: DO THE FUNKY ROBOT

the way that you play you can't just call yourself DJ Flash. Grandmaster sounds great, man. You should put it on top of that.' After I took the title I knew I had to start going to a laboratory, so to speak, and invent new ideas.

Grandmaster was an appropriate name for the extremes of concentration, dexterity and physical precision required to stay on top of the competition. As Flash had said elsewhere, if you made too many mistakes you could get yourself shot!

In the barren setting of a school gymnasium the fantasy level of the music invoked a mythical battle between the DC Comics superhero Flash, the fastest man alive, and the Shaolin grandmasters with their Mantis Fists, Drunken swordplay and Hawk's Paw Kung Fu. A crazy cast of one-armed boxers, deaf and mute heroines and white-eyebrow monks merged with the strangely costumed alter ego of police scientist Barry Allen, The Flash. When the smoke cleared a new superhero emerged – Grandmaster Flash – and a host of imitators followed in his wake – The Ghost of Flash, Grandmaster Caz, Grand Wizard Theodore and, the final ignominy, a fake Grandmaster Flash appearing with Melle Mel after the split of the group in late 1983.

Hong Kong martial arts films took over from the craze for blaxploitation movies in the early '70s. Even now, Grandmaster films are still shown in the cinemas lining Times Square, alongside Japanese ninja pictures, the latest Clint Eastwood Dirty Harry instalment and a mixed bunch of porno productions. In his book *Black Film*

CHOREOGRAPHY OF VIOLENCE

as Genre, Thomas Cripps assesses the appeal of Chinese films to black youth in America:

> The young black audiences who had originally supported 'blaxploitation' films soon lost interest and shifted their allegiance to other genres including science fiction or martial arts films, which traded on violent revenge themes set in Oriental locales. Black youth, then, recoiled from fantasies of lust and power, choosing instead symbols from another culture that provided metaphors for Afro-American experience despite their Oriental settings. Martial arts films offered blacks comic strips of pure vengeance dramatized in a choreography of violence unobtainable within the literal context of American social realism.

Sharing the twilight zone of 42nd Street movie houses, drug dealers and seedy subterranean record stores are the video arcades. Video games have had a big influence on latter day hip hop – the arcades are bleeping, pulsing, 24-hour refuges for the obsessive vidkids with nowhere else to go. Since the Japanese exploitation of American Nolan Bushnell's original games, a major part of the populated world has been saturated with Space Invaders, Gorgars, Missile Commands, Dragon's Lairs and Ms Pacmans. Along with their addictive properties, their imagery and their insatiable appetite for coins goes an e-z-learn induction into the world of computer technology.

On side two of the notorious 'Death Mix', recorded live at James Monroe High School in the Bronx, Afrika Bambaataa and Jazzy Jay can be heard cutting up YMO's (Yellow Magic Orchestra's) 'Firecracker'. 'Firecracker' is an electronic cover version of a Martin Denny tune (Denny, a white American based in Hawaii, specialises in exotic easy-listening music), and on the 1979 album from which it is taken it segues out of a track called 'Computer Games', a maddening simulation of video-

PLAYLAND ARCADE, TIMES SQUARE

machine beeps, rumbles and banal tunes.

Along with YMO, Bambaataa had a taste for Gary Numan ('Cars' is enjoyed by other hip hoppers, for some unknown reason) and Kraftwerk. Kraftwerk managed to invade almost all record-buying markets in America, from easy-listening to R&B. Bam recalls their influence:

Kraftwerk – I don't think they even knew how big they were among the black masses back in '77 when they came out with 'Trans-Europe Express'. When that came out I thought that was one of the best and weirdest records I ever heard in my life. I said, 'scuse the expression, this is some weird shit! Everybody just went crazy off of that. I guess they found out when they came over and did a performance at the Ritz how big they was. They had four encores and people would not let them leave. That's an amazing group to see – just to see what computers and all that can do. They took like calculators and added something to it – people pressing it and start playing it like music. It was funky. I started looking at telephones – the push-button type – they really mastered those industrial type of machines.

Kraftwerk were the most unlikely group to create such an effect among young blacks. Four be-suited showroom dummies who barely moved a muscle when they played, they were nonetheless the first group using pure electronics to achieve anything like the rhythmic sophistication of quality black dance music. They were fascinating to kids who had grown up with the incursion of microchip technology into everyday life. The George Clinton funk empire and its theatre of excesses had taken sex, sci-fi and comic-book abandonment about as far it could go on stage; four Aryan robots pressing buttons was a joke at the other extreme.

The album version of 'Trans-Europe Express' is extremely long – 13 minutes 32 seconds in total. With its eerie dramatic atmosphere, constant changes of texture and vocoder-type vocals on absolutely regular medium-tempo beats, it was unwittingly a b boy classic. Bambaataa was overlaying speeches by Malcolm X and other Nation of Islam ministers or Martin Luther King, and for Flash it was one of the very few records he was prepared to leave running for its entire length without cutting or scratching: ' "Trans-Europe Express", that was one record you couldn't too much cut – it was cutting itself. That shit was jumping off – leave that shit alone – smoke a cigarette. You can go cool out – go to the bathroom.'

For a Tommy Boy Records follow-up to 'Jazzy Sensation', Afrika Bambaataa took musical elements from 'Trans-Europe Express' – specifically the rhythmic feel and the simple melody line – as well as rhythm ideas from Kraftwerk's 'Numbers' and Captain Sky's 'Super Sperm'. Another inspiration was a record called 'The Mexican', a rock guitar treatment of Ennio Morricone's theme for Sergio Leone's film of greed and retribution, *For a Few Dollars More*. In his book *Spaghetti Westerns*,

Christopher Frayling describes Morricone's film scores as being 'as if Duane Eddy had bumped into Rodrigo, in the middle of a crowded Via Veneto' – very hip hop.

'The Mexican' was released on a West End Records Euro-disco album called *Bombers*. A 12-minute track with extremely long percussion breaks, it was 'interpolated' by guitarist Alan Shacklock, the main mover behind an English progressive rock band called Babe Ruth. Babe Ruth recorded their own limp dancebeat version of 'For a Few Dollars More' in 1972 and Bambaataa had been cutting between these two records and Kraftwerk on the turntables. The feature they shared in common was the tension of a melodramatic, drawn-out melody laid over a beat – also the most unusual aspect of 'Planet Rock', the name of the record which

emerged from this Frankenstein process.

'Planet Rock' was so strange on first hearing that it was hard to believe anybody would buy it. Not only one of the massive hits of 1982, it also shifted dance music into another gear. Produced by a team of Bambaataa, MC group Sonic Force (Mr Biggs, G.L.O.B.E. and Pow Wow), producer Arthur Baker and keyboardist John Robie, it combined a party atmosphere with propulsive electronic percussion or loud scratch-effect accents which sounded like an orchestra being rocketed into outer space. From the opening moments of Bambaataa shouting, 'Party people, party people – can y'all get funky?', 'Planet Rock' is as addictive and as hypnotic as a two-screen miniature Donkey Kong.

It was the first record to feature Soul Sonic Force properly. G.L.O.B.E. was the

inventor of the delayed-action rap called MC popping – like the Turtle Man in the Flash comic, you leave gaps in between words and phrases (not necessarily in the most obvious places). The writer of many of the Soul Sonic lyrics, G.L.O.B.E. met Bam when he was at Bronx River High School. He originally wanted to join the Funky Four but as they were already established he tried Bambaataa:

> I met up with Pow Wow. He always used to hear me rapping in the park and we would rap together. We were really friends. So then Pow Wow said, 'Okay, let's go to Bronx River' with a song that I wrote. Bam heard it and liked it and they put me on. It began with eight rappers. Then, when I came on, everybody dropped off except Mr Biggs, Pow Wow, Lisa Lee, Hutch and Ice Ice. As time went on Ice Ice fell off, then Hutch Hutch fell off then Lisa Lee fell off into The Cosmic Force. Ever since then it's been Mr Biggs, Pow Wow and G.L.O.B.E. in Soul Sonic Force.
>
> I don't even call my stuff rapping. I call it MC popping. It came along on just practising every day. For hours I was just walking around the house. I'd rap when I was washing the dishes. In the shower – like people will always sing in the shower. This was before rap records were even thought of – around '76, '77.

At the Funhouse on 26th Street, 'Looking For the Perfect Beat', Soul Sonic's follow-up to 'Planet Rock', is crashing out its idealistic message at terrific volume. The lights are flashing on and off, highlighting the fairground atmosphere of the place. The clientele are extremely young, mostly Hispanic and Italian (blacks are said to be discouraged) and the music they come to dance to is the jittering electric funk that has followed in the wake of 'Planet Rock'. Inside the DJ booth – a huge clown face – is John 'Jellybean' Benitez, yet another DJ turned producer. Jellybean's talent for creating commercial mixes out of tapes with a video-game aesthetic has been one of the factors responsible for bring hip hop downtown and, by extension, into the international marketplace. Afrika Bambaataa talks about the percolation through to lower Manhattan:

> Cassette tapes used to be our albums before anybody recorded what they called rap records. People started hearing all this rapping coming out of boxes. When they heard the tapes down in the Village they wanted to know, 'Who's this black DJ who's playing all this rock and new wave up in the Bronx?' and I was the only one who was playing all these different forms of music. They invited me downtown to play and I started in this club – The Mudd Club – then somebody called Malcolm McLaren visited us up in my home in the development projects at Bronx River. He liked what he saw so he invited my group to be on a show with Bow Wow Wow at The Ritz.
>
> That's the time the scene was really getting to know about rapping down there. They knew Grandmaster Flash already 'cos Flash had a better manage-

ment team that always looked out for him. The press jumped behind him so they always look to him like he was the first thing out there. I didn't trust nobody at the time. I was more independent than the other DJs. I didn't let nobody touch me. I guided my own career along with Soul Sonic Force and all the other groups that were under my Zulu Nation. I always worked from the streets. I made a following within the street itself – that's how I built on Zulu. I didn't have to worry about going downtown. I had my own steady crowd.

When they heard the tapes they started inviting me to play The Mudd Club, The Ritz, The Peppermint Lounge and I started getting a large white following. I ended up in Negril with Michael Holman and Lady Blue. Thursday nights there became one of the biggest nights downtown. Then it got too big for Negril. One time the fire marshalls closed the whole place down so we moved it to Danceteria. Then it got too big for Danceteria. Finally, we made home at The Roxy. It started slow building at The Roxy, and now Friday nights it's always 3,000, 4,000. Then it became a big commercial thing. Movie stars were coming, singers, everybody was coming to The Roxy and it just started stretching and stretching.

Other events which moved hip hop out of the Bronx and Harlem were shows like The Ritz rap party in March of 1981, The Funky Four's participation in a video and tour organised by The Kitchen (an art venue),

GIRLS IN THE BATHROOM AT THE FUNHOUSE

THE FUNHOUSE

and the white rap records from groups like Blondie and Tom Tom Club. Rap was irresistible as a genuine street culture created by disaffected youth. It had the double virtues of being romantic and daring yet easily packaged. Mostly it packaged itself as a self-contained show with DJs, MCs, on-the-spot graphics from graffiti artists, electric boogie and breakdancing, and maybe some double-dutch skip-rope routines.

Press coverage was unprecedented and rap tunes began to appear from all corners of the entertainment field – music, comedy and politics. The major problem with copying black music – the vocals – was largely sidestepped as almost anybody could be coached into talking their way through a rhythm.

Even the notorious entrepreneur Malcolm McLaren, previously manager for The New York Dolls, The Sex Pistols and Bow Wow Wow, took a hip hop-inspired melange of rap, Latin, Appalachian and Zulu music and with the help of WHBI radio rappers and scratchers The World's Famous Supreme Team and producer Trevor Horn, made himself a solo success. In 1983 the fad was spread even further by Charlie Ahearn's immensely likeable dramatised documentary film *Wildstyle* and the eminently dislikeable blockbuster movie *Flashdance*, and in '84 came the *Breakdance*, *Beat Street* deluge. Ten years on, hip hop had finally reached the mass international market.

The all-electronic sound of 'Planet Rock' was to become the new sound of the streets. The extraordinary advances in electronic music technology in the late '70s and early

DOUBLE DUTCH *Photo: courtesy of Stuart Cosgrove*

JUST ROCK: THE FEARLESS FOUR AT THE COPA CABANA

'80s radically transformed the possibilities for making music. Drum machines like the Roland 808, an analog machine with a microprocessor memory, along with more sophisticated (and costly) digital machines like the Linn Drum and the Oberheim DMX, compact polyphonic synthesisers and Simmons electric drums made it simple for one musician to lay down high-quality tracks without moving from the recording studio control room.

One of the records which followed quickly in the wake of 'Planet Rock' was The Fearless Four's 'Rockin' It' on Enjoy. Their previous release for Bobby Robinson was a tune called 'It's Magic', a suspended riff based on a Cat Stevens song, but it was 'Rockin' It' which really distinguished them from the crowd. From its spooky opening, 'They're here' – a catch phrase and advertising slogan from the Tobe Hooper/Steven Spielberg horror movie *Poltergeist* – it was obviously something special. A lopsided synthesiser riff stolen from Kraftwerk's 'The Man Machine' and repeated 137 times (as usual played by Pumpkin) and a battering electric drum beat were just about the only constituents other than the rap, but it was a compelling sound that captured the mood of the twitching would-be androids and vid-kids doing the electric boogie. The Fearless Four unravel their convoluted history:

Master O.C. It was about eight years ago – it started with me and Tito. We was doing home tapes, selling them for $10 in the streets. People liked Tito's voice and my cutting at that time.

Tito We had auditions to see who could be

135

down with our group. We were selling tapes and the tapes were giving us clientele, which means being known well.

Master O.C. We were known as The Houserockers Crew.

Tito We were selling them in Manhattan, Queens, The Bronx and our tapes was real familiar until we started really getting juice, which is people knowing us. We had got somebody else – Mike Ski – he was good. He had a different style of rap than I have. As time went by we bumped into Peso, and Peso came with a singing style of rap.

Master O.C. At that time, when Peso got down, we had Troy B from The Disco Four with us also and that's what made it four at the time. We got rid of Troy B and we found DLB when we did a talent show. We sounded good together so it was the four – me, Tito, Peso, DLB and Mike Ski at that time. At one time it was The Fearless Five.

Mike C Mike Ski had left the group. He got married and his married life couldn't cope with his career so it was The Fearless Four. We've been together ever since – pushing hits.

When rap groups call themselves the Four or the Five it doesn't always mean that there are four or five of them. The DJs tend to get left out of the numbering process – The Fearless Four feature The Mighty Mike C, The Devastating Tito, The Great Peso and DLB, The Microphone Wizard, upfront. Working the turntables behind them they have Krazy Eddie, named after the

retail store with the lunatic commercials, and the Master O.C., who also produces groups like The Fantasy Three, with their 'Biters In the City'. They talk about the records they were using for beats before they recorded:

O.C. We was using jazz records. Bob James, Grover Washington, Herbie Hancock – *Headhunters* – Isaac Hayes. We was using all the old records that we could make a beat out of.

Peso Kraftwerk – that's our soul group.

Tito We were always looking in all the music – jazz and pop and all that. We were looking at records just by name like on *Headhunters*. *Headhunters*? Maybe it's got some beat on it. We bought *Headhunters* and found that the beat on it was something that we started loving, making songs and routines to it. We used one cut. All we did was just cut up that one part – tik tik-atik boom da boom chh doom da doom chh. We had two turntables and just kept cutting up that one beat. It sounds like a whole different record.

Following 'Rockin' It' they moved from Enjoy (as did everybody else) and went to Elektra. If they thought that moving to a bigger label would break them worldwide they were in for some disillusionment. Their first record for the company was re-mixed by Larry Levan. Larry was more of a disco than hip hop mixer, known for records such as Instant Funk's 'I Got My Mind Made Up' or Skyy's 'First Time Around'. For one reason or another, 'Just Rock' (based on Gary Numan's 'Cars') was a flop.

ROCKIN' IT: THE FEARLESS FOUR AT THE FUNHOUSE

The Fearless Four feel that the most commercial rap comes from the ideas of the rappers and DJs themselves. As soon as the company feels it knows best then the records lose their street appeal. They claim 'Just Rock' as the first punk-rock rap (an unholy alliance if ever there was one). Their friends, The Cold Crush Brothers, added to the new genre with 'Punk Rock Rap' on Tuff City Records, a record which combines the renowned Cold Crush rhymes with a self-consciously 'English' feel – icy synthesisers, rock guitar and fake British accents. The notion of punk is so exotic up on Washington Avenue where the Cold Crusher Supreme EZ AD lives that it's no surprise that punk rap turns out to be a hilarious multiple pile-up of heavy metal, synthesiser rock and hip hop. The white boys got their own back with a nasty porno-

graphic scratch record called 'Cookie Puss' on Ratcage. 'Cookie Puss' was by Beastie Boys, a white hardcore group whose favourite band turned out to be Kiss. Inspired by a Mr Carvel soft ice-cream promotion (Cookie Puss – ice-cream sandwich from outer space), it brought together oral sex, telephone violence, food and sexually transmitted diseases as well as an implied racism. Back in the cage, Beastie Boys.

Cold Crush and The Fearless Four may well feel that their rock rap is new but black rock has been around for a long time. Jimi Hendrix and Sly Stone provided models for it, pursued during the '70s by groups like The Jimmy Castor Bunch, Funkadelic, Sons of Slum, War, The Barkays and The Skullsnaps and more recently by Prince and Rick James. Two musicians on the edges of the rap scene worked together in Detroit in

the middle '70s in the crossover area of funk rock. Dennis Weeden, who has worked with Ms DJ, Kenton Nix and Lenny White, came to New York in 1977 with Bill Laswell, a bass player. Weeden and Laswell played together in a group called Solar Eclipse in Michigan and after sharing a loft for a year both branched out in their own directions.

In 1979 Laswell teamed up with synthesiser player Michael Beinhorn, drummer Fred Maher and guitarist Cliff Culteri to form a group called Material – the original core of a floating aggregation of musicians drawn from free jazz, free improvisation and dance music. Through an association with a French-run record label called Celluloid, sited near Times Square, Laswell and Beinhorn came to produce a number of mainly electronic rap records. Bill gives the story:

> It was through this label we have called Celluloid. They were gonna do some records for France. I had heard the music before but I wasn't directly involved in doing tracks like that. We were doing dance tracks which all the kids who were doing these rap records had heard and were playing in clubs and stuff already. It came about as an obligation to a label to produce really quickly five rap records. At the time they were very easy to make 'cos I had already been through the process of making funk records so it was just minimalising and emphasising certain elements more than others. I didn't think

the music meant really anything. It was just kinda fun to do. It was more fun to make than it was to listen to.

Of the five records that resulted, one was produced by The Clash, a feeble and amateurish history of graffiti by spray-can artist Futura 2000; The Smurfs' 'Smurf For What It's Worth' involved members of The Peech Boys and is laughably bad; 'Une Sale Histoire' by Fab Five Freddy is dispensable but for its B side featuring Beside, a white woman from California who raps in French; 'The Roxy' by Phase II has a strong minimalism, and 'Grandmixer Cuts It Up' by Grandmixer D.ST and the Infinity Rappers (KC Roc and Shahiem) was deep in video wars – sequencer blips, vocoder vocals, random-fire electric percussion and Smart Bomb blasts. Defender comes to your turntable.

Grandmixer D.ST's favourite video game is Ms Pacman; his favourite TV show is *Star Trek*. The full-colour sleeves for these five Celluloid releases were ikons of the hip-hop scene – graffiti artworks on the back and personality portraits on the front. The Grandmixer (real name Derek Showard, whose home is Delancy Street on the lower east side – hence the D.ST tag) is posing in his room wearing a variant on the b boy uniform complete with white gloves. Behind him are his two turntables, mixer and headphones, coloured vinyl discs and a pair of 3-D glasses. To his right is his TV, his briefcase and his shades. B boying is about being cool.

The weakness of the records is that none of the featured artists was doing anything reflecting his own talents. Fab Five Freddy, Futura and Phase II are graffiti artists and D.ST is a DJ and scratch mixer. Freddy (Braithwaite) is candid about his own role in the scene, upsetting the frequent collusion between the media and hip hop that all b boys and b girls were born in burnt-out tenements. Born in Brooklyn, he admits, 'I was a voyeur at the time hip hop was created but I was a catalyst in bringing it to a wider thing.' His parents were lawyers (his father managed jazz musicians like drummer Max Roach and trumpeter Clifford Brown) and he studied logic in college for a while but moved on to graffiti, making a reputation for himself by spraying the side of an IRT train with his own version of Andy Warhol's silkscreen soup cans. Freddy was a founder member of the Brooklyn graffiti squad, The Fabulous Five, along with Lee Quinones.

With rap being consumed with such voracity by a worldwide audience largely unfamiliar with black music tradition, it is inevitable that distinctions should become blurred. In pop music, stars tend to be represented as images rather than as human beings with specific abilities. Therefore, it's hardly surprising that Afrika Bambaataa, Grandmaster Flash and Fab Five Freddy are regarded as rappers. Only gradually has hip hop come to be seen as an *attitude* which made its mark on forms of expression that had been around for years – dancing, fashion, graffiti, disc jockeying and schoolyard rapping.

Most graffiti artists claim that their movement was started by a teenager tagged

CRAZY CUTS: GRANDMIXER D.ST AT THE EARTH'S EDGE

TAKI 183, a Greek boy named Demetrios from West 183rd Street. TAKI was king of the Magic Markers from 1970 to 1972, yet graffiti was already a subject of study in the '60s. R. Lincoln Keiser's study of the Chicago Vice Lords has numerous photographs of wall writing – territorial markings with club names – and Herbert Kohl's essay, 'Names, Graffiti and Culture', is an analysis of both the reasons behind graffiti and the tags used by artists in place of their legal names. Kohl noted the changes taking place in graffiti as anti-poverty programmes in the late '60s legitimised wall writing by bringing together the youthful black and Puerto Rican artists with socially motivated painters. This sanctioned outdoor art led to more elaborate forms growing out of basic chalk or Magic Marker scribbling. Each borough shouted its identity with a distinct calligraphic style – bubble letters in the Bronx, a Manhattan style, a Queens style and a Brooklyn style called 'Wildstyle'. Artists formed into clubs, an extension of the established neighbourhood gangs – in Brooklyn The Ex(perienced) Vandals, The Vanguards, Magic Inc, The Nod Squad, The A Last Survivors – and bombings upped their daring from nervously scribbled tags into inconceivably detailed wall-size murals or completed trains, painted at night in the yards.

In no other city in the world has vernacular art impinged so fiercely. For a decade and a half the City has been at battle with its teenage art community. Herbert Kohl puts it into perspective: 'Graffiti is not a particularly durable form of expression . . . It is

DOUBLE TROUBLE, CHARLIE AHEARN AND FAB FIVE FREDDY MEET BACKSTAGE AT DANCETERIA

different for the rich and powerful who express their territorial claims and social identities in more durable forms. A gang can paint its name on the walls of its turf, but that is nothing compared to a corporation that stamps its emblem on its buildings or a rich man's club that embodies in stone its claim to power and importance.'

Even more transitory than graffiti are the dance styles that form a part of hip-hop subculture. The south Bronx dance known as Breaking was usurped by the Freak when Chic released 'Le Freak' in 1978, and it was only the intervention of tradition-conscious dancers Crazy Legs (aka Ritchie Colon) and Frosty Freeze (aka Wayne Frost) which kept it alive. Breaking originally concentrated on the legs and feet (bell-bottom trousers pulled up to reveal white socks which showed off steps to advantage in the darkness of the clubs) but Crazy Legs, Frosty Freeze and The Rock Steady Crew added an acrobatic element – worked out in the sandlots of Central Park then moving onto grass and finally concrete – which made Breaking the prime competitive dance as well as giving it a sensational flavour perfect for media fodder.

Through The Rock Steady Crew and countless other dance groups – Incredible Breakers, Electric Force, The Magificent Force, ABC, UTFO – Breaking became a dazzling display of body-punishing spins on the back, shoulders, hands and head. Combined with the west coast invention of Electric Boogie (like electric shock waves jerking through the limbs), Moonwalking (the illusion of gliding across the ground), Joint Popping, Freezes, Mime and Robot Imita-tions, Breaking became a freestyle dance that actualised all the key imagery of space age, video age, computer age, comic book and superhero America.

According to Afrika Bambaataa, Breaking started as a dance to James Brown's 'Get On the Good Foot':

I said the long hair hippies and the Afro-
blacks,
They all get together across the tracks and
they party,
Ho – on the good foot.
Ain't nothing going on – but the rent-a,
A whole lotta bills and my money's spent,
And that's on my bad foot.

In a deeply traditional ritual dating back to Southern customs and beyond to West Africa, the dancers would form a circle and take turns to solo in the centre. The word *break* or *breaking* is a music and dance term (as well as a proverb) that goes back a long way. Some tunes, like 'Buck Dancer's Lament' from early this century, featured a two-bar silence in every eight bars for the break – a quick showcase of improvised dance steps. Others used the same device for a solo instrumental break: one of the most fetishised fragments of recorded music is the famous four-bar break taken by Charlie Parker in Dizzy Gillespie's tune 'Night in Tunisia'.

Many of the dance moves used in current freestyle hark back to American dances from the past. In Marshall and Jean Stearns's *Jazz Dance*, Pigmeat Markham recalls the dancing of Jim Green in AG Allen's Mighty Minstrels tent show during

PAPO, MIGUEL AND CHRIS ON THE 6 TRAIN
GRAFFITI ON THE 6 TRAIN

the early 1920s: ' "Green had a speciality I'll never forget. He'd dance awhile and then fall on the floor and spin around on his backside in time with the music." '

Other dancers from vaudeville and minstrel shows had routines that show a mysterious continuity with all the 'new' tricks: a white dancer called Joe Bennett could move across a stage with his body held in a rigid sitting posture; flash dancer (no, that's not a new term, either) Ananias Berry from The Berry Brothers (who worked together from 1925 to 1951) could strut across a stage in a manner described by the authors of *Jazz Dance* as ' "freezing and melting" like frames in a film strip'; Albert

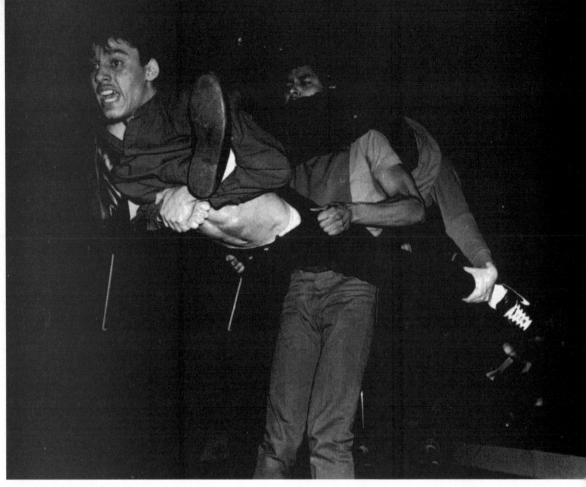

'Pops' Whitman, from Pops and Louis, spun like a top back in the 1940s; Tip Tap and Toe could slide in any direction; Jigsaw Jackson the Human Corkscrew danced with his chin on the Cotton Club stage to the accompaniment of Duke Ellington's Jungle Band. He could also point his face and toes in opposite directions.

Many of the eccentric and comedy dances like Scratch or Itch dancing, Rubberlegs, or Legomania, and Shake dances, also prefigure Breaking and Popping, while the acrobatic element of modern Breaking goes back to before 1900. *Jazz Dance* offers the following comments on early acrobatics: 'The earliest and best-known Negro acrobats were tumblers, who worked *on the ground* performing somersaults, cartwheels, flips and spins ... Tumbling is geared-to-the-ground, do-it-yourself acrobatics, which anyone can afford. It also lends itself readily to the dance'.

Acrobatics are not just easily applied to dance. They are also extremely dramatic and like all the other forms of hip-hop style they take the most limited resources from an impoverished environment and raise them to extraordinary heights of creativity.

In the early days, most rappers, dancers, DJs and graffiti artists lost sleep trying to figure new ways of crushing the opposition. Competition was relentless but the invention was high.

The more straightforward steps that didn't lead to concussion, fractured bones and Robbie the Robot tics – the kind of dances that are recycled every decade with new names – were still around. This time they had names like the Patty Duke, the Smurf and the Webo. With the latter two came a music that took the final warp out into hyperspace.

BREAKING THREE-UP AT THE ROXY

YOUNG BREAKERS AT THE ROXY

11. Wotupski, bug byte?

'Planet Rock' was like a light being switched on. The black music charts of 1982 were peppered with electronic records – space-breaking releases included Planet Patrol's 'Play At Your Own Risk', 'Nunk' by Warp 9, Tyrone Brunson's 'The Smurf', 'Message 2 (Survival)' by Melle Mel and Duke Bootee, The Fearless Four's 'Rockin' It', 'Hip Hop Be Bop (Don't Stop)' by Man Parrish, George Clinton's *Computer Games* album, 'Scorpio' by Grandmaster Flash and the Furious Five, 'Pack Jam' by The Jonzun Crew, and Whodini's 'Magic's Wand'. Although these records were parallel with the electronic soul of D Train, Kashif, The Peech Boys and The System or the late Patrick Cowley's hi-energy production for Sylvester (derived from Giorgio Moroder's sequencer disco), they differed in being militantly juvenile. Pop culture is inspirational and electro is craze music, a soundtrack for vidkids to live out fantasies born of a science-fiction revival (courtesy of *Star Wars* and *Close Encounters of the Third Kind*) and a video games onslaught.

Nobody can play Defender or Galaxian for long without being affected by those sounds – sickening rumbles and throbs, fuzzy explosions and mindless melodies – and when Gorf and Gorgar began to talk, the whole interactive games phenomenon took on a menacing aspect. Do they know that you've just spent all your mother's money? Do they care that your fantasies are

CHILLING OUT AT THE FUNHOUSE

saturated with deep blue space wars and glowing violet electronic insects? All the electro boogie records that flew in the 'Planet Rock' slipstream used a variant on imagery drawn from computer games, video, cartoons, sci-fi and hip-hop slanguage. Just as The Cuff Links defined boy/girl relationships through nuclear war images in their doo-wop ballad 'Guided Missiles' (recorded in the A-bomb-conscious 1950s), so Warp 9 sang 'Girl, you're looking good on my video' in the Casio keyboard-powered 'Nunk' (a hybrid of New wave and fUNK).

The whole electro genre fell under the appellation of hip hop, even if it was only distantly related to original Bronx style. Saturday morning TV cartoons were a rich source for b boy/girl source material. The Smurf, for example, was a dance named after the Hanna-Barbera cartoons developed from an adaptation of characters in an early '60s French comic called *Spiro*. The Smurfs had a fetching slang – very hip hop – which substituted verbs, as in 'My potion is wearing off. We'd better smurf out of here.' Washington-born bass player Tyrone Brunson made a record called 'The Smurf' which was pure dance-craze instrumental. It outraged the Smurf copyright holders. Dance discs that followed included 'Letzmurph Acrossdasurf' by the Micronawts (The Micronauts were Marvel Comics' 'heroes minute in size . . . but mighty beyond measure' who came from a sub-atomic solar system called the *Microverse*). On this Tuff City release, dub-mixed by Afrika Bambaataa, they were the alter ego of *Village Voice* music critic Barry

Michael Cooper. Since Micronauts, like Smurfs, are very small they have squeaky voices – a fact seized upon by critics of the electro genre as a sign of weakness and a throwback to David Seville's Chipmunks. They forget that dance music has always had a fondness for small creatures with high voices: the parents of The Micronawts were The Chubukos, who in 1973 recorded their tribute to Seville's 1958 US number one, 'Witch Doctor', with a thinly disguised version of Manu Dibango's 'Soul Makossa' called 'Witch Doctor Bump'. Another smurf record was 'Salsa Smurf' by Special Request – a collaboration on Tommy Boy between two contributors to NYC radio station 92KTU, Carlos DeJesus and Jose 'Animal' Diaz. Diaz also mixed Rhetta Hughes's electro hi-energy 'Angel Man', a paean to the subway Guardian Angels, and the Jonzun Crew's 'We Are the Jonzun Crew'. There was also 'Smerphies Dance' on Telestar Cassettes by Spyder D, a young man named Duane Hughes who produced the nightmarishly claustrophobic 'Get Into the Mix' by DJ Divine.

'Get Into the Mix' was inspired by the soundtrack of an Italian porno movie called *How Funny Can Sex Be* and its theme, 'Sesso Matto', released on West End Records. Like *Cooley High* and *Willie Dynamite*, *How Funny Can Sex Be* was a soundtrack with beats that could be cut by DJs. 'Get Into the Mix', along with a very few other records, was a new sub-genre of hip hop pornography.

Another dance craze of the period, along with the Smurf, was the Webo or Huevo (Spanish for egg). It, too, had its very own audiotrack, typical of '82–'83 madhouse dub mixes. Called 'Huevo Dancing' and released on Catawba, it was a creation of veteran soul producer George Kerr and keyboardist/guitarist Reggie Griffin. Its Latino/black soap opera intro, violent electric drums and seemingly random attacks on the mixing-desk faders made it the perfect illustration of the direction dance music was taking. Both Kerr and Griffin were associated with the Sylvia and Joe Robinson empire, and Reggie Griffin went on to make his own electro boogie record, 'Mirda Rock', for Sweet Mountain Records, a Sugarhill subsidiary.

Also doing some uncredited session work at Sugarhill was a Florida-born multi-instrumentalist named Michael Johnson, the periwigged force behind The Jonzun Crew. The Jonzun Crew mixed electronic drums, keyboards and vocoders with an image based on a black composer who gave proto multi-media concerts in Europe in the eighteenth century. 'Pack Jam' (originally called 'Pac Man' and released on the Johnson Brothers' own label, Boston International) was a video-game record, take it or leave it. Like 'Mirda Rock ('I am a computer') or Tilt's 'Arkade Funk' ('I am an arcade funk machine') there was no beating about the bush. These records were an invitation for kids to plunge themselves Tron-like into a world of freeze-frame See Threepios, and if adults wanted to run scared then that was their business – it was the reality of new technology that they were running from.

Many of the electro musicians and producers recognise their music as the fusion that it is – street funk and hip hop mixed with influences from British synthesiser music (Gary Numan, Human League, Thomas Dolby and Yazoo were all played on WKTU, the radio station that switched from rock to disco in 1978, and on WBLS by Frankie Crocker), Latin music, Kraftwerk and jazz fusion, all written into the breaker, robot, pop, wave and moonwalk meltdown. The music of Miles Davis and Herbie Hancock was an important antecedent. Davis's *Filles De Kilimanjaro* is a cool, infinitely subtle pre-echo of electro, and his *Bitches Brew* and *On the Corner*, along with Herbie Hancock's *Headhunters*, gave currency to the image of tribal Africa combined with state-of-the-art electronics. Hancock even stole a touch of rain-forest pygmy music (the polyphonic alternation of vocal yodelling and one-note whistle) for the intro of his 'Watermelon Man' remake. This was exactly a decade before the *Future Shock* album with its hit single 'Rockit'. 'Rockit' was a Material production obliquely inspired by *Headhunters*. In among the Fairlight, Chroma, Emulator and alphaSyntauri, the bata drums and the DMX, the Led Zeppelin guitar chord and the Vocoder, Grandmixer D.ST is featured cutting in rhythmic fills with turntable scratching of a record of the Ketjak Balinese Monkey dance. *Plus ça change*.

All music has a history, shameful or illustrious, but for a 14-year-old chilling out in Playland, white nylon anorak with the hood pulled tight and maybe a pair of Nike kicks with the tongues stuck out, what matters in the mini-phones plugged into the Walkman (or one of its cheaper variants) is the post - NASA - Silicone Valley - Atari - TV Break Out - Taito - Sony - Roland - Linn - Oberheim - Lucas - Speilberg groove. With his use of the Fairlight, a (very expensive) microcomputer system which samples sounds that can be used musically by means of either a keyboard or a light pen acting directly on a VDU, the English producer Trevor Horn has sidestepped the issue of having worked in the desperately unhip Buggles and Yes and gone straight to the hearts of the Bronx techno-warriors.

Lotti Golden and Richard Scher, Warp 9 producers, are equally unlikely as progenitors of the new-wave funk but their commitment to a medium generally considered junk food is disarming. Warp 9 are the perfect instance of hip hop's contemporary ramifications. Their second record, 'Light Years Away', was a 'when gods were space-people' sci-fi tale of alien visitation partially inspired by 'The Message'. It was created by a team which typifies current music-making: two percussionist/singers – Boe Brown who worked with The Strikers, and Chuck Wansley previously of The Charades; singer Ada Dyer who went on to work in the stage show of *The Wiz*; mixer and Funhouse DJ Jellybean; producer and ex-jazz fusion keyboard player Richard Scher, and producer/lyricist/vocalist Lotti Golden. Lotti explains her background:

I was an artist first. I had a record on Atlantic Records a while ago (1969) and it was a street record of its time. It was called 'Motorcycle'. Stream-of-consciousness rapping, singing about life in New York. It's a collector's item – you can still

WARP 9 AND LOTTI GOLDEN: THE 'BEAT WAVE' PLAYBACK

get it. And then I drifted into jazz for a while. I was very fascinated by jazz. I wanted to sing jazz because to me that was the epitome . . . then starting in the late '70s back to writing R&B. Years ago, Patti LaBelle and the Bluebelles recorded one of my songs. You never heard of it! It was called 'Dance To the Rhythm of Love'. It was a big hit in the Bahamas.

I've been doing music for a real long time and I do what I wanna do at the time that I wanna do it. I stay with what I believe in and I really believe in what Richard and I are doing.

Divine, The Beat Box Boys, The Boogie Boys, The Disco Four, Pumpkin, Captain Rock and Davy DMX. Focused down hard on the beats, these records are a black metal music for the '80s – a hard-edge ugly/beauty trance as desperate and stimulating as New York itself.

Davy DMX lives in Queens Village. His basement is crammed with electric keyboards, a drum kit, timbales, guitar, twin turntables, tape machines, records, photographs of his family and the ubiquitous Oberheim DMX. All of it is the reward for a spell as DJ with Kurtis Blow, an association which ended with a degree of bitterness on both sides. Originally a guitarist, Davy – whose real name is David Reeves – started in a group called Rhythm and Creation at the age of 16. He explains how economics affected his attitude to music-making:

> If you have a group of eight people in a band – it was hard to get work, you know? If you did get work it wasn't for a lot of money . . . When the DJ thing came out you can get the same money – you can just bring turntables and speakers and take the place of a band. I DJed for about two years. I used to go to the Bronx a lot and see people scratching. We didn't call it scratching. We called it cutting and mixing.
>
> I was the first DJ in Queens to do the quick mixing and stuff like that – cut turntable to turntable real fast and to play beats. They didn't like it at first – there wasn't no words, no melody into it. It was just drums. I played drums for hours with records . . . I was too young

The big start to their partnership came with writing 'I Specialise In Love' for Sharon Brown on Profile Records. Since then they have produced other electro hip-hop records with similar gorgeous textures and multiple layers to those of the Warp 9 productions – Chilltown's 'Rock the Beat' and 'Girl's Night Out' by Ladies Choice among them.

With the musicality of their productions they make a markedly different kind of electro boogie from the austere and increasingly freakish end of the genre occupied by Run-D.M.C., The B Boys, DJ

to play clubs – I had to go mobile and just play anywhere I could – neighbourhood bebop clubs. I had a DJ organisation called Solar Sound – we never made a record or nothing, it broke up before the record scene started because I was working with Kurtis Blow. Worked with him for five years.

As well as DJing for Kurtis, Davy played guitar in Orange Krush, playing beats-based music with bassist and co-writer Larry Smith and drummer Trevor Gale. Both Davy DMX's first solo release, 'One For the Treble (Fresh)' on Tuff City, and the reconstituted Orange Krush productions for Profile group Run-D.M.C. reflect the new sound – like an electronic update of Mississippi fife and drum music fed into a breaker's yard.

In Run-D.M.C. Joseph Simmons is Run and Darrel McDaniels ls D.M.C. Their records, 'It's Like That', 'Sucker MCs' (one of the biggest rap records of 1983), 'Hard Times' and 'Wake Up', are direct-to-disc wall poems rapped in a doggerel style over an unwavering piston beat. The minimal embellishments are restricted to a few rhythmic keyboard stabs or a bass tied in with the kick drum, sound effects and scratch sounds. Despite its initially bleak surface the music employs a cunning use of hooks – its danceability, wit and overall optimism distinguish it from the despair school of rock.

The concurrent fashionability of scratch mixing and sampling keyboards like the Emulator and Fairlight has led to creative pillage on a grand scale and caused a crisis for pre-computer-age concepts of artistic property. The B Boys' 'Cuttin' Herbie' on Vintertainment makes kamikaze raids on Herbie Hancock's 'Rockit', Howard Johnson's 'So Fine' and a voice that could be James Brown. The Beat Box Boys scrape beats from a screaming rock guitar for 'Punch'. The concept of the pop hook – a musical phrase that sticks in the mind – is pared down to a single noise that flashes up like an English word in Japanese script. The Imperial Brothers use a cough on their 'We Come To Rock' and The Boogie Boys use a Tarzan yell, a cuica, a single word – 'certainly' (pronounced New York style 'soyt'n'ley' – some 'classical' music, some 'heavy metal', mixed kitchen-sink method for their exhumation of the rap obsession with astrology, 'Zodiac/Break Dancer/Shake and Break'. The Awesome Foursome use the Tarzan yell for 'Funky Breakdown', and the classical music returns for The Beat Box Boys' 'Give Me My Money'. What next – Beethoven's Fifth? Soyt'n'ley – here comes Vincent Davies's Vintertainment label with 'Beethoven's Fifth Street Symphony'! The stick-up kids are on the loose.

To phone Tommy Boy Records in February '84 was a treat. For as long as you were kept on hold there was the legendary 'Payoff Mix' in your ear – the double D and Steinski mastermix of G.L.O.B.E. and Whiz Kid's 'Play That Beat Mr. D.J.', taking hip-hop cutting one step further into the realm of endless potential. It used the irresistible base of 'Play That Beat' to cut in fragments of 'Adventures On the Wheels of Steel', some James Brown soul power, 'Buffalo Gals', Funky Four's 'That's the Joint', West Street Mob, The Supreme Team, Culture Club, Starski's 'Live At the Disco Fever', Little Richard's 'Tutti Frutti', exercise routines (heel-toe, heel-toe), Humphrey Bogart in *Casablanca*, 'Rockit', The Supremes' 'Stop In the Name of Love', 'Planet Rock', Indeep's 'Last Night a DJ Saved My Life' and more. Like a long subway ride with the doors opening onto a different kind of music at every stop, it perfectly expressed the spirit of G.L.O.B.E.'s words:

> *Punk rock, new wave and soul*
> *Pop music, salsa, rock & roll*
> *Calypso, reggae, rhythm & blues*
> *Master mix those number one tunes*

Hip hop was the new music by virtue of its finding a way to absorb all other music. I.R.T. (Interboro Rhythm Team) sum up the New York mix with their subterranean journey across the city. At Times Square Julio is Breaking to his radio. The beats are electro boogie, the music is a classy salsa montuno from the piano, the dogs are barking, the words are the rap attack. 'Watch the Closing Doors!'

HARD TIMES: RUN - D.M.C.

154

WATCH THE CLOSING DOORS

12. Crush the groove

I don't really know but somebody said, some musical rhythms can mess with your head.

'84 moves into '85. Screams. Slashes of noise. A fat 808 bass drum with a whiplash snare – dough and breaking concrete – booms in a New York club called Area. 'It's Yours', by T La Rock and Jazzy Jay is the first release to sport the logo of Rick Rubin's label, Def Jam, and Rick is in the DJ booth, waiting to hear it drop.

The results are spectacular. 'One of the best moments I've ever had,' says Rick, with a typical lack of restraint. 'Someone who worked at the club came running up to the booth and said, "Turn it down! Turn it down!" They have these big Richard Long bass speakers, these huge floor model horns. One of the speakers actually caught on fire. They had to put it out with fire extinguishers. The best.'

This quest for fire, the desire to make a groove so hard and heavy that it crushed and burned everything in its path, was the key to rap after breakdance and the creative exhaustion of old-school rappers. Feature films like *Breakin'* and *Beat Street* had helped to fuel the mainstream acceptance of rap yet failed to transcend the artifice of Hollywood musicals. Breakdancing was the marketing gimmick needed to draw hip hop into the consumer arena; it appealed to young children – regardless of skin colour, class, education, economic status, language, and, to some degree, gender – and it was irresistible to ideas people within advertising agencies. Exotic and spectacular, divorced from its origins in Latin and African-American streetdancing, breaking could sell crisps, beer, cereal, batteries. For the breakdancers, lockers and poppers, their street dancing now had the potential to evolve into a conventional Hollywood career; pinned to the walls of Los Angeles cafés you can still find autographed photographs of the breakdancers that time forgot.

By February 1985, the pendulum had swung in the opposite direction, towards a harsh, upfront, seemingly uncommercial music. Some people saw this as the ultimate soundtrack for young urban African-Americans. In an office looking down onto Broadway, words pour out of Russell Simmons in a torrent – his history, his philosophy, his angle on life. 'The most commercial rap records, the ones that radio is so happy to play,' he says, 'they don't sell. Most of the rap that's selling is the most rebellious and the loudest.'

Rick and Russell had become partners in a venture which would grow into a small empire. Def Jam and Rush Productions raised the financial stakes for many rap acts, created moral panics, merchandising deals and crossover acceptance in the white suburbs, then finally splintered in disharmony and controversy. By the end of 1988, Russell was juggling with an increasingly complex rap empire in New York City and Rick had scooped up his cut of the kingdom and relocated to Los

RUSSELL SIMMONS '89 *Photo: Oliver Lim*

Angeles, overseeing a predominantly rock label called Def American.

On a sunny, pre-spring day in '85, they still worked from separate headquarters. Russell had his frantic management company, Rush Productions, looking after 16 acts including Kurtis Blow, Run-D.M.C., Whodini, L.L. Cool J, and rap veteran Jimmy Spicer; Rick, meanwhile, was still a student at New York University. His tiny room in the halls of residence served as an office of sorts, a flotsam of Def Jam T-shirts, twin turntables, crates of records, day-glo posters for Washington D.C. go-go shows, copies of *Hustler* and the sonic assault of AC/DC's 'Back In Black'.

Rick's philosophy was based on the idea that music should be hardcore. 'I think the way to go about really knowing what's going on,' he explained, 'is just being in tune with everything. You can't do it by listening to music. Pro wrestling is real important. Movies. You know, everything. You have to make records the way you live your life. I never try to make something that I think someone will like.' As it later transpired, this attitude generated plenty of material for rival forces in America's escalating censorship war; speed metal band Slayer ('Sadist of the noblest blood/destroying, without mercy/to benefit the Aryan race'), stand-up comedian Andrew Dice Clay ('I'm an old fashioned guy. I think women look good scrubbing toilets') and Houston rappers The Geto Boys ('Play pussy, get fucked') all had releases on Rubin's Def American label and upset anti-censorship libertarians and pro-censorship Christian fundamentalists equally. The tension between Rick's initial desire to make hardcore, radio-resistant records and Russell's wider ambitions (to make hardcore records *and* great black movies, to produce fabulous old-fashioned R&B and to drive a wedge into the mainstream music industry) heated their collaboration to boiling point.

The music that crossed the bridge between the confused rap scene of '84 and the tough, vibrant renewal of '85 was made by Run-D.M.C. At the tail end of the electro era, Run-D.M.C. records like

'Sucker M.C.'s' and 'Hard Times' sounded sparse, brutal and slow; the bare drum machine beats and interlocking, shouted raps sounded too strange and wonderful, perhaps, to make a lasting impression. However, this was to be the sound that redefined rap.

A trio with two rappers – Darryl McDaniels and Russell Simmon's younger brother Joe – and a DJ – Jam Master Jay – Run-D.M.C. had its origins in the New York neighbourhood of Hollis, Queens. This hard music from 'picturesque' surroundings raised questions that remain at the centre of the continuing debate about so-called gangster rap. As Nelson George commented in his *Village Voice* profile of Russell Simmons: 'What's always been surprising – at least to me when I attended St. John's University in the late '70s – is how fascinated with street culture the children of Hollis were. I came from Brownsville, an area that could easily have been Melle Mel's model for "The Message"; I knew "the ghetto" was nothing to romanticise. Yet here were kids like Russell who grew up in their own houses, with access to cars, furnished basements, both parents and more cash than my friends ever knew, acting (or trying to) as cool as any street kid.'

Run-D.M.C.'s involvement in rap was helped by Russell's early attempts as an entrepreneur. As Run describes it, 'I started with Kurtis Blow in '77 as The Son of Kurtis Blow. I would perform with him

ON BROADWAY: RUN-D.M.C. *Photo: Derek Ridgers*

at the weekends and in the summer I toured with him. We did a couple of Commodores dates and once I got out of high school I went on my own. My brother was managing Kurtis Blow. This was before records, even. Russell was pushing Kurtis when he was playing clubs in the area and Kurt used to come to my house and spend the night. In the morning I'd wake up and let him hear a little bit of my rap. He liked it a little bit so he said, "I could take you on as a sidekick and call you The Son of Kurtis Blow."'

While Run was playing the role of apprentice to Kurtis Blow, Darryl was learning to be a DJ. Basketball brought the two together and Run tried out his raps in Darryl's basement. 'Then I wrote my first rhyme,' says Darryl, 'and I already knew most of his raps. Then we needed a DJ. Jay would always be doing the parties in the park, the back gardens and the schools.'

'They always used to come and ask me for the mike,' explains Jay. 'I always had the equipment so they'd come and rap for me.' One of their innovations, an important one for rap's acceptance among young whites, was the use of rock breaks. 'Rock Box', from the first album, was a little too slick and contrived to launch a rock/rap fusion but with their second album, *King of Rock*, this unlikely genre collision smacked into place. 'We always rapped over rock records in the '70s,' says Run, 'but we didn't let the guitar come in too much.' Their producer, Larry Smith, contributed some ideas to the rock/rap fusion but Smith, who also produced for Whodini, was essentially an R&B man. *King of Rock* still sounds tough, if uneven,

RUN-D.M.C. AND WHODINI LIVE ON STAGE *Photo: David Corio*

but its layered mixes and fat, clean drum machine sounds have dated and the rock angle now seems like an over strenuous attempt to establish an image. The real b-boy Run-D.M.C. album was their third, *Raising Hell*, released in 1986 and produced by Jay and Run with Russell and Rick.

Raising Hell was a demonstration of the self-confidence that the rap industry (since that is what it had become) was discovering. Out went the keyboard hooks and all other lame attempts to be commercial. Russell had cut his teeth on '82/'83 tracks like 'Action' by Orange Krush and 'The Bubble

Bunch', followed by 'Money (Dollar Bill Y'all)', by Jimmy Spicer, working with Larry Smith and Jellybean Benitez; they were semi-disco, semi hip hop singles and despite failing to change the world they contained that kernel of low-budget honesty that Def Jam wanted to throw into the mainstream. The first single release from *Raising Hell* encapsulated the new policy. 'My Adidas', a praise song to sneakers which led, as these things do, to a sponsorship deal with the praised company, had a new swing beat and a backing track stripped to naked drum machine beats and jagged chunks of noise from Jam Master Jay's turntables. The other track, 'Peter Piper', was possibly the first track on which a DJ dared to employ a beaten-up breakbeat straight from his record box. Jay cut up 'Mardi Gras' by Bob James in masterly fashion under Run and D.M.C.'s snappy exchange of adapted nursery rhymes, and the crackles and pops of damaged vinyl were clearly audible.

This may seem trivial, a mere detail of production, but thousands of records based on scratchy samples have followed in the wake of 'Peter Piper'; by parading the fact that they use stolen fragments of ancient vinyl, all these tracks have emphasised the importance of this disregard for recording studio conventions. Paradoxically, by making such a practice commonplace they have also made us forget how revolutionary it once was. Rap was finally returning to its origins in the sweat and dangerous chaos of live jams, the adrenalin rush of slamming a scratched-up breakbeat onto the turntable just at the right moment. For the future, rap no longer had to ask musicians to create bogus hip hop music. As Rick Rubin once said about music, 'We don't go for that.'

One other track stood out from the consistently high standard of *Raising Hell*, which went against the trend of eliminating musicians from rap productions. From Run-D.M.C.'s earliest days, Jay had always cut up Aerosmith's 'Walk This Way', a b-boy rock classic, and there was an MTV-friendly angle to Rubin's suggestion of a rap remake which actually involved Aerosmith's Steven Tyler and Joe Perry, both of them back in business after a sharp descent into rock 'n' roll excess. 'Walk This Way' was one of the breakthrough records of rap, its metal guitar riffs, rock chorus, hard beats and raps fusing into an ultimate in rebel music that MTV and radio programmers, along with a lot of white rock fans, found impossible to resist.

Optimists interpreted this as a manifestation of utopian racial harmony, but racial divides were widening and black on black violence, some of it concentrated on rap events, was rising. Media reports blurred the distinction between the violence, whatever its cause, and the music. At the *Krush Groove Christmas Party*, held at Madison Square Garden on 27 December 1985, a packed and wildly enthusiastic crowd of over 20,000 rap fans screamed for Doug E. Fresh, Slick Rick, Whodini, L.L. Cool J, Lovebug Starski, Dr. Jeckyll and Mr. Hyde and Kurtis Blow. The scene inside the Garden was boisterous, occasionally cantankerous, but it was possible to walk back uptown after the show without suffering the harassment which later reports suggested was inevitable. 'So we gonna dedicate this one to God no matter what,' announced the Bible reading human beatbox Doug E. Fresh at the beginning of his set. 'Drugs, muthafucka!' somebody shouted from behind my left ear. 'Dedicate it to drugs!'

The following day, the *New York Post* final edition was barking CONCERT VIOLENCE FELLS 5 AT GARDEN. A man had been shot in the back on the sixth floor, among other incidents, all of which contributed to a growing panic about rap, guns, drugs and, as an unspoken undercurrent, young black men. Having attended the concert, I decided to see *Krush Groove*, the feature film which had been celebrated at the Christmas party. Inevitably a compromised and only sporadically interesting movie, *Krush Groove* was loosely based on the life of Russell Simmons, Def Jam and Rush Productions. Run-D.M.C. played themselves, Blair Underwood played the part of Russell, Sheila E was miscast as the love interest and The Fat Boys almost stole the show by eating themselves sick. In years to come, like the rock and roll features of the '50s, the only reason for watching will be the brief musical performances – in this case by L.L. Cool J, Run-D.M.C. and the Beastie Boys. Also reminiscent of those '50s films was the fact that a number of disturbances had been sparked at cinemas when *Krush Groove* opened. Concern in New York was running fairly high and after sharing this dull film with a total audience of four people at a Times Square cinema I was accosted at the exit by a TV reporter, looking for a soundbite to explain the connection between rap and violence.

The following year, Russell Simmons told me that he had been astonished to see an English journalist of his passing acquaintance pop up on Channel Two news with a defence of rap. Rap films and concerts were proving to be the chosen gathering point for people hostile to authority, people whose involvement with drugs, guns or gangs would incline their minds towards violence whatever the setting; rap was at most the soundtrack, not the cause, I told the TV reporter.

As the '80s wore on, however, media focus intensified on issues like gang violence or the spread of drugs. Police brutality directed at African-Americans, censorship, inept political 'solutions' to the drug problem, a lack of gun control, racial bitterness and all the other intractable problems that beset young blacks growing up in America today were tightly interwoven.

The responsibility for some of these problems was loaded onto the shoulders of Run-D.M.C. during their Raising Hell tour. Along with L.L. Cool J, the group traversed the great divide that lay between pop music and black street culture. The tour celebrated that achievement with a strong bill that included L.L., Whodini and the Beastie Boys. Although many concerts passed without incident, dates in Pittsburgh, New York and Long Beach, California were marred either by scare stories in the press or genuine violence. The Long Beach concert, scheduled for 17 August 1986, became the focal point for a Los Angeles gang battle which prevented Run-D.M.C. from performing. L.A. gang rivalry has been extensively documented since the 1940s, particularly prior to the Los Angeles Olympic Games of 1984. Why, then, were rappers repeatedly forced into explaining that gang wars and inner city shoot-outs were not new phenomena? The visibility of rap had drawn these age-old confrontations out into the open.

Being people who had hauled themselves up into the land of the haves without too much compromise, many rappers were reluctant to accept the idea that such destructive, self-destructive behaviour had any connection with a lack of opportunity or the frustratingly elusive nature of the American dream. In January 1986 I asked L.L. Cool J for his opinion of this view. 'Not necessarily,' he answered. 'Was it a black kid who was unemployed who shot the Pope? That doesn't have anything to do with it. It was just the fact that you put a lot of urban kids together in the same place and a lot of them are interested in seeing how tough they can be. Rap doesn't mean violence. How can rap mean violence? That's real dumb. They have rock concerts and people get killed and stomped. Does rock mean violence? I dare any critic to call it noise or say it causes violence. Do doctors make people commit surgery on people? That's just media.

'You don't hear a rap record and wanna go out and kill somebody. It's keeping kids out of trouble. That's what they don't like. They wanna see black kids running around with no money 'cause they like that shit. It's all stereotype. They get a kick out of that shit. You know how the press is. Things happen and they blow it all out of proportion 'cause it's black kids and it's rap and they don't understand neither. They wanna comment on how you wear your sneakers. They ain't concerned about what you're doing. Some bullshit reporter in the basement complaining with a typewriter. Black kids is doing it. You know that. It's black teenagers doing it. I'm not even a racist. Being black, man. They don't wanna see you with money. Money makes you equal. Rap brings unity. It puts a lot of black people in one place at one time. They don't want a lot of black people in the same place because then they can think about

I'M BAD: L.L. COOL J *Photo: David Corio*

some shit besides rap. They don't like that. Keep 'em spread out so they don't get to congregate too much and think. That's all that is. It's a way of putting brakes on somebody. But you see it's not working because the music's being exposed and it's becoming loved.'

It was indeed becoming loved, and as Barry Michael Cooper pointed out in a landmark essay about the drug-fuelled gun lore of young blacks in Baltimore, 'The priest, the rabbi, the Dalai Lama of this religion is L.L. Cool J, using mouth and beat box like stone and mortar, reducing these kids to fine powder . . . this is a cat with sharp verbal claws, and his rhymes are weapons. Like the kid who probably started shooting at the stage at 4604 [a Baltimore rap club], L.L. has something to prove, and he will never be disrespected. His rage caricatures the anger of black male teenagers, a rage that makes punk rock's tantrums look like something from *Captain Kangaroo*. L.L. shrinks the airwaves, the disco, the world into this insecure little room of his generation, the room with no exit. The only way out is scratching and clawing and maybe shooting.' (*In Cold Blood*, *Spin* magazine, May 1986).

Cooper's parallel between the vehemence of L.L.'s first records and the claustrophobic, angry world of many of his listeners poses a difficult question. Is violence endemic within rap, simply because rage boils in every young American black, whether they grew up with a car, a furnished basement and both parents or not? It's a point that L.L. has implied himself, in rejecting the ghetto music stereotype. 'They're hipped on that ghetto from the streets shit,' he said in exasperation. 'I ain't from the ghetto. I'm from Queens. The beat is from the street. The hardcoreness. Just being real ill and live and hard but I'm not from the ghetto. I live with my grandmother. Shit.'

Music, whether honky tonk country, hardcore, disco, rock 'n' roll, bubblegum pop or Stravinsky's *Rite of Spring*, has always been a catalyst, one stimulus among many that levers people's wild side over their inhibitions, helps them get crazy, inflames them to riot when they feel like rioting; it goes with getting drunk, having sex, destroying concert halls and driving cars too fast. Without the need for that side of music we would all be in rocking chairs, listening to Bing Crosby. L.L. discovered exactly how important the 'hardcoreness' was to his audience when he attempted to go soft on his second album with a ballad called 'I Need Love'. In London, the crowd booed him for this transgression, forgetting that L.L.'s formula had always been a mixture of hard and soft.

His first record on Def Jam (the first official release, since T La Rock's 'It's ours' was released in collaboration with Partytime/Streetwise), 'I Need A Beat', was punchy enough to match anybody's definition of hard. The second single, however, was a cute, minimalist rap ballad called 'I Want You'. The DMX drums still punched your chest, slapped your face, jabbed your ears, but L.L.'s fluent rap, addressed to his ex-babysitter, was teenage desire encapsulated.

The album that followed in '85, *Radio*, with its urgent expositons of b-boy life like 'I Can't Live Without My Radio' and 'Rock the Bells', remains a classic of b-boy music. When I first met L.L. he was 17 years old, fine tuning his Kangol hat and check shirt in a dressing room backstage at Madison Square Garden. Knowing there was an audience of 20,000 waiting for him, his attitude was cool to the point of arrogance. As Russell Simmons had warned me, a year before, 'I'm on a 'plane with Jeckyll and Hyde and L.L. walked over to us to tell us his new song and I think Hyde it was who said, "Just get the fuck out.

He's talking too much shit." They couldn't believe the lyrics – the way it flew. It's very different. A whole new style of rap. The new generation.'

The arrogance became his undoing. Both the second and third albums, produced by L.L. and his friends, were uneven. They seemed to need an outside ear to sharpen then up. Part of the problem lay with the rhymes, which had become uninspired enough to return again and again to the same theme: the consummate brilliance of L.L. Cool J. The strength of his rapping was its precise articulation, the way in which he could deliver complex lines with such poise that it sounded like perfectly structured, intimate conversation. Bragging and 'dissing' (disrespecting) were fundamental to L.L.'s style but these elements seemed to overtake him once he became as successful as he believed he should be. Time marches at a breathtaking rate in rap and nobody, no matter how successful, can afford to believe Barry Michael Cooper's assertion that 'he will never be disrespected'. L.L. was disrespected in the most humiliating manner when audiences turned away from him but he recovered to release the Marley Marl produced *Mama Said Knock You Out* in 1990 to positive reactions from both critics and fans. As Tyrone Woods from California wrote in a letter to *The Source* magazine: 'When I first heard "Boomin System" I could just imagine L.L. in his video, rollin' down 125th street or the Boulevard frontin' hard in front of people or some club.' The 'dissing' aspect of rap, the put-down of other rappers, enemies or imaginary objects of contempt, the parading of pure ego and malice, became one of the enlivening features of rap during the mid-80's. After L.L. had rapped about his monstrous, trademark radio with its volume set way past 10, Steady B came back at him on a Philadelphia label, Pop Art, with 'I'll Take Your Radio': 'Walking down the street, a JVC I see so I can snatch it up, throw it against the concrete.'

Also on Pop Art was Roxanne Shanté from the Queensbridge Projects in Long Island City. She was 14 years old in 1984, and her first record, 'Roxanne's Revenge', was an early episode in a vinyl soap opera that expanded pop music's answer record tradition into a minor war and gave a taste of future rap battles between boroughs (Brooklyn versus Long Island) and egos (L.L. Cool J versus Kool Moe Dee).

The opening salvo in this particular battle of rhymes was 'Roxanne Roxanne', recorded by Brooklyn's UTFO. With lines like 'Your mother her name is Mary, I heard everywhere that your father was a fairy,' this was an insult record with a story contrived around a young woman called Roxanne who snubbed the group's advances. UTFO's producers, Full Force, were smart enough to realise that a female audience would buy a female response and so recorded 'The Real Roxanne', by Joanne Martinez. From the point when she was 'discovered' while waitressing in a Brooklyn diner, Joanne became known as The Real Roxanne. Her dis track was positively refined, however, by comparison with Shanté's, who lashed out at the individual members of UTFO with a squeaky, breathless delivery while Marley

Marl lashed cavernous echo onto a drum track grabbed from UTFO's original.

Like rocket attacks, law suits were launched against this new practice of stealing a complete backing track. The insults grew rougher, the music grew tougher, the language got stronger, the drums got louder. This was the beachhead that Shanté won and defended. Through 'Queen of Rox', 'Bite This' to 1989's 'What's On Your Mind' and 'Independent Woman', she faced down all opposition. Rap might not be violent in itself, might not cause violence, but it had become intoxicatingly venemous, defiant, flamboyantly piratical, living out the traditions of the dirty Dozens or Yoruban abusive songs within an urban soundscape. This was music of collapsing buildings, steam horns, metal industry, all secreted within the microchip, scissoring its way across town. Bring the noise.

QUEEN OF ROX: ROXANNE SHANTE *Photo: David Corio*

13. Bring the noise

Got kinda high, and, uhh, kinda drunk,
so I had to beat up this little punk,
Forgot my key had to ring the bell
my momma came down she said 'Who
the hell?'
'Wait momma, wait, it's me, your
little son,'
Before I know it my ma pulled a gun.
Schoolly-D, 'Saturday Night'

It's Saturday night alright. The air on Key West's Duvall Street is heavy with the tropical perfume of frangipani, bougain-villea and hibiscus, thick with the bass that booms from gloss black Toyota jeeps and satanic crackmobiles, their matt-black window glass rattling in the door frames. Jeep music they call it, bumper to bumper cus-tomised loudspeaker rigs on four wheels. The boomin' system. Cars with the boom.

The music? For spring '88, Miami bass, Latin freestyle, 'The New Style' by the Beastie Boys: 'Kick it over here baby pop and let all the fly skimmies feel the beat, mmmmm, drop . . . Coolin' on the corner on a hot summer's day, just me and my posse and MCA, a lotta beer, a lotta girls and a lot of cursing, 22 automatic on my person.'

In 1990 a report was published in the *New England Journal of Medicine* which gave evidence to suggest that a black man living in Harlem has less chance of reaching his 65th birthday than a man living in Bangladesh. Louis Sullivan, Secretary for Health and Human Services, has said, 'I do not think it is an exaggeration to suggest that the young black American male is a species in danger.'

The intensity in many American cities is palpable. There are places – Southcentral Los Angeles, Miami's Overtown, Chicago's Cabrini Green, north Philadelphia, south-east Washington D.C., whole areas of New York City and Detroit – where you could touch this intensity but if you had the choice you would walk away. Those unable to walk away, the endangered species, are not listening to new age music to calm themselves down; they are listening to Ice Cube and Public Enemy. They need to hear rap about street life, black pride, shotguns. They have a paranoiac suspicion that women are climbing over their bodies to reach their money. They want music and words that are dense, cluttered, harsh, discontinuous, hallucinatory, hypnotic, a perpetual motion of screams, shouts of 'fuck the police'.

Within this new music, fragments of a more settled past – a sonic flashback museum of digital samples grabbed from old 45s – mix with a dismembered future. B-movies, Schoolly-D has called them; tracks on a 12-inch single (itself an endan-gered species as tape and CDs supercede vinyl) carrying layers of content, a whole archeology of ideas and musical develop-ment, condensed into throbbing capsules of violent energy.

The accusation increasingly levelled at rap is that the music has become amoral in its celebration of lowlife, firearms, misogyny, drugs, aggression and noise. Yet the environment of rap has become extreme and surreal in its decay, its disregard for human life and dignity. The pejoratively named Mole People live in the disused railway tunnels of Manhattan, like the underground ambients of Jack Womack's science fiction novel *Ambient*, and many urban districts look worse than the chaos of post-apocalypse films. As Mike Davis wrote in his scintillating study of Los Angeles, *City of Quartz*, 'Hollywood's pop apocalypses and pulp science fiction have been more realistic, and politically perceptive, in representing the programmed hardening of the urban surface in the wake of the social polarisations of the Reagan era. Images of carceral inner cities (*Escape From New York*, *Running Man*), high-tech police death squads (*Blade Runner*), sentient buildings (*Die Hard*), urban bantustans (*They Live!*) Vietnam-like street wars (*Colors*), and so on, only extrapolate from actually existing trends.' In the fourth world of American cities, science fiction has become science fact, though as Living Colour guitarist Vernon Reid has asked, where are the black people in science fiction?

Children carry automatic weapons like Uzis and sell crack on the streets. Babies are born with Aids and teenagers are shot dead for their shoes. Music may be powerful and influential but no music is strong enough to create this kind of social decay. The raps are fictions, and whether these fictions have their basis in lived reality or an overcharged imagination, the world they reflect is moving fast, out of control,

too fast to have a mere rap record as a navigator. To quote Public Enemy, 'Black to the bone my home is your home, so welcome to the Terrordome.'

The most brutal music of the mid-1980s was created by Schoolly-D and DJ Code Money. As Schoolly said on 'I Don't Like Rock 'n' Roll', 'Rock 'n' roll livin' is uh thing of the past so all you long-haired faggots can kiss my ass.' His first album, untitled, was released on Schoolly-D Records

SCHOOLLY-D: DUSTED? *Photo: Oliver Lim*

with the telephone number conveniently handwritten on the label. It was full of all those wealth and poverty contrasts of black streetlife that began to fill the newspapers in the late '80s when Washington D.C. murders rose to a rate of one death every 16 hours and drug dealers were fitting gold-plated hub caps to their cars. 'Put Your Filas On' and 'Gucci Time' or lines like 'sucker ass nigger I shoot you dead' – glamour or true grit? Just like the inhabitants of Beverly Hills and Jackie Collins novels, black homeboys were beginning to mix up Italian brand names with abstract concepts like time; like everybody else, they found themselves enjoying the blur between fantasy and reality.

Not everybody believed that Philadelphia's Schoolly-D was as tough as he made out; was he just the musical equivalent of a hardboiled crime novelist? Everything about the packaging of his records suggested that one of the fundamental qualities of his work was an amused irony. Subtract that essential ingredient and the music was ponderous, grim and nihilistic, awash with echo and stuttering crash cymbals, drums of doom and Schoolly's emotionally impervious drawl. The extremism made it thrilling, of course. After telling everybody that he had once been a member of a gang called the P.S.K., or Parkside Killers, Schoolly-D failed to live up to the sociopathic image that he had fashioned for himself.

Mike D of the Beastie Boys expressed everybody's dismay: 'I was disappointed with Schoolly-D. I wanted him to be really dusted and sort of not on the same plane as the rest of us y'know? Somebody with a purple Isaac Hayes *Shaft* suit on with a huge collar, but naw, he's a really nice guy' (from *Hip Hop*, by Nick Smash). The same sentiments could be applied to the Beastie Boys themselves.

From an unpromising beginning on records like 'Egg Raid On Mojo' and 'Cookie Puss', the Beastie Boys became pop stars. Being white helped, naturally. Rap was drawing young whites into black music by virtue of its fierce energy, its promulgation of an exclusive, if downbeat, lifestyle. As *Los Angeles Times* staff writer Bob Sipchen put it, 'In the past year or so, young people who would seem to be at no risk of becoming gang members have begun to imitate gang behaviour. Their inspiration comes in part, youth workers say, from the movie *Colors*, with its graphic depiction of inner-city gang life. Another factor, they say, is the growing popularity of rap music' (*Los Angeles Times*, 'Call of the Wild', 25 June, 1989). These 'young people' are the white sons of affluent Agoura Hills and Westlake Village residents, who spend good money on keeping Bloods and Crips out of their neighbourhoods. Commenting on the fashion for wearing beepers in imitation of crack runners, L.A. County Sherrif's deputy John Cater was quoted as saying, 'The only time they'd get beeped is when their mothers wanted them home for dinner.'

This challenge to musical and attitudinal (if not geographical) apartheid was precipitated by the Beastie Boys as much as anybody. Michael Diamond (Mike D), Adam Yauch (MCA) and Adam Horovitz

BEASTIE BOYS ON THE JOE FRANKLIN CABLE SHOW

(Adrock) all grew up in New York City. With parents whose jobs included architect, New York City schools administrator, interior designer and playwright (Israel Horovitz), these were not ghetto kids, neither were they comparable with the Hollis, Queens rappers like Run-D.M.C. or L.L. Cool J. They were bohemians, making phoney gangster music that was calculatedly obnoxious and guaranteed to offend every liberal tenet, every right wing terror. A lot of it was also very good.

'Rock Hard' followed L.L. Cool J's 'I Need A Beat' on Def Jam and was one of the noisiest tracks in living memory. Based on the chords of AC/DC's 'Back in Black', the rap was silly but the beat was massive. This was, incidentally, the record that persuaded The Cult to approach Rick Rubin for help with production on their *Electric* album of 1987. At the time, The Cult's vocalist, Ian Astbury, said, 'We didn't know who the Beastie Boys were. We didn't know who Rick Rubin was. We just heard this sound – booom/kkkhh/booom/kkkhh. An amazing drum sound with, like, Led

Zeppelin, AC/DC mixed over the top and these other guitars added. We thought that was just such a basic raw sound, really exciting and stimulating.'

Many of the rock/dance hybrids of the early 1990s can be traced back to influences from the early Def Jam and Run-D.M.C. records. Within the bigger record companies, black artists were assumed to be dance/R&B orientated and white artists could do more or less as they liked. The stereotyping began to dissolve during the late '80s and although this more often benefited white rappers and dance musicians rather than black rock bands, the trend still felt positive.

'I kinda think of it like I think of the Rolling Stones playing the blues, stuff like that,' said Adam Yauch during the Beasties first visit to London, 'and Led Zeppelin coming and playing like New Orleans jazz and stuff.' After 'Rock Hard', Beastie Boys tracks were released through Def Jam/Columbia, following a deal in which Def Jam was rumoured to have signed with CBS for $1,000,000. Whatever the true figure, the Beastie's *Licenced To Ill* turned out to be the fastest selling debut album in Columbia's history. Clever, funny and stupid, it mixed pop hits like 'Fight For Your Right' with b-boy tracks like 'Hold It Now Hit It' and 'Slow and Low'. Briefly, the group was the scourge of worldwide decency, accused in the media of a broad variety of unsociable activities. As a conclusion to the panic, Horovitz ended up in a court in England, accused and then cleared of injuring an audience member with a beer can.

A second album, *Paul's Boutique*, appeared on Capitol in the summer of 1989 after the association with Def Jam ended in an acrimonious dispute over unpaid royalties. The Beastie Boys had taken a break, partly because of this dispute, partly due to the exhaustion that comes from non-stop touring and controversy. Horovitz acted in a movie during this period and the group went in a different direction by working with an L.A. production duo called the Dust Brothers.

Pacing around the Los Angeles apartment of Horovitz, dressed in maroon leather trousers, a white towelling pimp hat, a yellow ochre string vest and a pair of unlaced Adidas sneakers, Mike D explained the working principles behind the album. 'You know,' he said, 'this brings up a term we've used before. Bouillabaisse. Okay? In making the bouillabaisse you might have fishermen from all around the village bringing in different fish. You might have a coupla farmers bringing in some tomatoes to just *thicken* the stew. Alright?'

The lyrics on *Paul's Boutique* were beatnik, surreal, free associative; more crime, more sex, more profanity. Tight little tales of urban madness, populated by Greek burger sellers, alcoholic rockabilly singers, turbanned deli owners, grubby American celebrities like Bernard Goetz, David 'Son of Sam' Berkowitz, Ed Koch, Bruce Willis, and Geraldo Rivera. Underneath, there were terrific breaks, bass, banjos, Burundi drums. It was an inspired comeback from the dead but few cared. Competition was too fierce and a new noise had spirited away the initiative.

Two years earlier, rap had been in a period of transition. Despite the uncertainty, there were good releases in 1987 from Brooklyn's Stetsasonic, the Marley Marl productions on Cold Chillin', Boogie Down Productions, Eric B & Rakim, Fresh Gordon, Just-Ice, King Sun-D Moet, Sweet Tee & Jazzy Joyce, UltraMagnetic M.C.'s and others. The future of R&B was evident, also, for anybody who perused the small print on record labels. Teddy Riley was the stepson of Gene Griffin, the man who released one of the earliest rap tracks – Trickeration's 'Rap, Bounce, Rockskate'. Rap records provided the apprenticeship for Teddy's vision of a new hyperkinetic, swinging soul music called jack swing or swingbeat. After helping to introduce the Washington D.C. go-go shuffle to hip hop via some uncredited work on 'The Show' (1985) by Doug E. Fresh, Teddy Riley refined his pre-swingbeat techniques, later to dominate R&B radio in America, with veteran rapper Kool Moe Dee, once a member of The Treacherous Three.

Kool Moe Dee was one of the last of the old school to stay afloat. Grandmaster Flash had attempted a comeback on a series of increasingly directionless albums and then faded into sporadic production work; Melle Mel fell into drugs and petty crime until rescued by Quincy Jones for the Grammy winning *Back on the Block* project; Afrika Bambaataa's recordings with James Brown, John Lydon and subsequent odd collaborations looked intriguing on paper but fell short of their potential; Spoonie Gee released a superb track called 'The Godfather' but then suffered personal problems; Jimmy Spicer and Lovebug Starski, both unsung pioneers from the early days, had their 15 minutes of fame with single releases but obscurity reclaimed them with the sudden brutality of a guillotine; Kurtis Blow slid from view as his congenial, commercial style started to look dated; The Cold Crush Brothers had released tracks on Elite, Smokin', Tuff City and B-Boy Records to little effect and at one point were rumoured to be joining Def Jam. Singles like 'Fresh, Wild, Fly and Bold' were very strong but the group's rapping style sounded too eager to please, too cheerful, too fixed in an era of innocence.

Rap's lack of focus in '87 was perhaps inevitable. Stream of consciousness self-praise/dissing lyrics, exemplified in the awesome 'Cold Gettin' Dumb' by Just-Ice – 'so try to convince me to believe all of your stupid nonsense' – or the endless word wars launched by 'Roxanne Roxanne', recalled Barry Michael Cooper's image of the claustrophobia of a generation. The insults stretched ahead like a narrow dark tunnel, restricting any kind of creative verbal expansion, blocking a clear view of the wider issues in which rap was a player.

Beyond the internal workings of the music the rap audience had grown and divided. There were now regional variants, not only in America's northern cities but in sunbelt locations like Miami and Los Angeles; many of these were influenced more by Run-D.M.C. than by the old school originators but the African-American and Hispanic audiences had also divided. The Hispanics stayed faithful to the old electro sound of 'Planet Rock', adding Latin percussion elements and an overlay of teenage romance. Their emphasis shifted towards young female singers and, for a time, girl groups like Exposé and The Cover Girls charted with records that were hybrids of pop, hip hop, disco and even salsa. The electro era of hip hop also contributed to the new house sound, mostly germinating in Chicago, via New York tracks like Strafe's 'Set It Off', also to the techno music of Detroit, via Cybotron, and to the emergent Miami bass music of Maggatron. In other words, there was pop rap, hardcore rap, reggae rap, soul rap, black rap, white rap, regional rap, multi-national rap, Latin hip hop and various mutations of disco. The market had fractured and rap briefly lost a sense of direction, either looking for a marketing niche, looking for crossover sales in the opening created by Run-D.M.C. or temporarily withdrawing into the underground to compose rhymes loaded with serious purpose and music devoid of commercial sweetening.

If a radio show began touting the achievements of Western Civilisation over civilisations of others there would barely be a letter to the station from anyone, anarchist or Calvin Coolidge Republican.
Ishmael Reed, *Mumbo Jumbo*

Hotel muzak bubbles with unstoppable gaity as Richard Griffin, notorious among rap fans, Jewish activists, black nationalists, white liberals and white supremacists as Professor Griff, counters the mood with an ominous message. 'Today,' says Griff, neatly dressed, courteous, flanked by two silent companions, 'if a black man's walking round in America blind, deaf and dumb, that's his fault. There've been too many teachers, too many warnings from God to the people. Now the whipping has to come. I'm sorry, how many teachers they want? How many teachers does the world have to get? The world has murdered the best teachers. No, I'm sorry, I think God is saying to the world, 'specially to the entertainers, that I'm sending you teacher after teacher. I'm even waking some dead ones up. Like KRS-One. He came from *Criminal Minded* to *Edutainment*. I think that's beautiful, but God had to wake him up from that criminal mind, out of that criminal state, to bring him to an educational point where he could teach the people. I think that's wonderful. But how many warnings and teachers the music industry going to get? They need to take heed and heed the call before it's too late.'

The group that pulled rap into focus in 1987, offering a vision that outstripped simple music business ambitions, was Public Enemy. *Yo! Bum Rush the Show* was again released on Def Jam, but put together by a team that included Bill Stephney, Hank Shocklee, Chuck D and Eric 'Vietnam' Sadler, rather than Rick Rubin. Stephney, Shocklee and a design and communications student named Carl Ridenhour (Chuck D), convened at Long Island's Adelphi University where they pooled their tal-

PROFESSOR GRIFF AND THE LAST ASIATIC DISCIPLES *Photo: Oliver Lim*

ents to create a group that would move beyond rap's nightmare of materialism and directionless hostility into that recurrent dream of agitation and propaganda with a funky beat.

When every other rapper was bowed under the weight of thick gold chains, Public Enemy countered the trend by dressing down. The qualities that distinguished the group from the rest of the rap scene were a new militancy of image and message, aligned with a ferocious, crowded sound dominated by busy drumbeats and mantric digital sample loops of '70s funk guitars, rock riffs and archaic synthesiser squeals. Buried within the name Public Enemy were cross-references to the work and influence of James Brown, who had once recorded an anti-heroin track called 'Public Enemy #1', and the notion of young blacks as enemies of the state, caught in the crosshairs of a gun sight.

At times, there seemed a distinct possibility that strong image would translate into hard reality. In 1989, lead rappers Chuck D and Flavor Flav, DJ Termina-

BRING THE NOISE: PUBLIC ENEMY *Photo: David Corio*

tor X and the dismissed so-called Minister of Information, Professor Griff, were deluged by protests from Jewish organisations, warnings from panicky retailers that they might refuse to stock Public Enemy records, censorship by CBS Records, even death threats and a sniper incident. Ejected from Public Enemy as a punishment for the repercussions that followed an interview in the *Washington Times* in which he suggested that Jews are responsible for the majority of the wickedness in the world, Griff gives his version of the formation of the group:

'Chuck and Flav had a radio programme in the college, WBAU, that gave the little man in the street the opportunity to send in tapes and get 'em played on the air. It gave Chuck and Flav a chance to recognise new talent. The thought and the idea of Public Enemy came out of the head of Hank Shocklee. They wanted to do something real different in the music industry. He was my partner. We had a mobile DJing unit. We went around and DJ'd at clubs, banquets and bar mitzvahs, high schools, block parties – Roosevelt, Hempstead, Freeport, Long Island. We called it Strong Island. Me and Hank was partners and Chuck and Flav was partners. Terminator was this local DJ. Like I said, the idea came from Hank and Chuck. Basically, what had happened was they offered Chuck a record contract from Def Jam. He turned it down once or twice because he never did want to make "it's all about me" kinda records. I respect that. When we put the concept together, he thought the concept would last a lot longer than individuals. And that stands to be true, because Public Enemy's a lot bigger than Griff. You understand what I'm saying? It's a lot bigger than Chuck. It's somewhat of an institution in the black community.'

If Public Enemy encouraged a new wave of support for black nationalism and Afrocentrism among young African-Americans, the group also caused many observers (black, white and other colours) to indulge in an orgy of uncertainty and dismay; some of it was brought on by microscopic examination of the metaphors within Chuck D's lyrics, some of it by Griff's apparently anti-Semitic indiscretions, some of it by the revival of Black Panther styling, complete with berets, camouflage fatigues, on-stage military manouvres and weapons drill by the Security of the First World.

Were tracks like 'Miuzi Weighs A Ton' advocating violence? Was 'Sophisticated Bitch' yet another example of rap misogyny? Pulled out of context, many lines

MIUZI WEIGHS A TON: PUBLIC ENEMY LIVE
Photo: David Corio

from Public Enemy raps could be used to prove conflicting arguments, but this arises not from incoherence but from flirting with dangerous juxtapositions; the nature of their music is that it can be sliced many ways. The droning loops, screams and word-blitz of the second album, *It Takes A Nation of Millions To Hold Us Back*, elevated the art of rap onto a level that was simultaneously abrasive and seductive; the texture of its noise and the polysemic, labyrinthine maze of imagery were relentless. Constant movement, sirens, slang stretched into the realms of the surreal; anger, perplexity and paranoia, tapes running backwards, cyclical high shrieks of an alto saxophone, fragments pulled from the James Brown/JBs/Meters/Kool and the Gang funk archive, party talk, revolutionary rhetoric, all threaded into an intricate web of sound, designed to instruct, to awaken, to energise, to provide catharsis or just to speak.

Who knew what Flavor Flav was talking about? 'Live lyrics from the bank of reality, I kick da flyest dope manouver technicality, To a dope track, you wanna hike git out ya backpack, Um in my Flav-mobile cole lampin, I took dis G upstate cole campin, to da poke-a-nose, we call da hide-a-ways, A pack of franks and a big bag of frito lays.' Roughly the same lines turned up when Flav and Chuck D guested on George Clinton's 'Tweakin' ' in 1988. 'Hey yo, Chuck!' said Flav. 'They don't know what I'm saying', you know what I'm sayin'?' A translation might be possible but as Chuck D and 'media assassin, hip hop activist' Harry Allen wrote for

Spin, 'My whole thing is that a whole lot of black people, and especially those white liberals, they get so fuckin' *booked*, they don't know how to bring it down to a practicality.' (*Spin, Black II Black*, October 1990)

The base-line, or bass line, is glimpsed again on 'Tweakin'': 'Remember the livin', Remember the dead, Speakin' in drum, Drummin' it into a tweak, drowning out the voices in my head. Follow follow, (do you) follow follow.' Public Enemy's music is like voices in the head, multiple personalities that won't coalesce, language that won't lie still, a clamouring madness.

Darkness was invading the evening, shrouding figures in shadows, and the streets were becoming less crowded as the elderly hurried to the shelter of their small rooms or, if more fortunate, their small homes. Areas where children had played happily now became darkly ominous spots that women walked around with hurried steps.

Donald Goines, *Street Players*

In 1964, when William Burroughs wrote in *Nova Express* about the Subliminal Kid, who 'brought back street sound and talk and music and poured it into his recorder array so he set waves and eddies and tornadoes of sound down all your streets and by the river of all language – Word dust drifted streets of broken music car horns and air hammers – The Word broken pounded exploded in smoke . . .' he could have been hearing pre-echoes of Public Enemy's *Fear of a Black Planet*, Ice Cube's *AmeriKKKa's Most Wanted*, even the Anthrax/Chuck D thrash metal version of 'Bring the Noise'. Burroughs saw a future in which images spread and replicated like a virus, languages merged, images of reality and reality itself melted in the escalating schisms created by propaganda and counter-propaganda.

As an expression of propaganda feedback, N.W.A., otherwise known as Niggers With Attitude, were hard to beat. Here was a group, straight out of the Los Angeles neighbourhood of Compton, that understood that the Vietnam of the late '80s was being enacted on the streets of Los Angeles, then fed back to the rest of America via violent, atmospheric media coverage. 'We're like reporters,' Ice Cube has said, and the first release on Ruthless Records, launched by rapper Eazy-E and producer Dr. Dre in 1986, was like a tabloid report from the crime beat fed through a paper shredder. In its chopped-up vignettes of gangbanger life, 'Boyz-N-The-Hood' ran with the ball thrown by Schoolly-D: 'Take him up the street to call a truce, the silly motherfucker pulls out a deuce deuce, little did he know I had a loaded twelve gauge, one sucker dead *L.A. Times* front page.'

N.W.A. – Eazy-E, Dr. Dre, Ice Cube, Yella and M.C. Ren – formed the following year and their first single, 'Dope Man', sold despite a lack of airplay. The logical way to follow N.W.A.'s career was to trace it through the media virus, since sensational media coverage was central to the group's escalating notoriety, vital to N.W.A.'s exploitation of their own image. On-site reports began to flood in from TV networks like CNN, once N.W.A.'s promotional video for 'Straight Outta Compton' was banned by MTV for contravening a charter designed to '. . . prohibit videos that glorify violence and/or show gratuitous violence.' On Channel 4 News, Dr. Dre repeated the reporter line, saying, 'We're not on the good side of violence, we're not on the bad, we're in the middle,' and on Channel 7 KABC TV, a newsreader asked his colleagues, 'I wonder if they wrote a book about it, whether that book would be banned at the library.'

The problem with N.W.A.'s projection of themselves as objective reporters was that their music, at least on a few tracks, was exhilarating stuff. Should crime reporting make your heart pound, make you want to dance? The dividing line between news as information and the thrill of voyeurism has always been fragile; it is not uncommon for journalists to become novelists and since Truman Capote's *In Cold Blood*, Weegee's photographs of New York crimes and disasters and 'realistic' feature films like Jules Dassin's *The Naked City*, faction has become a desirable element in both fiction and documentaries within all media. Even Barry Michael Cooper, whose *Spin* pieces like *In Cold Blood* (a title which obviously reflects the depth of this factional confusion) and *Crack* documented the barely controlled spread of guns and drugs in America cities, put his experiences to commercial, fictional use by co-writing the screenplay for a Hollywood film, *New Jack City*. When Gabriel Williams, a 19

year old New Yorker died in a cinema gunfight during a screening of *New Jack City*, Cooper must have reached for the anti-feedback button. To quote again from *Nova Express*, '. . . nobody knew whether he was in a Western movie in Hongkong or The Aztec Empire in Ancient Rome or suburban America whether he was a bandit a commuter or a chariot driver whether he was firing a "real" gun or watching a gangster movie.'

Much of the moral panic sparked by N.W.A. may have stemmed from the realisation that large numbers of teenagers were buying a record released on an independent young black label without being hyped into it by a major record company or radio play. Initially, this was an underground, word of mouth phenomenon. The album *Straight Outta Compton* went gold after six weeks, no thanks to the fearful attitude of black radio and a censorious MTV. Inevitably, the controversy magnified sales and increased the general lever of punditry on rap and violence.

N.W.A. made some exciting records but while the drug dealing, gangbanging, car thieving autobiographies they sketched for themselves were accepted at face value, their motivations were as mercenary as any other reporter. Rap was finally making a lot of money for its practitioners, allowing them to move beyond the tough stereotypes. Ruthless Records gleefully taped all the news reports about N.W.A. but also released records by a self-consciously cute, pop/hip hop female trio called J.J. Fad.

N.W.A.'s 'Fuck The Police' track generated a letter of protest from Milt Aerlich

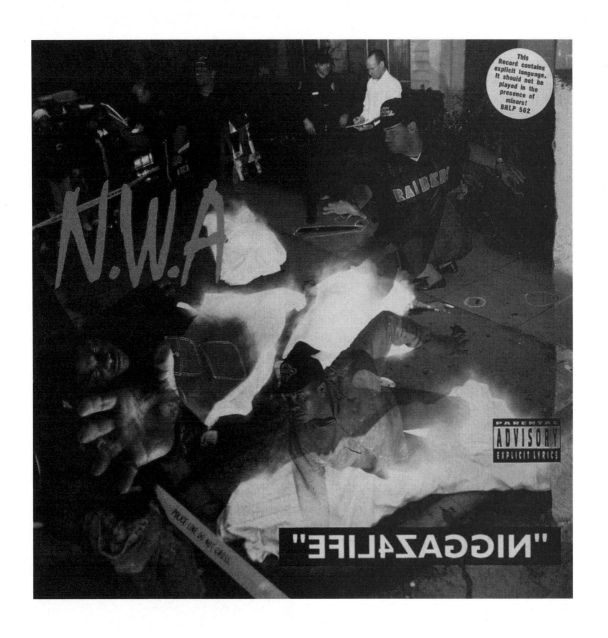

PARENTAL ADVISORY: N.W.A.

of the FBI's public affairs department, who accused the group of 'encouraging violence and disrespect' towards the police. Police forces around the country used their fax machines to warn other departments in cities due for a visit from N.W.A. but new technology also had a hand in putting the entire overblown issue into chilling perspective. When an onlooker tested his new video camera by filming white police viciously beating a 25 year old black man, Rodney King, after a high speed car chase, the results were shown on television repeatedly. Both in shock value and political effect, N.W.A.'s videos were tame by comparison and for *Efil4zaggin*, their next album, the group resorted to even more offensive subject matter. They were rewarded with runaway sales and immediate seizure of copies from record company offices in Britain. Censorship of rap was still alive as an issue.

The group's most talented member, Ice Cube, left to go solo after a money dispute with manager Jerry Heller. To judge from his album, *AmeriKKKa's Most Wanted*, Ice Cube's appreciation of the televisual quality of postmodern life seemed to run deeper than N.W.A.'s. Going east to work with Long Island's Bomb Squad – Hank Shocklee, Keith Shocklee, Chuck D and Eric 'Vietnam' Sadler – Ice Cube produced an album that crackled with tension. This was a naked city for the '90s – tapes of radio DJs refusing to play rap, white supremacists ranting 'you gold teeth, gold chain wearin' fried chicken and biscuit eatin' monkey' tirades, police raids, phone-ins, newsreaders, drive-by shootings, snatches

of *The Flintstones*, a short story about picking up a girlfriend from a crack house in the projects, a nasty argument about men versus women, titles like 'The Nigga Ya Love To Hate' and 'Endangered Species (Tales From the Darkside)'. Tracks cut at random points into explosions or different music, dissolving into interference, as if Ice Cube was sitting on the couch, flicking channels with the remote control. This was television structured music, influenced as much by tabloid news dramatisations as by the fragmentation of TV narrative by over-frequent commercial breaks.

On stage, Ice Cube is one of the most powerful performers in rap. His co-rapper, T-Bone, takes a break and Ice Cube and DJ Sir Jinx slow down their hyper-energetic show to deliver a withering rap about

TALES FROM THE DARKSIDE: ICE CUBE

gullibility and exploitation over a cool blaxploitation break: 'You knew the game and you still ended up on your back, now ax yourself, who's the mack? Mackin' is a game and everybody's playin' an' as long as you believe what they sayin', consider them a M.A.C.K. and with no delay they are gonna get off the play, but when it comes to me sayin' a drama for ya mind, it's Ice Cube and you know that I'm a mack in my own right, when it comes to rhymin' rap 'cause all I do is kick facts, I'm like Iceberg Slim and all of them be claimin' P.I.M.P., no, I'm not goin' out that way, I'm just a straight up N.I.G.G.A.'

There is a strong probability that as new young black heroes come to centre stage, they will neither seek nor welcome the universal approbation and love of white America . . .

Robert Beck (Iceberg Slim),
The Naked Soul of Iceberg Slim

Iceberg Slim, author of *Pimp*, *Death Wish* and other books in a similar vein, is a recurrent name in the context of so-called gangster rap. When Ice-T went to high school in Southcentral Los Angeles he would use words he had learned from Iceberg Slim's books and was eventually given a nickname which combined the Ice from Iceberg with the T from his own first name. Inspired by the writing of Beck and crime novelist Donald Goines (the author of black streetlife books like *Dopefiend*, *Black Gangster* and *Daddy Cool* who was shot dead in his late 30s by two white men), as well as black comedians like Rudy

Ray Moore and Redd Foxx, Ice-T wrote his own stories of Los Angeles life for *Freedom of Speech . . . Just Watch What You Say*, *Rhyme Pays*, *Power* and the 1991 album, *O.G.*

These included 'I'm Your Pusher', based on Curtis Mayfield's *Superfly* song 'Pusherman'. The blaxploitation connection has been a key element in Ice-T's career. His first movie involvement was with the worst rap film of them all, *Breakin'*. This was followed by Dennis Hopper's *Colors*, for which he wrote the brooding title song, and then, finally, serious acting roles in Mario Van Peebles's *New Jack City* and *Ricochet* with Denzel Washington.

In 1989, I spoke to Isaac Hayes, veteran blaxploitation composer and bad guy actor. His attitude to the entire genre was ambivalent, despite the fact that his music for *Shaft* has become legendary and his performances in a number of films, including John Carpenter's *Escape From New York* and the revival blaxploitation spoof *I'm Gonna Git You Sucka* have been excellent. 'The only gripe I had during those times about those films,' said Isaac in his sepulchral voice, 'is there was only one kind. If there had been more variety to offset some of the stereotypes, then it would have been okay. We as blacks wanted to see some other images. We just needed to see more films about other sides of our life, but, finally, we didn't have too much to say about it. As they say, he who pays the piper calls the tune.'

With the emergence of new waves of African-American film directors and the sweeping success of rap, the payers are becoming somewhat unsure of just what

DADDY COOL: ICE-T *Photo: Oliver Lim*

Many Hollywood business people would deny the necessity of a hand grenade, since their ability to wreck havoc with a contract is far greater. Films like *Lethal Weapon* and *Die Hard* proliferate, and in rap there is what *The Source* magazine has called 'a musical crime wave,' citing Too Short, Mob Style, Compton's Most Wanted, Kool G Rap and DJ Polo, King Tee, Poison Clan, Above The Law and the Boo-Yah T.R.I.B.E. as some of the most prominent hip hop gangsters.

Los Angeles is deceptive, however. The sun shines and before dusk, battlegrounds can look uncannily like the suburban American dream. In Carson, a tranquil south Los Angeles community divided from Compton by the Artesia Freeway, a formidable Samoan extended family and funk/rap crew called the Boo-Yah T.R.I.B.E. lives with a basement full of guns and a daily routine that is close to red alert. Most of them being ex-gangbangers, their raps are written in hardcore prison slang, with joy, pleasure, identity and emergence expressed in metaphors of death, violence, intimidation, fear and imprisonment.

Like Public Enemy's dangerous juxtapositions, these images have been frequently misconstrued. 'We can't talk about girls,' a member of the Boo-Yah T.R.I.B.E. told me as we sat out at the front of their house, watching the dusk roll in and Christmas lights transform Carson into Disneyland. 'We can't talk about happy things. Our life was never happy. It was a lot of frustration. We just lived in the darkness, man. It's like crazy. We don't want our kids to live like us.'

tune they should call. There are new markets out there to be unlocked and rap is the skeleton key. Certainly the stereotypes remain, but Ice-T's raps about pimps, drugs and gangsters should not be confused with Ice-T off-stage – articulate, witty and an ambitious businessman. As he told a rap video magazine, 'I've got a 'phone, answer machine, TV set, computer, hand grenade – everything you need to run a business in Los Angeles.'

14. Native tongues

You know how the Egyptians told their stories on the walls of the pyramids? You know how the Chinese teach their children stories in kung fu, karate, by telling different stories with different moves? This move your great great grandfather did because he fought these people over here during this period – they told that history. So you put 50 of these moves together, you can tell somebody's life story. With black people, I think that's what [rap's] doing. It's taking the place of writing on walls. It's taking the place of the kung fu moves.

Professor Griff interview,
11 October, 1990.

Hip hop may have taken giant steps since the middle of the '80s, buying its practitioners status symbols or financing their business ventures, but the rise of rap as the unofficial language of Jesse Jackson's 'rainbow coalition' or New York mayor David Dinkins' 'gorgeous mosaic' was a trend with some disquieting aspects. Had rap become the musical equivalent of boxing? Was it an escape route from the underclass realities of American (and British) cities that promised the successful an uneasy brand of celebrity, big cheques at irregular intervals and a short career?

KICKIN' IN THE HOOD: BOO-YAH T.R.I.B.E. *(Brad Fierce)*

By the beginning of the '90s there were Samoan, Cuban, Mexican, Korean, Haitian, Dominican, Jamaican, Vietnamese, Puerto Rican, Ecuadorian, Chinese, Indian and British rappers in America, while Professor Griff, considered to be one of the more extreme black nationalists in rap, was half African-American, half Blackfoot Indian. More women were rapping. There were Jewish rappers like the Beastie Boys and 3rd Bass, even a group of white rappers calling themselves Young Black Teenagers.

All of the utopian metaphors used to describe the multiracial character of America – from melting pot to gorgeous mosaic – were being outflanked by developments that nobody quite understood. Already, you could hear on the streets the *Blade Runner* polyglot tongues, slipping in and out of Spanish, English, Black English and all kinds of regional slang. Chicano rapper Kid Frost flipped between Spanish and English on 'Ya Estuvo' and 'La Raza', giving name checks to other Hispanic rappers. Mellow Man Ace's 'Mas Pingon' was like a lethal customised lowrider cruising through East L.A. while LA Cubano, Skatemaster Tate, mixed reggae, jazz, go go and salsa break beats into the urban bouillabaisse.

As Hank Shocklee told London newspaper *The Voice*, 'New York and L.A. are totally different. I had to spend two weeks to learn about getting "gaffled", getting "smoked", you know?' In Miami, rap is strongly influenced by the closeness of Cuba and Jamaica; in Orange County, young Vietnamese-American girls are forming gangs like the Dirty Punks, following an age-old tradition of new immigrants but expressing it in a form that Hollywood tells us is exclusively Black and Hispanic. Bill Adler – rap archivist, writer and publicist – has written that, 'Hip hop's present-day cultural nationalists argue that so-called "blackness" is as much a matter of cultural identification as it is of skin color and that, by that measure, there are *millions* of suspiciously light-skinned young black teens roaming around *right now*, undetected and unsupervised.'

This is the fourth world in progress. Some fourth world inhabitants want racial separation, some want to give up their own race and join another, some look for racial identity, racial roots, some embrace the cultural merging inevitable in a world of high speed, omnipresent communications. Some, the white supremacist fans of Andrew Dice Clay, can't cope with any of it and blankly wonder who all the 'piss coloured people' are.

Epitomised in one way by the blistering, fractured assault of Public Enemy, the current broadness of rap, its simul-cast of a complex post-screenie culture, its understanding of new technology, has been advanced by a new wave of rappers, known under the collective heading of Native Tongues. On the one side, rap is a spoken newspaper, a fax from the wax; on the other side, rap fits into the storytelling tradition of oral history and symbolic teaching.

In April 1988, overshadowed by the smokescreen of controversy thrown up by Dennis Hopper's contentious L.A. gangwar film, *Colors*, two singles crept onto the market, loaded with future potential. From the Brooklyn label Idlers came a track called 'Because I Got It Like That' by the Jungle Brothers, and from out of the quiet that had descended upon Tommy Boy Records came a Long Island group called De La Soul with 'Plug Tunin' '.

With its organ sample and relaxed, chantalong rap, 'Because I Got It Like That' had a carnival feel, while 'Plug Tunin'' slowed old R&B breaks down to a rock steady crawl. With lines like 'wind vocal flow brings it all down in ruins' and 'words are sent to the vents of humans then converted to a face called talk,' delivered in a conversational style, De La Soul lived up to their claim that this was 'the new speak'.

YA ESTUVO: KID FROST *Photo: Brad Fierce*

Both groups set new trends in all aspects of rap – the vocal sound, subject matter, musical samples, beats, clothes, hair and philosophy. Sitting in Tommy Boy Records' First Avenue offices in October '88, Posdnous and Trugoy the Dove, De La Soul's public speakers, wore baggy clothes in black or flowery fabrics, their hair cut in radical fades, peace signs etched into the close crop above Posdnous's ears. 'We're the bringing of a Daisy Age,' said Pos. 'Daisy Age stands for – DA represents The. I is Inner. S is Sound and Y is Y'all. The inner sound y'all. Everything is coming from within us. It's time to pull down that front, trying to be like somebody else. You come out with what's inside you.'

We sat and listened to the music of their first album, *3 Feet High and Rising*, put together with Stetsasonic's Prince Paul and their DJ, Pasemaster Mase. On first hearing, the closest parallel was perhaps the vintage recordings of Lee Perry – concise collages with rough edges and obscure meanings but masterful hooks and rhythms. Tracks like 'The Magic Number', 'Transmitting Live From Mars', 'Eye Know' and 'Dela Orgee' sped by, leaving fleeting impressions of vaguely familiar tunes by The Detroit Emeralds, Sly Stone, Johnny Cash, Cymande, The Turtles, Otis Redding and even Tommy Roe; easy listening, gospel organ, '60s soul, doo wop, reggae and early rap records, all structured within the format of a TV game show.

'Our music turns out that way, with a different sound to everyone else,' said Trugoy, 'because of our backgrounds. Pos, his father would listen to old jazz and stuff like that. My mother and father would listen to a lot of reggae and calypso and Mase's mother listened to a lot of R&B.' Guesting on the album were the Jungle Brothers and Q-Tip from the Queens based group A Tribe Called Quest. This convergence of like minds caused a turnaround in rap. No more gold chains, gold teeth, huge gold rings; after a period of sartorial extravagance, taken to the maximum by Eric B & Rakim with their colossal gold chains, plate sized pendants and Dapper Dan personalised black and gold jackets, many rappers followed the change to leather Afrika pendants,

POS AND TRUGOY: DE LA SOUL *Photo: Bart Everly*

beads, braids, African fabrics and baggy clothes.

KISS FM DJ Red Alert, a colleague of Afrika Bambaataa from back in the old-school days of rap, took over management of the core groups with his Red Alert Productions and De La Soul, the Jungle Brothers, A Tribe Called Quest, in company with Queen Latifah, British rapper Monie Love, DJ Mark the 45 King and the long-established KRS-One with Boogie Down Productions offered a serious challenge to the violence of gangster rap and a complementary angle on Public Enemy's educational shock treatment.

Elsewhere in New York there was the Blackwatch Movement of X-Clan and Isis, along with Nation of Islam and Five Percent Nation rappers Brand Nubian, Poor Righteous Teachers, Rakim and Lakim Shabazz. In San Francisco there was the new Black Panther, Paris; in Oakland, California, the Digital Underground rappers were creating a surreal, Clintonesque sex-universe and, commuting between Los Angeles and Brooklyn, Divine Styler was writing convoluted lines such as 'Chuck a 'flip copy cat try to jock watch your back when you buck up on Cokni Dreadlocks who live under Selassie I orthodox.' In Toronto there were The Dream Warriors and in England, MC Buzz B, Black Radical MkII, Red Ninja and others, all seeking to find new ways of using the spoken word. Some of these artists, X-Clan and Paris, for example, used their music to

DREAM WARRIORS *Photo: David Corio*

promote black nationalism. Others, like Downtown Science, were simply searching for ways in which to expand rap into more individualised form of expression, aiming to attain the standards of fractured meaning and open-ended music set by Rammelzee's 'Beat Bop' back in 1983.

That was certainly De La Soul's intention, although after the runaway success of *3 Feet High and Rising* (over 2 million sales worldwide) the point was misconstrued so often that they titled the follow-up album *De La Soul Is Dead*. 'People weren't paying attention to what the Daisy Age meant,' Posdnous complained in March '91. 'They were looking but not touching. We died and now we're alive again, rejuvenated into a new form.' The new album was slicker than the first and slightly more downbeat. Three years in the music business was enough to dampen even the most ebullient spirits.

One other noticeable difference about *De La Soul Is Dead* was the clearance and listing of all breaks and samples used in the music. There they all were on the album cover for copyists to peruse: Serge Gainsbourg, Bob Marley, Brother Bones, Parliament, Frankie Valli, Wayne Fontana, The El Dorados, Taana Gardner and 'The Three Little Pigs'.

Tommy Boy Records and De La Soul found problems with the first album's cavalier approach to sampling when The Turtles sued for $1.1 million for the unauthorised use of a looped section from their 1969 track 'You Showed Me'. The law suit was settled out of court for a sum said to be in 'the low 5 figures' but companies were getting less inclined to take chances on infringing copyright.

Posdnous was not entirely happy about this move into legality. 'It definitely takes the mystery out of it,' he said. 'It gives the competition a taste of our buying habits.' These were buying habits .that had expanded dramatically when De La Soul's world tours got under way but the attention given to the issue of sampling expanded to match. Some music business lawyers were now instructing their older clients to listen to rap, just in case their work was being sampled.

The reason why rap changed its sound so dramatically in the latter half of the '80s was due to the development of relatively low priced digital samplers with enough memory to hold and loop a few bars of music. By the '90s, these samplers could run multiple loops of long or short sections of music simultaneously, along with drum sound samples and other noises, all of which could then be saved onto floppy disc to be kept as the producer's personal library of 'signatures'. This was a massive progression from Grandmaster Flash cutting up 'Adventures on the Wheels of Steel' in the studio, or Jam Master Jay running one section of Bob James's 'Mardi Gras' under a drum machine beat.

Now layers could be built up, using a rhythm loop from, say, 'Funky Drummer' by James Brown, augmented by new drum beats from a drum machine, a bass line from a Funkadelic record, some atmospheric strings from a blaxploitation soundtrack like *Cotton Comes to Harlem* and synthesiser squirts from a J.B.'s funk track. The emphasis on early '80s sampling with expensive machines like the Fairlight was high quality, but rap demands a raw, xerox feel. As DJ Mark told *Music Technology* magazine, 'I don't use too many synth sounds, 'cos to me they sound fake and they sound too clear.' The new samplers could provide high quality but they also allowed producers like Prince Paul, Mark the 45 King and Eric B to mix different textures from their vast record collections, sometimes cleaning up a fragment to give it more punch, sometimes retaining all the crackles and pops or making the joins between a rhythm loop and a drum fill clearly audible. Painstaking hours could be spent, using state-of-the-art technology, to make a new track sound authentically old. Somehow, in all the waffle about morality and legality that arose around the subject, the fact that this was an extraordinary way to compose music was bypassed.

Experience the Old World for a day without actually having to go there.
(Disneyworld TV commercial)

There has always been a strong element of fetishism in this aspect of hip hop. The artwork for DJ Mark the 45 King's Tuff City album *45 Kingdom* displayed the labels of collectable 45s by Funky Four Corners, Rimshots and The Honey Drippers over a Disney style castle. Mark's best known track, 'The 900 Number', was named after the sampler that changed everything, the Akai S900, and simply looped 2 bars of baritone saxophone and drums (with added drum machine) from Marva Whitney's 1968 single, 'Unwind Yourself'.

James Brown productions like 'Unwind Yourself' or 'Funky Drummer', also pictured on the sleeve of *45 Kingdom*, were the central core of any producer's or DJ's collection of breaks. One of the first tracks to exploit James Brown classics like 'Funky Drummer' and 'Sex Machine', along with Aretha Franklin's 'Rock Steady' was a bootleg on T.D. Records called 'Feelin' James', later released officially on Tommy Boy in 1987 in a cleaned-up, 'safe' version with its creator, Fresh Gordon, pictured on the label. The original 'Feelin' James' followed the artistic path of discontinuity laid down by 'The Adventures of Grandmaster Flash on the Wheels of Steel', 'Death Mix' and 'Fusion Beats'.

When 'Feelin' James' was first released, caution was the word. Nobody seemed too sure about how many rules and copyright legalities they could overlook. Quote records were briefly the rage. Doug E. Fresh and Slick Rick quoted from The Beatles' 'Michelle' on 'La-Di-Da-Di', M.C. Craig 'G' reworked 'Shout' by Tears For Fears, The Kartoon Krew reworked Doug E. Fresh's reworking of the *Inspector Gadget* theme, Joeski Love did 'Tequila' on 'Pee-Wee's Dance' in a salute to the dancing of Pee Wee Herman and The Real Roxanne quoted The Isley Brothers' 'For the Love of You' on 'Bang Zoom! Let's Go Go!'. The dissing wars also generated a degree of sample sampling, as when Pretty Ricky & Boo-Ski stole the basic beats of 'It's Yours' and claimed 'It's Mine'.

So who did it belong to? The Mantronik/

track. The emphasis on early '80s sampling with expensive machines like the Fairlight was high quality, but rap demands a raw, xerox feel. As DJ Mark told *Music Technology* magazine, 'I don't use too many synth sounds, 'cos to me they sound fake and they sound too clear.' The new samplers could provide high quality but they also allowed producers like Prince Paul, Mark the 45 King and Eric B to mix different textures from their vast record collections, sometimes cleaning up a fragment to give it more punch, sometimes retaining all the crackles and pops or making the joins between a rhythm loop and a drum fill clearly audible. Painstaking hours could be spent, using state-of-the-art technology, to make a new track sound authentically old. Somehow, in all the waffle about morality and legality that arose around the subject, the fact that this was an extraordinary way to compose music was bypassed.

Experience the Old World for a day without actually having to go there.
(Disneyworld TV commercial)

DOUBLE D AND STEINSKI *Photo: Patricia Bates*

There has always been a strong element of fetishism in this aspect of hip hop. The artwork for DJ Mark the 45 King's Tuff City album *45 Kingdom* displayed the labels of collectable 45s by Funky Four Corners, Rimshots and The Honey Drippers over a Disney style castle. Mark's best known track, 'The 900 Number', was named after the sampler that changed everything, the Akai S900, and simply looped 2 bars of baritone saxophone and drums (with added

Beats and *Break Beats* (with an octopus drawn on the label) formed the basis of many subsequent rap tracks, alongside legitimate releases like *Drum Drops* (illustrations of drum rhythms) or three volumes of TV themes on the TeeVee Toons label *Television's Greatest Hits*.

The serious record collectors like Eric B regarded this unmasking of the underworld as a gift to the lazy, a betrayal of the DJ's detective abilities, yet the wide availability of these rare grooves changed hip hop in a positive direction. Crashing drum machine beats were superceded by a more funky, live feel. The music wasn't live, since it came from old records, but the effect was the same. 'Hip hop is such a beats orientated music', DJ Jazzy Joyce told me in 1987. 'It's just beats and a bass line. If you put anything else to it like keyboards and guitars and a whole bunch'a other stuff it becomes *music*!' Her record with Sweet Tee, 'It's My Beat', along with infectious tracks like Big Lady K's 'Don't Get Me Started', Traedonya's 'The Boogaloo' and D.J. Jazzy Jeff & Fresh Prince's 'Touch Of Jazz' had a loose, R&B feel which made a refreshing change from the obsessively heavyweight music of the Run-D.M.C. school.

Consensus shatters. On a personal level we are all besieged and blitzed by fragments of imagery, contradictory or unrelated, that shake up our old ideas and come shooting at us in the form of broken or disembodied 'blips'. We live, in fact, in a 'blip culture'.
Alvin Toffler, *The Third Wave*

Sample 'n' scratch records were a mixed blessing. Consummate illustrations of postmodern theories about our cannibalistic, self-referential culture, in which 'all the divergent spaces of the world are assembled nightly as a collage of images upon the television screen' (David Harvey, *The Condition of Postmodernity*), the actuality of listening to an electronic viral blip-storm of cartoon voices, commercials, bursts of movie and TV dialogue, scratches, funk fragments, power chords, brass stabs, frantic percussion breaks and vaguely familiar two bar segments from obscure old records could leave you with a hangover. After Double D and Steinski's 'The Payoff Mix' and 'History of Hip Hop', Doctor Funnkenstein & D.J. Cash Money's 'Scratchin' to the Funk', Steinski's 'We'll Be Right Back', 'Pump Up the Volume' by MARRS, Coldcut's 'Say Kids What Time Is It?', the Coldcut remix of Eric B & Rakim's 'Paid In Full', Criminal Element Orchestra's 'Put the Needle on the Record' and Dynamix II's 'Just Give the DJ a Break', the genre had driven itself into hyperspace. DJ Extraordinaire and the Bassadelic Boom Patrol's 'Drop the Bass (Lower the Boom)' was perhaps the ultimate in the disintegration aesthetic, being little more than a fast beat and a stream of decentred info-bites. In the end, sampling needed a framework, a context, to enhance the strangeness of its sound world.

Eric B & Rakim constructed that framework with tracks like 'I Know You Got Soul', 'In the Ghetto' and 'Follow the Leader'. On stage, their music was a massive boom, Rakim's menacing voice devoured in the jaws of bass; on record, Eric B created moody soundstages, dramatising Rakim's hypnotic monologues, sweeping urgent drums in and out of distant landscapes, using samples like windows that opened and shut onto adjacent

FOLLOW THE LEADER: ERIC B & RAKIM
Photo: David Corio

194

soundscapes. 1988's 'Follow the Leader', in particular, was a breathtaking record, its grumbling bass and swirling flutes and strings quite unlike anything else in rap.

This was music as cinema. Stuttering wah wah guitar, threatening drums and a Funkadelic chorus created the same disturbing, brilliant effect on EPMD's 'So Wat Cha Sayin' ', a year later. The message was typical of rap's sometimes parochial tendency to talk about itself, like a community newsletter or an in-house business memo. Erick & Parrish used their single to sneer at the people who doubted them, bragging about the fact that their album had gone gold. Was this an example of Professor Griff's black oral history or merely a fixation on dollars? Bearing in mind that EPMD stood for Erick & Parrish Making Dollars, probably both.

The man who bridged the gap between all extremes of the rap audience was Kris Parker, better known as KRS-One. The first rap crew he was involved with was 12:41, whose sole release, 'Success Is the Word', focused on the subject of pink champagne and caviare. His actual lifestyle was somewhat different, since he had left home at the age of 13 and lived on the streets.

Talking to me in 1990, he said, 'From aged 13 to about 19, 20, those were like the best years of my life. Living in the street, living by myself. It was the best time. It was a different time to this but I enjoyed every minute of it. As I look back on it I can say, damn, that looked like a rough childhood but it didn't really feel like that when I was actually living like that. It was very relaxing.' His reasons

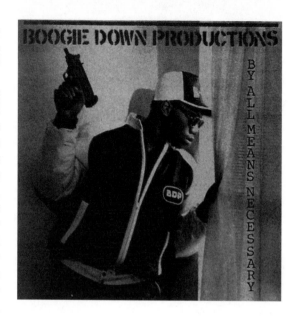

STOP THE VIOLENCE: KRS-ONE

for leaving home, he claims, were 'to study metaphysics, basically to find myself, and to be a rap artist.' His mother taught him and his brother African history when they were both still small and by the age of 13, he says, 'I knew exactly where I wanted to go and what I wanted to do.'

This precocious sense of destiny was fuelled by DJ and counsellor Scott LaRock, who he met at the Franklin Avenue men's shelter on East 166th Street in the South Bronx. In 1987, working under the name of Boogie Down Productions, the two of them recorded a controversial album, *Criminal Minded*, a record dressed in the images of gun culture; later that year, Scott LaRock became the victim of the same gun culture, shot dead in a South Bronx street while trying to mediate in an argument.

The contradictions have not stopped. The following year, KRS-One illustrated his *By All Means Necessary* album with a new version of the famous photograph of Malcolm X peering through a crack in the curtain, gun ready to shoot. He then launched the Stop The Violence movement, hoping to influence rap fans away from shootings and stabbings. 'In California, they have gangs driving by with that record on,' he admitted. How much of the message penetrates, then? 'About 10 to 20 percent gets through to people,' he said. '20 percent is high. I'd love it to be a higher percentage but it's not a goal of mine. I mean, you want everybody to act right but in this world we're living in it's not like that.' As well as recording raps about violence, eating beef, blacks trying to be white, the homeless and drug dealing, all aimed at potentially unreceptive listeners, he has also delivered lectures in American colleges, using extracts from these talks to punctuate the tracks on *Edutainment*.

Rap music is 'the last voice of black people', KRS-One claimed in one of these lectures. Some of the new 'educated science rap', the spiritual revolutionary wing of hip hop, was, as he has said, false bandwagon jumping; the best of it, however, managed to align commercial music with anti-materialism without creating too much of a paradox. The music helped to further, as well as reflect, an emergent political militancy, a rebirth of Black Nationalism and a new found interest in the African roots of black American culture. The millennialist word of the Jungle Brothers, intoned over chants, congas, gospel, wah wah guitars and monkey cries on their complex, layered album *Done By the Forces of Nature*, was 'Good news everyone, the Last Day is right around the corner. Down the block, and up the boulevard. The oppressed will be saved from oppression. The ghetto will be TransAfriKanedExpressed to the heavens, the "Righteous Playgrounds".'

The advance guard of the spiritual wave distanced itself from entertainment altogether. For X-Clan (Professor-X, Brother J, Sugar Shaft and Paradise) Isis and Queen Mother Rage, rap was 'verbal milk', the music 'vanglorious'. Lines like 'Sweet tongue grand vital scrolls, now behold let the legend unfold, born in the cosmos, where no time and space do exist, vibeing the mist of chaos,' were inspired by Malcolm X, Marcus Garvey, H. Rap Brown, Adam Clayton Powell and various Egyptian gods, along with influences closer to home like the Zulu Nation, Afrika Bambaataa and Lumumba 'Professor X' Carson's father, '60s black activist Sonny Carson. The mystical was mixed with the practical, as X-Clan organised events like 'The Taking of Brooklyn Bridge', a protest at the shooting of Yusef Hawkins, or registration drives and anti-crack talks in schools.

This combination of grassroots activism and musical weirdness was very reminiscent of the 1960s. Eclecticism and experiment broke out all over. MC 900 Ft Jesus with DJ Zero gave hip hop an industrial noise slant, using treated and whispered vocals, Laquan was sampling blues singer Robert Johnson and working with a live band in preference to sample loops while Long Island group Son Of Bazerk pushed

X-CLAN, ISIS, SONNY CARSON *Photo: David Corio*

the blip culture syndrome to the limit by changing musical styles from funk to dancehall reggae and thrash metal in a restless, hyperventilating frenzy. Droning montage tracks like the Dream Warriors' 'Tune From the Missing Channel' or Gang Starr's jazz samples on 'Jazz Thing' were contrasting examples of the diversity of hip hop in the early '90s.

The extremes of that diversity were not difficult to find. On the one hand, there was the mellow, tender rap of A Tribe Called Quest on 'Bonita Applebum', with its sitar sample and gentle guitar octaves. 'Do I love you? Do I lust for you? Am I a sinner because I do the two? Can you let me know? Right now please,' pleaded Quest, swathed in psychedelic '60s phasing. And down in Miami, 2 Live Crew were coming up with lines like, 'It's the only way to give her more than she wants, like the doggy style you get all the cunt, 'cause all men

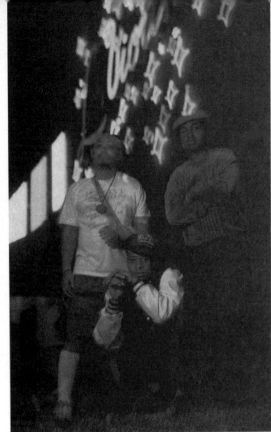

A TRIBE CALLED QUEST *Photo: Bart Everly*   **2 LIVE CREW** *Photo: Bart Everly*

try real hard to do it, to have her walking funny we try to abuse it.'

Prior to the April 1987 arrest of 18 year old Laura Ragsdale, a part-time shop assistant at Starship Records & Tapes in Callaway, Florida, 2 Live Crew's album *2 Live Crew Is What We Are* had sold 250,000 copies for the Skyywalker label. These figures were concentrated mostly in Florida, the Carolinas and Georgia, so Ragsdale must have experienced quite a

shock to find that it had become an offence to sell it.

By 1990, 2 Live Crew and Luther Campbell's, the owner of Luke Records (retitled after George Lucas won a law suit preventing Campbell from using the *Star Wars* name), were embroiled in an international debate on censorship, under attack from the Tipper Gore's Parents' Music Resource Centre, Miami lawyer Jack Thompson, Florida governor Bob

Martinez, music retailers who refused to stock their records and a variety of police officials, politicians and entertainment licencing officials. In June 1990, a federal court ruled that 2 Live Crew's 'As Nasty As They Wanna Be' could not be sold legally in southeast Florida because it violated community standards but in October of the same year, a Florida jury acquitted the group on charges of performing obscene songs. A statement from the Recording Industry Association of America said: 'This judgement should serve as notice to others trying to find music obscene that Americans believe very strongly in our First Amendment rights. Whether they find it vulgar or obnoxious or lewd still does not mean that it is criminally obscene.'

During the furor, a strange alliance of free speech supporters flocked to the defence of 2 Live Crew, including Atlantic Records; their release of a Luke album called *Banned in the U.S.A.* included a 2 Live Crew version of Bruce Springsteen's 'Born in the U.S.A.' The whole issue caused discomfort all round, except perhaps for 2 Live Crew, suddenly the most famous rap group in the world. As Martha Frankel wrote in *Spin*, 'So we'll push real hard for 2 Live Crew's right to make this shit, but that doesn't mean we have to like it.'

A career in rap was difficult enough for a woman without 2 Live Crew's nasty rhymes or Ice Cube and his 'Get Off My Dick and Tell Yo Bitch To Come Here.' As women reacted against a prevailing brutal misogyny in rap, there were slight signs of change. After six years of releasing records, Def Jam finally recorded Nikki D's 'Daddy's Little Girl', their first track by a female rapper, and Public Enemy recruited Sister Souljah to the ranks. In Los Angeles, Ice Cube put his support behind Yo Yo, co-producing her scorching *Make Way For the Motherlode* album with DJ Sir Jinx. Yo Yo, who had already showed her capacity for fightbacks on Ice Cube's 'It's A Man's World', founded the Intelligent Black Woman's Coalition, hoping to reverse the low status and self-esteem that women were clearly suffering in the face of such a concerted shut-out by men.

(DON'T PLAY WITH MY) YO YO *Photo: Brad Fierce*

All these tracks, good or indifferent, as well as X-Clan's production of Isis, bore heavy handed signs of male direction. Added to this, women were often directed or took their own route into softer, more commercially orientated hip hop, thus confirming the prejudices of their male counterparts. The casting couch was still a factor in the career hazards of aspiring female rappers. Describing producer Hurby Luv Bug, also the guiding force behind Salt 'n' Pepa, Sweet Tee said, 'He's good with the female acts. I've run into some characters who think they can get sexual favours to get the record out. Hurby's not like that. He's a good person.'

There were exceptions to the Catch 22 syndrome, but for every serious act, there was a group like Hoes With Attitude or Bitches With Problems to compound the difficulties. The situation was similar to reggae, in which men were traditionally expected to chat hardcore rhymes about sex, guns or culture over tough rhythms and women sang the romantic material. Ragga star Shabba Ranks, speaking in early '91, said it all: 'The ladies, they cannot be ragga, dealing with the rough patter all through their life, because they are not males. They are females, OK?' Sweet Tee expressed it from the other side in 1987. 'Everybody's runnin' so noisy,' she complained. 'I said, "let's run it smooth and slow".'

Despite the powerful example of Roxanne Shanté's longevity in the business, one of the few female rappers to develop a career beyond a few isolated singles was Queen Latifah. Latifah is an Arabic name meaning 'delicate and sensitive', which, by rap's standards, would make a fair description of her style. Living in East Orange, New Jersey, and working with Mark the 45 King, Latifah tracks like 'Dance For Me' and 'Inside Out' were hard without being boneheaded, light without being lightweight, mixing warm reggae with a forthright rapping approach that sidestepped the dissing clichés. As she said on 'Inside Out', 'Rhymin's not a question of one's superiority but rather how you delegate the use of your authority.' Gaining authority was clearly the next step.

QUEEN LATIFAH *Photo: Bart Everly*

15. How ya like me now?

During a visit to Jim and Tammy Bakker's Christian amusement park, Heritage U.S.A., P.J. O'Rourke discovered Christian rap music cassettes. 'I was witnessing a miracle, I was sure, or auditing one anyway,' wrote O'Rourke. 'Here was something that sounded worse than genuine rap' (from P.J. O'Rourke, *Holidays in Hell*).

At the beginning of the 1990s, considerable numbers of music consumers discovered a form of rap which, to them, sounded better than genuine rap. After all those years on the outside track, rap suddenly overtook the competition. Speaking for the Christians, M.C. Hammer sold huge quantities of his *Please Hammer Don't Hurt 'em* album, and speaking for the phoney gangsters, Vanilla Ice's *To the Extreme* was said to be the fastest selling rap album in history.

Whatever the truth in the statistics that record companies provide, Hammer and Ice dominated the *Billboard* charts. The music may have been thin but the images were perfect for an MTV generation. Although those hordes of pop-rap fans found these two stars easier to digest than Public Enemy or even De La Soul, the rap industry reeled. 'They are they and we are we,' wrote Kim Green in

FAT BOYS *Photo: David Corio*

The Source. In other words, rap had split off into the authentic faction and the showbusiness wing.

Hip hop had always had its share of entertainers. Setting aside the showbiz aspects of Public Enemy and Ice Cube, there were groups like the Fat Boys, Salt 'n' Pepa, Mantronix, DJ Jazzy Jeff & Fresh Prince, Kid 'n' Play, L'Trimm, 2 In A Room, J.J. Fad and Heavy D & The Boyz or solo artists Redhead Kingpin, Tone Loc, Young M.C., Doug Lazy, Gerardo and Candyman. In Britain there was the Cookie Crew, Kiss AMC, Wee Papa Girl Rappers, She Rockers and M.C. Tunes, along with all the anonymous hip-house crews or the adventurous groups like Massive Attack, Definition of Sound, Unique 3, Krispy Three and First Offence, concocting an eccentrically British brew of rare groove soul, house, reggae and even punk. In Germany there was Snap and from Sweden to Japan, Paris to Bangkok, Milan to Hong Kong, wannabee rappers forged slick hybrids of pop music, house, techno, soul and hip hop.

The Fat Boys and Salt 'n' Pepa were both examples of acts that started out tougher than they finished. 'Fat Boys', the Disco 3's second release, appeared in 1984 on Sutra and was produced by Kurtis Blow, in a variant of Larry Smith's Whodini sound. The subject matter was a little different, however, with lines like, 'Now, it started off when I was very small, I devoured chocolate cakes, plates, candles and all,' being fairly typical. Working with an astute manager and publicist, Charles Stettler, the group was persuaded into the obvious step of becoming a walking joke, changing their name from the Disco 3 to the Fat Boys.

From then on, their career was a foregone conclusion. The first album went gold in 10 weeks and after the Swatch Watch commercials came a series of albums, each less fun than the last, records with The Beach Boys and Chubby Checker, the *Krush Groove* eating extravaganza, a part in *Miami Vice* and finally their very own contribution to the slapstick rap genre of movie making, *Disorderlies*. Also worth noting was the fact that the Fat Boys began an unfortunate trend, now fairly common, of using backing tapes on stage in preference to a DJ. By 1991, most people had forgotten the group until Darren 'Human Beat Box' Robinson, the fattest Fat Boy of the three, was put on trial in Pennsylvania for sexual abuse of a minor.

Printed on the back of Salt 'n' Pepa's 1986 album, *Hot, Cool & Vicious*, was a potted history of the group. Cheryl 'Salt' James and Sandy 'Pepa' Denton met at Queens Borough College where they were studying nursing. Their DJ, Spinderella, used to hang out with them at Laces Skating Rink in Long Island and became part of the group when Hurby 'Luv Bug' Azor decided she was the best candidate for the job. Like Roxanne Shanté, they began their career with an answer track, in their case a response to Doug E. Fresh's 'The Show', called 'Showstopper'. On record they were witty and forthright, reacting against the prevailing trend of portraying women as dangerous sluts, 'skeezers', bitches, easy lays. 'Push It' and 'Shake Your Thang' were both clever and successful pop records which mixed up break beats with go go in a smooth hip hop style. By 1990 they seemed to have lost it. *Black's Magic*, despite some ambitious lyrics, sounded over-polished and uninspired, as if the group's natural evolution had been knocked off course by the pop hits.

With Salt 'n' Pepa and Jazzy Jeff & Fresh Prince established as the acceptable, MTV-approved faces of rap, the door was open to any rapper who could find the right formula in the studio. Redhead Kingpin did it with the Teddy Riley swingbeat sound of 'Do the Right Thing' but Tone Loc really hit the ball dead centre with 'Wild Thing'. Released on Delicious Vinyl, a Los Angeles label situated in amongst the Thai restaurants, postcard shops, biker jewellery and kitsch furniture outlets of Melrose Avenue, 'Wild Thing' was produced by the label owners, Matt Dike and Michael Ross. The most distinctive feature of this thumping, sleazy track with its Van Halen guitar riff and distinctive drum roll was Tone Loc's unique testosterone growl. For a simple record, the results were startling. Sales ran over 2 million and at one point 'Wild Thing' was the biggest selling single in rap history.

The track had another claim to fame. After the notorious Central Park gang rape of a jogger, the media claimed to have discovered a new phenomenon called 'wilding'. Wilding was supposedly named after the Tone Loc hit, and was

WILD THING: TONE LOC *Photo: Derek Ridgers*

said to involve packs of young (black) men, roaming the streets in search of rape, injury, looting, even murder. The MTV embrace of Tone Loc's video, a $500 take-off of Robert's Palmer's 'Addicted To Love' clip, seemed to go hand in hand with this particularly ridiculous moral panic. The more that mainstream America got to know about rap through its pop hits, the more convenient the genre became for shouldering the burden of urban collapse.

Perhaps films like *House Party*, starring Kid 'n' Play, or the Quincy Jones backed NBC sitcom *Fresh Prince Of Bel Air*, starring rapper Fresh Prince in a 'homeboy meets the buppies' scenario, redressed the balance slightly by being sweet enough for anybody to swallow. And perhaps the Quincy Jones album, book and film project, *Back On the Block*, also helped. Having already sold a young black man, Michael Jackson, to America and the world, Jones attempted to legitimise rap within the history of African-American music. Big Daddy Kane, Melle Mel, Ice T and Kool Moe Dee appeared alongside Ella Fitzgerald, Miles Davis, Ray Charles, Sarah Vaughan and Dionne Warwick. Regrettably, a potentially remarkable gathering of great black voices was buried under over-refined production and forgettable compositions, but sales of more than 3 million and a clutch of music business awards showed that the world was just about ready for Quincy's high aims.

M.C. Hammer's initial aims were fairly modest. *Let's Get It Started*, he called his first album, but once started, the Hammer proved hard to stop. Nobody took him seriously as a rapper, but perceptive observers like Nelson George predicted the eventual effect of Hammer's hyperkinetic dancing and video-perfect image. 'This man has an underground video,' George wrote in his February '89 *Billboard* column. 'His "Pump It up" suggests that this super-nimble dancer, backed with a crew of female and male dancers, is bringing new ideas and energy to hip hop performing. Hammer took the current catalogue of "new jack" moves and added some twists and turns. The "Pump It Up" video helped push Hammer's album into the top 10.'

Young America had been primed by artists like Bobby Brown, singers who used dancing and a hybrid R&B/rap style to grab a broad audience. The major record companies – CBS (now owned by the Sony Corporation), Atlantic, MCA, Warner Brothers, Capitol, Island/Polygram – had moved in on rap, scooping up most of the independents or signing important acts like Eric B & Rakim for advances in the region of $700,000. Some of these relationships were troubled, notably the one between Def Jam and CBS, which eventually frustrated Rick Rubin beyond his patience. Rap had been co-opted by the multinational music industry. That in itself was not surprising, considering the size of the potential worldwide market. What was surprising was the majors' apparently low level of intervention in a potentially controversial form of music.

Although the independents were there,

LET'S GET IT STARTED: M.C. HAMMER
Photo: Derek Ridgers

ready to release the extreme records that nobody else would touch, the majors were just as ready to absorb all but the most extreme of their efforts, creating a bigger market in the mainstream than a small independent could normally supply. Cable television shows like *Yo! MTV Raps* drew MTV's largest audiences and the hybrid genres multiplied. Artists like En Vogue, Soul II Soul and Bel Biv Devoe would have been straight R&B 5 years previously. Now they incorporated a hip hop crossover feel.

The creative future of rap also seemed assured due to the hip hop and reggae collaborations that began to flourish. Shabba Ranks was hanging with Big Daddy Kane, Rob Base and Slick Rick and recording with KRS-1; and reggae singer J.C. Lodge, with whom Shabba had recorded 'Hardcore Loving', had signed with Tommy Boy. As Shabba said in March, '91, 'Rapping and my style, we're brothers. If you go round now and ask rappers about Shabba, they know me as well as I know them. It's similar. The only difference is that they're using a funky beat. I'm on a reggae beat. I don't use the amount of lyrics that they use but it's definitely rapping.'

Despite all these developments, rap would have been just another niche in the devolved, multi-market society without its own megastars. The limited musical talent and conspicuous success of M.C. Hammer and Vanilla Ice caused some anger within rap, yet others were pleased to see hip hop lifted onto this level of the entertainment industry. Entertainment was, after all, an industry, and Hammer embraced all of its demands and possibilities, clearly believing

SHABBA RANKS *Photo: David Corio*

that the American dream was more than just a myth.

Born into a large family in Oakland, he tried college and then professional basketball, finally settling for a while in the navy. His first musical venture was a rap duo called the Holy Ghost Boys, but after this failed he launched himself into the punishing regimen that has since brought him success. Hammer could be fitted into the performing, rather than singing, tradition of James Brown, Rick James, Cameo, Michael Jackson and Prince. Like all of these artists, he had understood that there was more to life at this level of pop stardom than just music.

Tracks like 'U Can't Touch This' and 'Pray' may have been weak by comparison with the best rap but this was hardly the point. With his baggy harem pants, glasses and convulsive dancing style, Hammer was instantly recognisable as his own trade mark. This inherent marketability led to a reported $8 million advertising deal with Pepsi, two plastic M.C. Hammer dolls manufactured by Mattel, and the sale of rights to use the Hammer name and image for a variety of video games, the precursors of a future multi-media, screenie generation, pop world of integrated electronic products. Ten years earlier, hip hop had fused African roots and video game imagery as an act of surreal imagination. Now it fused the same elements in the service of marketing.

Whatever the disturbing implications of a digitised M.C. Hammer, the reality of Vanilla Ice caused far more distress. A tall white man with angular cheekbones, an American flag shirt and a Captain America look, Ice superficially appeared to be recreating the Elvis Presley syndrome all over again, though he lacked Presley's raw talent and charisma. While Hammer was strenuously living the life of a positive role model, espousing the virtues of prayer, straight living, hard work and dedication, Vanilla Ice was trying to come across as a hardboiled gangster, getting sweaty over guns, breasts, whips and chains, naming himself after a drug and plainly trying to be blacker than black.

His autobiographical yarns failed to persuade the rap community that he was Stagger Lee but, beyond that, few of his

LIFE IS A FANTASY: VANILLA ICE *Photo: Derek Ridgers*

young fans cared where he grew up or what his ethnic preferences were. Maybe they wanted to act black themselves and in Vanilla Ice they had their Thespian example. It had been only a matter of time before a young Caucasian-American sprang up to make serious money from their fantasy. Vanilla Ice had said it himself: 'Life Is A Fantasy' was the title of one of his worst tracks. His best effort, 'Ice Ice Baby', was a crafty single that stole a bass lick from the David Bowie/Queen hit 'Under Pressure'. Most of the other raps on his SBK released album *To The Extreme* were feeble but Ice was white, he danced, he made the right kind of videos, he had toured with M.C. Hammer; when Hammer's *Please Hammer Don't Hurt 'em* finally dropped off the number one spot after 21 weeks it was Vanilla Ice who displaced him. As ever, record companies jumped to supply the new demand. The string of imitators sported revealing names like Icy Blue, Fred Astaire and 4PM (four pale males).

Perhaps this was rough justice for the black rap artists who had struggled to establish the genre but popular music has no justice. The rise of Vanilla Ice was the final stage in rap's acceptance by the music industry. Another day, another dollar. Young Americans were continually lifting themselves out of nowhere into the electronic aether of late 20th Century celebrity and its slippery rewards. As Professor Griff warned with typical severity, 'When you finish chasing the American dream, you come to find it's not for you any old how.'

Elsewhere, radio, tape and TV loud-speakers were rattling their casings with messages that had rarely been so directly expressed in music before, a sound of urban absorption that had rarely been so finely articulated. 'I feel that a lot of cultures need to understand,' said Griff, 'that if you oppressed us and you kept us in this condition and you took our language from us then we would develop a language to communicate with each other.'

While one sector of America was struggling to reassert the values of 1950s America, fighting to maintain the illusory cohesion of a single unified culture, battling to limit the spread of information, the erosion of the old truths, rap was attacking and remoulding the fragments of the electronic age with a speed that was breathtaking. Knee deep in an intangible world of past, present and future. Saturated in bass vibrations, drumming out voices in the head, speaking in tongues, swinging and locating. Pass the plugs, pass the plugs.

Lightning swords of death

One Hundred Rap Attacks: these are all 12-inch singles with their American labels given in preference to those of the British releases. Some of them are in the list for historical importance, others because I like them. Strictly *not* in order of preference.

1. Afrika Bambaataa, 'Death Mix' (Winley)
2. Afrika Bambaataa and Cosmic Force, 'Zulu Nation Throwdown' (Winley)
3. Afrika Bambaataa and the Soul Sonic Force, 'Looking For the Perfect Beat' (Tommy Boy)
4. Afrika Bambaataa and the Soul Sonic Force, 'Planet Rock' (Tommy Boy)
5. Afrika Bambaataa and the Soul Sonic Force, 'Renegades of Funk' (Tommy Boy)
6. Beastie Boys, 'Cookie Puss' (Ratcage)
7. Beat Box Boys, 'Give Me My Money', 'Einstein', 'Yum Yum-Eat 'Em Up' (Memo)
8. Bobby Gilliom, 'Give Me a Break' (Clappers)
9. Bon Rock and Cotton Candy, 'Junior Wants to Play' (Tommy Boy)
10. Bon Rock and the Rhythem Rebellion, 'Searchin' Rap' (Reelin' and Rockin')
11. Brother D, 'How We Gonna Make the Black Nation Rise' (Clappers)
12. Captain Rapp, 'Bad Times (I Can't Stand It)' (Becket)
13. Captain Rock, 'Cosmic Glide' (Nia)
14. Captain Sky, 'Soap Opera City' (Jamtu)
15. CC Crew, 'CC Crew Rap' (Golden Flamingo)
16. Community People, 'Education Wrap' (Delmar International Inc.)
17. Count Coolout, 'Here to Stay (Me and My Double R.R.)' (WMOT)
18. Crash Crew, 'Breaking Bells (Take Me To the Mardi Gras)' (Sugarhill)
19. Davy DMX, 'One For the Treble (Fresh)' (Tuff City)
20. Dimples D. 'Sucker DJs (I Will Survive)' (Party Time)
21. Disco Four, 'Whip Rap' (Profile)
22. DJ Divine, 'Get Into the Mix' (West End)
23. Dr Jeckyl and Mr Hyde, 'Genius Rap' (Profile)
24. Fab Five Freddy 'Une Sale Histoire' (Celluloid)
25. Fantasy 3, 'Biters In the city' (CCL)
26. Fatback Band, 'King Tim III (Personality Jock)' (Spring)
27. Fresh Face, 'Huevo Dancing' (Catawba)
28. Fresh 3 M.C.s, 'Fresh' (Profile)
29. Funky Four Plus One, 'That's The Joint' (Sugarhill)
30. Funky Four Plus One More, 'Rappin' and Rockin' the House' (Enjoy)
31. Gary Byrd and the G.B. Experience, 'The Crown' (Motown)
32. George Clinton, 'Nubian Nut' (Capitol)
33. G.L.O.B.E. and Whiz Kid, 'Play That Beat Mr D.J.' (Tommy Boy)

34. Grandmaster and Melle Mel, 'Jesse' (Sugarhill)
35. Grandmaster Flash, 'Adventures of Grandmaster Flash on the Wheels of Steel' (Sugarhill)
36. Grandmaster Flash and the Furious Five, 'Flash To the Beat' (Bozo Meko bootleg)
37. Grandmaster Flash and the Furious Five, 'Flash To the Beat' (Sugarhill)
38. Grandmaster Flash and the Furious Five, 'Superrappin'' (Enjoy)
39. Grandmaster Flash and the Furious Five, 'The Message' (Sugarhill)
40. Grandmixer D.ST, 'Crazy Cuts' (Island)
41. Grandmixer D.ST and the Infinity Rappers, 'Grandmixer Cuts It Up' (Celluloid)
42. Hurt 'Em Bad and the S.C. Band, 'Martin Luther' (Profile)
43. Hurt 'Em Bad and the S.C. Band, 'The Boxing Game' (Profile)
44. I.R.T., 'Watch the Closing Doors' (RCA)
45. Jazzy Five/Kryptic Krew, 'Jazzy Sensation' (Tommy Boy)
46. King Tim III, 'Charlie Says (Roller Boogie Baby)' (Spring)
47. K9 Corp featuring Pretty C, 'Dog Talk' (Capitol)
48. Kurtis Blow, 'Party Time' (Mercury)
49. Kurtis Blow, 'The Breaks' (Mercury)
50. Lady B, 'To the Beat Y'All' (Tec)
51. Lady D, 'Lady D' (Reflection)
52. Love Bug Starski, 'You've Gotta Believe' (The Fever)
53. Malcolm X/Keith LeBlanc, 'No Sell Out' (Tommy Boy)
54. Men at Play, 'Dr Jam (In the Slam)' (Sunshine)
55. Nairobi, 'Soul Makossa Rap' (Streetwise)
56. Naomi Peterson, 'Sweet Naomi Rap' (Heavenly Star)
57. Nice and Nasty Three, 'The Ultimate Rap' (Holiday)
58. Paulette and Tanya Winley, 'Rhymin' and Rappin'' (Winley)
59. Pee Wee Mel and Barry B, 'Life On the Planet Earth' (12 Star)
60. Phase II, 'The Roxy' (Celluloid)
61. Planet Patrol, 'Play At Your Own Risk' (Tommy Boy)
62. Pumpkin, 'King Of the Beat' (Profile)
63. Rammelzee Vs. K-Rob, 'Beat Bop' (Profile)
64. Reggie Griffen and Techno Rock, 'Mirda Rock' (Sweet Mountain)
65. Rockers Revenge, 'Sunshine, Partytime Rap' (Streetwise)
66. Rock Master Scott and the Dynamic 3, 'It's Life (You Gotta Think Twice)' (Profile)
67. Ronnie Gee, 'Raptivity' (Reflection)
68. Sequence, 'Funk You Up' (Sugarhill)
69. Shango, 'Shango Message' (Celluloid)
70. She, 'Ms D.J. Rap It Up!' (Clappers)
71. Slim, 'It's In the Mix' (D.E.T.T.)
72. South Bronx, 'The Bottom Line' (Rissa Chrissa)
73. Special Request, 'Salsa Smurf' (Tommy Boy)
74. Spoonie Gee, 'Spoon'nin' Rap' (Sugarhill)
75. Spoonie Gee, 'The Big Beat' (Tuff City)
76. Spoonie Gee/The Treacherous

Three, 'The New Rap Language'/
'Love Rap' (Enjoy)
77. Spyder-D, 'Smerphies Dance' (Telestar Cassettes)
78. Sugarhill Gang, 'Rapper's Delight'
(Sugarhill)
79. Sula, 'Jungle Rap' (Starwave)
80. Sweet G, 'A Heartbeat Rap' (West
End)
81. Tanya Sweet Tee Winley, 'Vicious
Rap' (Winley)
82. The B Boys, 'Two, Three Break'
(Vintertainment)
83. The Beat Boys, 'Be Bop Rock'
(Sugarscoop)
84. The Boogie Boys, 'Zodiac/Break
Dancer/Shake and Break' (Capitol)
85. The Cold Crush Brothers, 'Punk
Rock Rap' (Tuff City)
86. The Disco Four, 'Country Rock Rap'
(Enjoy)
87. The Fearless Four, 'Problems of the
World' (Elektra)
88. The Fearless Four, 'Rockin' It'
(Enjoy)
89. The Force MDs, 'Let Me Love You'
(Tommy Boy)
90. The Last Poets, 'Long Enough' (Kee
Wee)
91. The Rake, 'Street Justice' (Profile)
92. The Treacherous Three, 'Feel the
Heartbeat' (Enjoy)
93. The Younger Generation, 'We Rap
More Mellow' (Brass)
94. Tilt, 'Arkade Funk' (D.E.T.T.)
95. Time Zone, 'Wildstyle' (Celluloid)
96. Trickeration, 'Rap Bounce Rockskate' (Sound of New York)
97. Trouble Funk, 'Pump Me Up' (Jam)

98. T Ski Valley, 'Catch the Beat' (Grand
Groove)
99. Wayne and Charlie 'Check It Out'
(Sugarhill)
100. Whodini, 'Magic's Wand' (Jive)

The following old-school albums are also re-
commended (even though rap was once music
for 12-inch singles):
Run-D.M.C. (Profile), Crash Crew Meets
Funky Four (Sugarhill/Vogue, French LP),
Warp 9 It's a Beat Wave (Prism), Wildstyle
(Animal Records soundtrack LP), Jonzun
Crew Lost In Space (21 Records/ Tommy
Boy), Genius of Rap (Island UK Sampler),
The Perfect Beat (Tommy Boy/Polydor UK
sampler), Live Convention '82, Vols 1 & 2
(Soul On Wax), Rapped Uptight, Vols 1 & 2
(Sugarhill/PRT UK samplers), Electro, Vol 1
onwards (Street Sounds UK samplers),
The Big Break Rapper Party, Vol 1 (Sound
of New York, USA/Queen Constance),
Grandmaster Flash and the Furious Five
The Message (Sugarhill), Enjoy (New York
Connexion UK sampler), Super Disco
Brakes, Vols 1 to 4 (Winley).

Lightning swords of death 2

Another 100 deadly singles, listed in alphabetical order and included for historical importance, artistic merit or personal whim:

101. A Tribe Called Quest, 'Bonita Applebum' (Jive)
102. Above the Law, 'Untouchable' (Epic)
103. B Fats, 'B Fats' (Rooftop/Champion)
104. Beastie Boys, 'Hold It, Now Hit It' (Def Jam/CBS)
105. Beastie Boys, 'Rock Hard' (Def Jam/CBS)
106. Big Daddy Kane, 'Raw' (Cold Chillin'/ WEA)
107. Big Lady K, 'Don't Get Me Started' (B/Ware Records)
108. Biz Markie, 'Pickin' Boogers' (Cold Chillin'/ WEA)
109. Boogie Down Productions, 'My Philosophy' (Jive)
110. Boo-Yaa T.R.I.B.E., 'One Time' (Villain)
111. Brand Nubian, 'Wake Up' (Elektra)
112. Busy Bee, 'Busy Bee's Groove' (Sugarhill)
113. Kurtis Blow, 'I'm Chillin'' (Polygram)
114. Choice M.C.s, 'Beat of the Street' (Tommy Boy)
115. Chris 'The Glove' Taylor, 'Itchiban Scratch' (Electrobeat)
116. Chubb Rock, 'Ya Bad Chubbs' (Select/Champion)
117. Cold Crush Brothers, 'Fresh, Wild, Fly and Bold' (Smokin')
118. DDS, 'History of Hip Hop' (RPM)
119. Def Jef, 'Droppin' Rhymes On Drums' (Delicious Vinyl/Island)
120. De La Soul, 'Plug Tunin'' (Tommy Boy)
121. Digital Underground, 'Underwater Rimes' (T.N.T./Macola)
122. Disco 3, 'Fat Boys' (Sutra)
123. DJ Extraordinare, 'Drop the Bass' (Lower the Boom)' (Jamarc)
124. DJ Jazzy Jeff & Fresh Prince, 'Girls Ain't Nothing But Trouble' (World Up/Champion)
125. D.J. Scott La Rock, Blastmaster KRS One & D-Nice, 'South Bronx' (B Boy Records)
126. Dream Warriors, 'Wash Your Face In My Sink' (Island)
127. Drum, 'Bite-It' (Jamar)
128. EPEE MD, 'It's My Thing' (Chrysalis)
129. EPMD, 'So Wat Cha Sayin'' (Fresh)
130. Eric B, 'I Know You Got Soul' (Zakia/ Chrysalis)
131. Eric B & Rakim, 'Follow the Leader' (MCA)
132. Eze 'T', 'Kickin' Butts' (Force Groove)
133. Fat Lawrence, 'Tina Tina (Have You Seen Her)' (Fourth Floor)
134. Feelin' James, 'Feelin' James' (T.D. Records, Inc.)
134. KC Flightt, 'Planet E' (RCA)
136. The 45 King, 'The 900 Number' (Tuff City)
137. Doug E. Fresh, 'The Show' (Reality)
138. Dougé Fresh, 'Just Having Fun' (Enjoy)

139. Dougy Fresh, 'The Original Human Beat Box' (Vintertainment)
140. Gang Starr, 'Jazz Thing' (CBS)
141. Professor Griff, 'Pawns In the Game' (Luke Skyywalker)
142. Heavy D & the Boyz, 'We Got Our Own Thang' (MCA)
143. Hollis Crew, 'It's the Beat' (Def Jam)
144. Ice Cube, 'AmeriKKKa's Most Wanted' (Priority/Island)
145. Ice-T, 'I'm Your Pusher' (Rhyme Syndicate/Sire)
146. Jazzy Jay, 'Def Jam' (Def Jam)
147. Joeski Love, 'Pee-Wee's Dance' (Vintertainment/ Chrysalis)
148. Jungle Brothers, 'Because I Got It Like That' (Idlers)
149. Just Ice, 'Cold Gettin' Dumb' (Sleeping Bag)
150. J.V.C. Force, 'Strong Island' (B Boy Records)
151. Kid Frost, 'La Raza' (Virgin)
152. Kid 'n' Play, 'Last Night' (Select/ Chrysalis)
153. King Sun-D Moet, 'Hey Love' (Zakia)
154. Kool Moe Dee, 'Go See the Doctor' (Jive)
155. Lifers Group, 'The Real Deal' (Hollywood Basic)
156. L.L. Cool J, 'I Want You' (Def Jam)
157. L.L. Cool J, 'Going Back To Cali' (Def Jam/CBS)
158. Mantronix, 'Bassline' (Sleeping Bag/ 10)
159. Massive Attack, 'Daydreaming' (Circa)
160. The Masters of Ceremony, 'Sexy' (Strong City/London)
161. MCA and Burzootie, 'Drum Machine' (Def Jam)
162. M.C. Craig 'G', 'Shout' (Pop Art)
163. MC 900Ft Jesus, 'I'm Going Straight To Heaven' (Nettwerk)
164. M.C. Shan, 'The Bridge' (Cold Chillin'/WEA)
165. N.W.A., 'Straight Outta Compton' (Priority/Island)
166. Original Concept, 'Can You Feel It?' (Def Jam/CBS)
167. PM Dawn, 'A Watcher's Point of View' (Gee Street)
168. Public Enemy, 'Bring the Noise' (Def Jam/CBS)
169. Public Enemy, 'Rebel Without A Pause' (Def Jam/CBS)
170. Queen Latifah, 'Dance For Me' Tommy Boy)
171. The Real Roxanne, 'Bang Zoom! Let's Go Go!' (Select)
172. Rob Base & D.J. E–Z Rock, 'It Takes Two' (Profile/Citybeat)
173. Roxanne Shanté, 'Bite This' (Pop Art)
174. Run-D.M.C., 'My Adidas' (Profile)
175. Salt 'n' Pepa, 'I'll Take Your Man' (Next Plateau)
176. Schoolly-D, 'Put Your Filas On' (Schoolly-D/Rhythm King)
177. Schoolly-D, 'Saturday Night' (Rhythm King)
178. Lakim Shabazz, 'Pure Righteousness' (Tuff City)
179. Sha-Quan, 'Don't Fess' (Midnight Sun)
180. Skatemaster Tate, 'Justice (To the Bass)' (Island)
181. The Skinny Boys, 'Rip the Cut' (Warlock)

182. Son of Bazerk, 'Change the Style' (SOUL/ MCA)
183. Spanish Prince, 'Maria' (4th & B'Way)
184. Jimmy Spicer, 'This Is It' (Def Jam)
185. Spoonie Gee, 'The Godfather' (Tuff City)
186. Steady B, 'Take Your Radio' (Pop Art)
187. Stetsasonic, 'Talkin' All That Jazz' (Tommy Boy)
188. Sugar Bear, 'Don't Scandalize Mine' (Coslit/ Champion)
189. Sugar Ray Dinke, 'Cabrini Green Rap' (Rhythm King)
190. Sweet Tee & Jazzy Joyce, 'It's My Beat' (Profile/Champion)
191. 3rd Bass, 'The Gas Face' (Def Jam/ CBS)
192. Tone-Loc, 'Wild Thing' (Delicious Vinyl/ Island)
193. Traedonya, 'The Boogaloo' (Tuff City)
194. Tricky Tee, 'Johnny the Fox' (Sleeping Bag)
195. T La Rock & Jazzy Jay, 'It's Yours' (Partytime/Def Jam)
196. 2 Live Crew, 'What I Like' (Macola)
197. UltraMagnetic MC's, 'Give the Drummer Some' (Next Plateau/London)
198. UTFO, 'Roxanne Roxanne' (Select)
199. Word of Mouth featuring D.J. Cheese, 'King Kut' (Beauty and the Beat)
200. X-Clan, 'Heed the Word Of the Father' (Island)

Since rap albums now proliferate, a list of recommendations is not practical, other than to say that Public Enemy, De La Soul, Ice Cube and other major rap performers have all produced albums that work in their entirety. Ideally, they need to be listened to as albums, which reverses my comments of the first edition of this book, that rap is music for 12-inch singles. Old school rap, the music of 1979 to 1983, is now hard to find but a new interest in the old school has resulted in some worthwhile archive compilations. These include 'Back To the Old School' (Republic), 'Old School Classics' (Tuff City) and 'The History of Rap' (Select).

Lightning swords of death 3

The good, the bad and the ugly

100 more liquid swords to take us through to the new millennium . . .

201. Arrested Development, *3 Years, 5 Months and 2 Days in the Life of . . .* (Cooltempo)
202. Beastie Boys, *Check Your Head* (Capitol)
203. Beastie Boys, *Hello Nasty* (Capitol)
204. Beastie Boys, *Ill Communication* (Capitol)
205. Big Punisher, *Capital Punishment* (Loud Records/BMG)
206. Black Star, *Mos Def & Talib Kweli Are Black Star* (Rawkus)
207. Busta Rhymes, *Extinction Level Event*The Final World Front* (Elektra)
208. Canibus, *Can-I-Bus* (Universal)
209. Clay, Cassius, *I Am the Greatest* (Rev-Ola)
210. Company Flow, *Funcrusher Plus* (Rawkus)
211. Company Flow, *Little Johnny From the Hospital* (Rawkus)
212. Cypress Hill, *Cypress Hill* (Columbia)
213. Da Lench Mob, *Guerillas In Tha Mist* (Street Knowledge Records)
214. The Disposable Heroes of Hiphoprisy, *Hypocrisy Is the Greatest Luxury* (4th & Broadway)
215. DJ Faust, *Man Or Myth?* (Bomb Hip-Hop)
216. DJ Shadow, *Endtroducing* (Mo' Wax)
217. DJ Shadow, *Influx* (Mo' Wax)
218. DJ Spinna, *Heavy Beats Volume 1* (Rawkus)
219. Downtown Science, *Downtown Science* (Def Jam)
220. Dr. Dooom, *First Come, First Served* (Copasetik)
221. Dr. Dre, *The Chronic* (Death Row/Interscope)
222. Dr. Octagon, *Instrumentalyst* (Dreamworks)
223. Dr. Octagon, *Dr. Octagonecologyst* (Dreamworks)
224. Eminem, *The Slim Shady LP* (Aftermath Ent./Interscope)
225. Fat Joe, *Don Cartagena* (Mystic/Big Beat/Atlantic)
226. Freestyle Fellowship, *Innercity Griots* (4th & Broadway)
227. The Fugees, *The Score* (Columbia)
228. Gang Starr, *Daily Operation* (Cooltempo)
229. Gang Starr, *Hard To Earth* (Chrysalis/ERG)
230. Genius/GZA, *Liquid Swords* (Geffen)
231. Ghostface Killah, *Ironman* (Epic)
232. Goodie Mob, *Soul Food* (LaFace)
233. Gravediggaz, *Diary Of a Madman* (Gee Street)
234. Gravediggaz, *Niggamortis* (Gee Street)
235. Gravediggaz, *The Pick, The Sickle and the Shovel* (Gee Street)

236. Lauryn Hill, *The Miseducation of Lauryn Hill* (Ruffhouse/Columbia)
237. Iceberg Slim, *Reflections* (Infinite Zero/American)
238. Ice Cube, *Death Certificate* (Priority)
239. Inspectah Deck, *Uncontrolled Substance* (Loud)
240. The Invisibl Skratch Piklz, *The Shiggar Fraggar Show* (Hip Hop Slam Records)
241. Jay-Z, *Vol. 2 . . . Hard Knock Life* (BMG)
242. Jeep Beat Collective, *Technics Chainsaw Massacre* (Bomb Hip-Hop)
243. Jeru The Damaja, *The Sun Also Rises In the East* (PayDay/FFRR)
244. Jeru The Damaja, *Wrath Of the Math* (Payday/FFRR)
245. Jungle Brothers, *J. Beez Wit the Remedy* (Warner Bros.)
246. Jurassic-5, *Jurassic-5 LP* (Pan)
247. Kool G Rap, *4, 5, 6* (Sony)
248. Kurupt, *Kuruption!* (Antra/A&M)
249. Lil' Kim, *Hard Core* (Big Beat/ Atlantic)
250. Main Source, *Breaking Atoms* (Wild Pitch Records)
251. MC Solaar, *Qui Sème Le Vent Récolte Le Tempo* (Polydor)
252. Me'Shell NdegéOcello, *Plantation Lullabies* (Maverick/Sire/Reprise)
253. Method Man, *Tical* (Def Jam)
254. Missy Elliot, *Supa Dupa Fly* (The Gold Mind Inc./EastWest)
255. Missy Misdemeanor Elliot, *Da Real World* (The Gold Mind Inc./East West)
256. Mixmaster Mike, *Anti-Theft Device* (Asphodel)
257. Nas, *It Was Written* (Columbia)
258. New Kingdom, *Heavy Load* (Gee Street)
259. New Kingdom, *Paradise Don't Come Cheap* (Gee Street)
260. The Notorious B.I.G., *Life After Death* (Puff Daddy Records)
261. Outkast, *Aquemini* (LaFace)
262. Ozomatli, *Ozomatli* (Almo Sounds)
263. Peanut Butter Wolf, *My Vinyl Weighs a Ton* (Copasetik Records)
264. Pete Rock & C.L. Smooth, *The Main Ingredient* (Elektra)
265. The Pharcyde, *Bizarre Ride II The Pharcyde* (Delicious Vinyl)
266. PhonopsychographDISK, *Ancient Termites* (Bomb Hip-Hop)
267. P.M. Dawn, *Of the Heart, Of the Soul And Of the Cross* (Gee Street)
268. Public Enemy, *There's A Poison Goin On* (PIAS/Atomic Pop)
269. Puff Daddy & the Family, *No Way Out* (Puff Daddy Records)
270. Quannum, *Spectrum* (Quannum Projects)
271. Raekwon, *Only Built 4 Cuban Linx* (Loud/BMG)
272. The Roots, *Things Fall Apart* (MCA)
273. Scarface, *The Diary* (Rap-a-lot Records/Noo Trybe Records)
274. Gil Scott-Heron, *Spirits* (TVT Records)
275. Prince Akeem, *Coming Down Like Babylon* (Chicago Tip Records)
276. Shyheim, *A/K/A The Rugged Child* (Virgin)

277. Will Smith, *Big Willie Style* (Columbia)
278. Snoop Dogg, *Da Game Is To Be Sold, Not To Be Told* (No Limit Records)
279. Snoop Doggy Dogg, *Doggystyle* (Death Row/Interscope)
280. Rob Swift, *The Ablist* (Asphodel)
281. 2 Pac, *All Eyez On Me* (Death Row/Interscope)
282. 2 Pac, *Strictly 4 My N.I.G.G.A.Z. . . .* (Interscope)
283. Van Peebles, Melvin, *X-Rated By An All-White Jury* (A&M)
284. Various artists, *Altered Beats* (Axiom)
285. Various Artists, *DJ Pogo Presents Block Party Breaks* (Strut)
286. Various Artists, *DJ Pogo Presents The Breaks* (Harmless)
287. Various artists, *Hi-Phat Diet: A Wild Pitch Compilation* (Wild Pitch/EMI)
288. Various artists, *Jimmy Jay présente 'Les Cool sessions'* (Virgin)
289. Various artists, *Lyricist Lounge volume one* (Rawkus)
290. Various artists, *New York Reality Check 101* (Payday/FFRR)
291. Various artists, *The Sugarhill Story: Old School Rap – To the Beat Y'all* (Sequel)
292. Various artists, *Rawkus Presents Soundbombing II* (Rawkus)
293. Various artists, *Return Of the D.J. Vol. I* (Bomb Hip-Hop)
294. Various artists, *Return Of the D.J. Vol. II* (Bomb Hip-Hop)
295. Various artists, *Tommy Boy's Greatest Beats: The First Fifteen Years 1981–1996* (Tommy Boy)
296. Justin Warfield, *My Field Trip to Planet 9* (Qwest/Reprise)
297. Warren G, *Regulate . . . G Funk Era* (Violator/RAL/Island)
298. The Watts Prophets, *The Black Voices: On the Streets In Watts* (Acid Jazz)
299. The Watts Prophets, *Rappin' Black In a White World* (ALA)
300. Wu-Tang Clan, *Enter the Wu-Tang (36 Chambers)* (Loud/BMG)

Bibliography

Abrahams, Roger D., *Deep Down in the Jungle: Negro Narrative Folklore from the Streets of Philadelphia*, second edition, New York: Aldine de Gruyter, 1970.

Adler, Bill, *Tougher Than Leather*, New York: New American Library, 1987.

Ali, Muhammad, with Durham, Richard, *The Greatest: My Own Story*, New York: Random House, 1975.

Anderson, Jervis, *Harlem: The Great Black Way*, London: Orbis, 1982.

Beck, Robert (Iceberg Slim), *The Naked Soul of Iceberg Slim*, Los Angeles: Holloway House, 1986.

Brown, H. Rap, *Die, Nigger, Die!*, New York: Dial Press, 1969.

Burroughs, William S., *Nova Express*, London: Jonathan Cape, 1966.

Courlander, Harold, *Negro Folk Music, U.S.A.*, New York: Columbia University Press, 1963.

Cripps, Thomas, *Black Film as Genre*, Bloomington and London: Indiana University Press, 1979.

Davis, Mike, *City of Quartz: Excavating the Future in Los Angeles*, London/New York: Verso, 1990.

Eshun, Kodwo, *More Brilliant Than the Sun: Adventures in Sonic Fiction*, London: Quartet Books, 1998.

Fernando Jr., S.H., *The New Beats: Exploring the Music, Culture, and Attitudes of Hip-Hop*, New York: Anchor Books Doubleday, 1994.

Finnegan, Ruth, *Oral Literature in Africa*, Oxford: Oxford University Press, 1970.

Fox, Ted, *Showtime at the Apollo*, New York: Holt, Rinehart & Winston, 1983.

Gillespie, Dizzy, with Frazer, Al, *Dizzy – To Be Or Not To Bop*, London: Quartet, 1979.

Goines, Donald, *Street Players*, Los Angeles: Holloway House, 1973.

Groia, Philip, *They All Sang on the Corner: A Second Look at New York City's Rhythm and Blues Vocal Groups*, New York: Phillie Dee Enterprises Inc., 1983.

Harvey, David, *The Condition of Postmodernity*, Oxford/Cambridge, Massachusetts: Blackwell, 1989.

Heilbut, Tony, *The Gospel Sound: Good News and Bad Times*, New York: Simon & Schuster, 1971.

Jackson, Bruce, *Wake Up Dead Man: Afro-American Worksongs from Texas Prisons*, Cambridge, Massachusetts: Harvard University Press, 1972.

Kochman, Thomas (ed.), *Rappin' and Stylin' Out: Communication in Urban Black America*, Urbana-Champaign: University of Illinois Press, 1972.

Kohl, Herbert, and Hinton, James, 'Names, Graffiti and Culture', in Thomas Kochman (ed.), *Rappin' and Stylin' Out* (see above).

Keiser, R. Lincoln, *The Vice Lords: Warriors of the Streets*, New York: Holt, Rinehart & Winston, 1969.

Labov, William, 'Rules for Ritual Insults',

in Thomas Kochman (ed.). *Rappin' and Stylin' Out* (see above).

Mailer, Norman, Kurlansky, Mervyn (photographer), and Naar, Jon (photographer), *Watching My Name Go By*; US title *The Faith of Graffiti*, New York: Praeger Publishers, 1974.

Oliver, Paul, *Savannah Syncopators: African Retentions in the Blues*, London: Studio Vista, 1970.

Reed, Ishmael, *Mumbo Jumbo*, London: Allison & Busby; USA: Atheneum, 1988.

Roberts, John Storm, *Black Music of Two Worlds*, New York: Praeger, 1972.

Ro, Ronin, *Have Gun Will Travel: The Spectacular Rise and Violent Fall of Death Row Records*, London, Quartet Books, 1998.

Smash, Nick, *Hip Hop 86–89*, Woodford Green, Essex: International Music Publications, 1990.

Toffler, Alvin, *The Third Wave*, London: Pan Books, USA: Bantam, 1980.

Wimsatt, William Upski, *Bomb the Suburbs*, Chicago, The Subway and Elevated Press Co., 1994.

Womack, Jack, *Ambient*, New York: Weidenfeld & Nicolson, 1987; London: Unwin Hyman, 1989.

Index

Please note: due to the frequency of nicknames and stage names in this book, all names are alphabeticised by the first name or title rather than the family name.

Page numbers in italics refer to photographs.

Other titles of interest published by Serpent's Tail

Exotica: Fabricated Soundscapes in a Real World

David Toop

'A virtuoso blend of biography, music criticism, interviews and poetic flights of fancy, all exploring the 20th century's obsessive fascination with the exotic . . . Toop must be the only writer around who can devote an entire chapter to the dramatic and musical structure of Lassie and remain intriguing. It is intoxicating stuff' *The Times*

'Toop's voyage through this largely untouched musical realm is gripping and aromatic. Wading through schlocky, esoteric terrain, he has produced a book which resembles an 18th century cabinet of curiosities' *Guardian*

'*Exotica* interweaves practicality with mysticism, the familiar with the unheard of and the trivial with the deadly serious . . . And it's in the gaps between intention and result, artifice and essence, the real and the fake, that *Exotica* plants its most fertile seeds' *Independent*

'An all enveloping and essential account of all that is musically taboo' *Mojo*

'Toop is a curator of sound of a rare catholicity. It's the outlandishness, the surrealism, the gap between Western constructs of exotic paradises that engages him . . . Good man, this Toop' *Time Out*

'Toop's ache for the healing, enlivening balm of "oceanic" sounds is the restfully beating heart of this strange study, which explores the West's centuries-long fascination with alien cultures . . . it sucks you in' *Uncut*

'Toop opens a network of communication between fiction and research, interview and drift . . . rigorously hallucinatory' *i-D*

'A wonderfully provocative book . . . Toop is spot-on in his analysis of stress-busting New Age music and scathing towards those who collect music like a tourist's mementos. For him, music, and more particularly sound, is a thing of infinite power. A superb book' *New Internationalist*

'An unusual and surprisingly rewarding book' *New Statesman*

Ocean of Sound

David Toop

'*Ocean of Sound* is as alien as the 20th century, as utterly Now as the 21st. An essential mix' *The Wire*

'This is a hugely optimistic book ... for all the talk of scents and shades, perfumes and tints, it is the capacity of sound to thrill the senses that comes across in these pages' *Independent*

'To put it starkly, Toop knows *far more*, about a *far broader* range of music, than any other critic in the non-specialist British press ... His sense of the absurd, of potential darkness and madness, is a bullshit detector never turned off' *New Statesman*

'It challenges the way we hear, and more importantly, how we interpret what we hear around us' *Daily Telegraph*

'A masterfully innovative and radical work ... a definite route forward for the pop book' *Melody Maker*

'*Ocean of Sound* is a challenging hymn to amorphousness in the echo-chamber of our future' *The Idler*

'An heroic endeavour brought off with elegance and charm ... no-one else has come close to placing the emergent sounds of post-acid music in such shimmeringly correct context' *New Musical Express*

'Extends ambient way beyond chill-out compilations into the compellingly alien zones of disco, dub soundsystems, bat radar, Japanese garden music, Yanomami shamanic ceremonies and dream theories ... like sonic fact for our sci-fi present, a Martian chronicle from this Planet Earth' *The Face*

'It's packed with astonishing ideas that linger for days after ... *Ocean of Sound* shatters consensual reality with a cumulative force that's both frightening and compelling. Buy it, read it and let it remix your head' *i-D*

'*Ocean of Sound* is brave in ambition and scope, exciting in execution ... The result is a book that, like no other, encompasses the way that people hear and produce music today' *Mojo*